Financial and Managerial Accounting

Debasis Mukerjee

ALTAR PUBLISHING HOUSE
NEW DELHI (INDIA)

Published by

ALTAR PUBLISHING HOUSE
L- 9 A, IInd FLOOR, STREET NO.42
SADATPUR EXTENSION
DELHI-110094 (INDIA)
CELL- 0-9899346553, 0-9868990429

Financial and Managerial Accounting

Edition 2010
ISBN 978-81-910524-5-9

Printed in India
at Asian Offset Printers, Delhi

Preface

Managerial accounting is concerned with providing information to managers—that is, people inside an organization who direct and control its operation. In contrast, financial accounting is concerned with providing information to stockholders, creditors, and others who are outside an organization.

Managerial accounting provides the essential data with which the organizations are actually run. It is also termed as management accounting or cost accounting. Financial accounting provides the scorecard by which a company's overall past performance is judged by outsiders. Managerial accountants prepare a variety of reports. Some reports focus on how well managers or business units have performed-comparing actual results to plans and to benchmarks. Some reports provide timely, frequent updates on key indicators such as orders received, order backlog, capacity utilization, and sales. In contrast, financial accounting is oriented toward producing a limited set of specific prescribed annual and quarterly financial statements in accordance with Generally Accepted Accounting Principles (GAAP).

Managerial accounting differs from financial accounting in a number of ways. Financial accounting reports are prepared for the use of external parties such as shareholders and creditors, whereas managerial accounting reports are prepared for managers inside the organization. This contrast in basic orientation results in a number of major differences between financial and managerial accounting, even though both financial and managerial accounting often rely on the same underlying financial data. In addition to the to the differences in who the reports are prepared for, financial and managerial accounting also differ in their emphasis between the past and the future, in the type of data provided to users, and in several other ways.

Designed for graduate students of accounting courses, this text presents balanced coverage of both financial and managerial topics. It focuses primarily on the use of accounting information in today's business world. Besides discussing the current accounting and business practices, greater attention also given to ethics, service enterprises and international issues. This concise volume, with accessible writing style, will destined to become an essential companion to students and professionals in the field.

Author

Contents

1

Introduction to Management Accounting

Managerial accounting may be regarded as a body of knowledge that is concerned with concepts and decision-making tools that enable management to make better decisions and to evaluate results. As a body of technical knowledge, management accounting primarily consists of certain decision-making techniques or tools drawn from financial and management theory and practice. A basic premise is that the primary task of management is to make decisions and that this task is greatly improved by the knowledge and skills of the management accountant.

What is accounting? A very old but frequently used definition states: "Accounting is the art of recording, classifying, and summarising in a significant manner and in terms of money, transactions, and events, which are, in part at least of a financial character, and interpreting the results thereof."

A more recent definition states: "Accounting is a service activity. Its function is to provide quantitative information, primarily financial in nature, about economic entities that is intended to be useful in making economic decisions–in making reasoned choices among alternative courses of action." This latter definition is more appropriate to managerial accounting because of its emphasis on decision-making.

Management accounting may be simply defend as a body of accounting knowledge primarily consisting of concepts and techniques useful to management in making better decisions and evaluating performance.

The subject matter of management accounting has little to do with transactions analysis and the preparation of statements from historical data. However, management accounting is not independent of financial accounting. Financial accounting is a foundation requirement for management accounting and a study of financial accounting must precede the study of management accounting. An understanding of how to analyse and record the effects of individual transactions of assets, liabilities, capital, and revenue is helpful but not essential.

The term management accounting obviously consists of two words each of which represents highly developed areas of study. The term management accounting suggests an important relationship between management and accounting. Furthermore, there is implied an area of common interests.

The student that is planning a professional career in accounting must develop an appreciation and understanding of management. It is management that guides the business and makes the decisions which determine the success or failure of a business. The accountant serves in a staff or advisory function under management. Although accountants use technical accounting expertise to prepare financial statements, it is management that receives and uses financial statements. Management, not accountants, has the need and responsibility to read and understand financial statements. Financial statements, in one sense, are summary reports of how well management has performed for a given period of time.

Certain concepts of management are essential to a study of management accounting. The following concepts will be employed throughout this text as important in understanding the technical aspects of management accounting.

Accounting as an Organisational Function

Management accounting techniques are useful in all types of businesses. Managers of service, merchandising, manufacturing, banks, insurance companies, etc. all can benefit from the use of management accounting. Management accounting is frequently associated with fairly large corporate businesses; however, it is equally useful to small businesses.

When a business reaches a certain size, then the accounting activity is of such a volume that the accounting activity must be organised and managed. Consequently, accounting in larger businesses can be thought of as a departmentalised function appearing on the organisation chart as a staff function. While the term management accounting implies to individuals possessing specialised knowledge of management and accounting, the term can also be applied to the accounting department as a whole.

From a departmental viewpoint, all accounting activities are management in nature. The accounting department exists to serve the financial data needs of management. The controller or head of the accounting department in many companies is considered to be a part of the decision-making team. The controller, the chief executive officer of the accounting department, is always serving as an management accountant, regardless of what type of accounting is being done. However, the majority of accounting activities he or she supervises would from an academic viewpoint be classified as financial accounting as opposed to management accounting.

The study of accounting is normally divided into two broad categories: financial and managerial. This division is somewhat arbitrary in that the study of managerial accounting requires a strong foundation in financial accounting.

Accounting exists in a network of complex business relationships both internal and external. In management accounting, the focal point is the role of management within the organisational structure. Both the financial accountant and the managerial accountant need a knowledge of external factors and relationships as well as a conceptual knowledge of accounting principles and procedures. Accounting as a function within a business organisation is service oriented.

In a broad sense, financial accounting, as a branch of accounting in general, serves all types of users. Financial accounting is concerned with the reporting of operations to external parties; whereas, management accounting is internal in direction and is primarily concerned with serving the decision-making needs of management.

Management accounting as a body of technical knowledge is, in fact, a synthesis of various disciplines. Many of the techniques such as capital budgeting models and EOQ models have been borrowed from other disciplines. The conceptual framework of management accounting, then, has building blocks in its foundation from:

1. Management theory
2. Financial accounting
3. Finance theory
4. Economic theory
5. Marketing theory
6. Mathematics

Therefore, an understanding of management accounting is greatly enhanced, if preceded by a knowledge of the fundamentals of management, finance, production, marketing, economics, and mathematics.

Environmental Structure of Accounting

Accounting is a complex body of knowledge and procedures that has evolved over the last few hundred years. The complexity of accounting in the last ffty years has greatly accelerated as more complex financial transactions have been developed and regulatory agencies, both private and non private, have come into existence. Voluminous rules and regulations, have been written and put into practice. Within accounting, there are highly developed specialised areas such as the following:

Tax accounting	Accounting Information Systems
Financial auditing	Internal auditing
Management accounting	Financial accounting
Not-for-profit accounting	Governmental accounting

Accounting as a profession employs hundreds of thousands of individuals who serve both in public accounting and private accounting. As of 2006, there were approximately 650,000 CPAs in the USA. Accounting is needed in every type of business and organisations including state and federal governments, banks, not-for-profit businesses, manufacturing and retail businesses of all types, and labor unions.

Comparison to Financial Accounting

The differences between financial and managerial accounting can be effectively illustrated by using (1) an input and output approach and (2) a financial statement approach. Both approaches will be illustrated.

Input/output Approach: Although narrower in scope of users, management accounting, nevertheless, is broader in scope in the type of data used in the models through which data is processed and analysed.

The methodology of processing data involves numerous types of mathematical model. The inputting, processing, and outputting of data in management accounting is not limited to a prescribed set of rules dealing only with historical data as is the case in financial accounting.

Financial Statement Approach

Both financial accounting and management accounting are concerned with financial statements. The financial accountant is concerned with analysing and recording the historical transactions of the business. A primary objective of the financial accountant is to fairly present financial statements based on past events. The management accountant is primarily concerned with desired future events. Future events will be the results of decisions to be made by management. The management accountant, then, is also concerned with financial statements that reflect the anticipated consequences of planned decisions.

Management Accountant

The management accountant is a professional accountant just like the CPA. He or she is likely to possess a degree in accounting. However, unlike the CPA, the management accountant is more likely to work for an industrial firm rather than an accounting firm. In a manner similar to the CPA, he or she may even be certified. The Institute of Management

Accountants which is the professional organisation of management accountants has over 70,000 members. The IMA gives twice a year a comprehensive three day exam over the knowledge expected of the management accountant. Individuals passing all parts of the exam are awarded a Certificate in Management Accounting (CMA). The exam is a difficult test with less than 20% of those taking the exam passing in one setting. The exam is given in five parts covering the following subject areas: (1) managerial economics and business finance, (2) organisation and behaviour, (3) public reporting standards, auditing and taxes, (4) periodic reporting for internal and external purposes, and (5) decision analysis, including modeling and information systems.

Management Accounting Conceptual Framework

The real business world is extremely complex. The environment in which the accountant and manager operates has myriads of components which are highly interrelated. A successful approach in dealing with complexity is to develop a model which contains the components of reality that need to be studied and understood. Most management accounting books have some underlying model; unfortunately, these authors' use of the model is seldom well-defend or clearly presented. This management accounting model will facilitate the understanding of how accounting and management are interrelated and how they have a mutual dependency upon each other. Furthermore, this model clarifies the relationship of financial and managerial accounting.

MANAGEMENT ACCOUNTING VIEW OF VUSINESS

Management accounting writers tend to present management accounting as a loosely connected set of decisionmaking tools. Although the various textbooks on management accounting make no attempt to develop an integrated theory, there is a high degree of consistency and standardisation in methodology of presentation.

The formulation of theory in terms of conceptual models is a common practice. Virtually all textbooks in business administration use some type of conceptual framework or model to integrate the fundamentals being presented. In economic theory, there are conceptual models of the firm, markets, and the economy. In marketing, there are models of marketing decisionmaking and channels of distribution. Even in financial accounting, models of financial statements are used as a framework for teaching the fundamentals of basic financial accounting.

Management accounting texts are based on a very specific model of the business enterprise. There is unanimity in assuming that the behaviour of variable costs within a relevant range tends to be linear. The consequence of assuming that variable costs vary directly with volume is a classification of cost into fixed and variable.

The management accounting view of business may be divided into two broad categories: (1) basic features and (2) basic assumptions.

Basic Features

The business firm or enterprise is an organisational structure in which the basic activities are departmentalised as line and staff. There are three primary line functions: marketing, production, and finance. The organisation is run or controlled by individuals collectively called management. The staff or advisory functions include accounting, personnel, and purchasing and receiving. The organisation has a communication or reporting system to coordinate the interaction of the various staff and line departmental functions. The environment in which the organisation operates includes investors, suppliers, governments bankers, accountants, lawyers, etc.

The organisational aspect of the business firm is illustrated. This descriptive model shows that there are different levels of management. A commonly used approach is to classify management into three levels: Top management, middle management, and lower level management. The significance of a hierarchy of management is that decisionmaking occurs at three levels.

Basic Assumptions

The framework of management accounting is based on a number of implied assumptions. Although no single work has attempted to identify all of the assumptions, the major assumptions will be detailed below. Five categories of assumptions will be presented:

1. Basic goals
2. Role of management
3. Nature of Decisionmaking
4. Role of the accounting department
5. Nature of accounting information

Basic Goal Assumptions: The basic goals or objectives the business enterprise may be multiple. Other goals could be to maximise sales, ROI, or earnings per share. Management accounting does not require a specific of type of goal. However, whatever form the goal takes, management will at all times try to achieve a satisfactory level of profit. A less than satisfactory level of profit may portend a change in management.

Role of Management Assumptions: The success of the business depends primarily upon the skill and abilities of management–which skills can vary widely among different managers. The business is not completely at the mercy of market forces. Management can through its actions influence and control events within limits. In order to achieve desired results, management makes use of specific planning and control concepts and techniques. Planning and control techniques which management may use include business budgeting, cost volume profit analysis, incremental analysis, fexible budgeting, segmental contribution reporting, inventory models, and capital budgeting models.

Decision-making Assumptions: A critical managerial function is decision making. Decisions which management must make may be classified as marketing, production, and financial. Decisions may also be classified as strategic and tactical and longrun and shortrun.

Accounting Department Assumptions: The accounting department is a primary source of information necessary in makingdecisions. The accounting department is expected to provide information to all levels of management. Management will consider the accounting department capable of providing data useful in making marketing, production, and financial decisions.

Nature of Accounting Information: In order for the accounting department to make meaningful analysis of data, it is necessary to distinguish between fixed and variable costs and other types of costs that are not important in the recording of business transactions. Some but not all of the information needed by management can be provided from financial statements and historical accounting records. In addition to historical data, management will expect the management accountant to provide other types of data, such as estimates, forecasts, future data, and standards.The accounting department will be expected to provide the information required by a specific tool. In order for the accounting department to make many types of analysis, a separation of costs into fixed and variable will be required.

Implications of the Basic Assumptions

The assumption that there are three types of decisions, requires that management identify the specific decisions under each category. The identification of specific decisions is critical because only then can the appropriate managerial accounting technique be properly used.

An understanding of financial statements is critical to the ability of management to make good decisions. Financial statements, although prepared by accountants, are actually created by management through the implementation of decisions. The reader and user of financial statements is not primarily the accountant but management. From a management accounting point of view, it is management rather than accountants that needs to have the greater understanding of financial statements.

The income statement and the balance sheet can be viewed as a descriptive model for decisionmaking. Financial statements reflect success or lack of success in making decisions. Management can be deemed successful when the desired income has been attained and financial position is considered sound.

The basic balance sheet equation, of course, is $A = L + C$. A management accounting interpretation is that the assets or resources come from the creditors and the owners. It is management responsibilities to manage both sides of the equation. That is, management must make decisions about both the resources and the sources of the assets.

Each item on the balance sheet is an area of management. Stated differently each item on financial statements represents a critical area sensitive to mismanagement. Cash, accounts receivable, inventory, fixed assets, accounts payable can be too large or too small. Given this fact, then, for each item there must be the right amount or optimum. Gross mismanagement of any single item could either result in the failure of the business or the downfall of management.

The statement that the management accountant will be required to furnish information not of a historical nature means that the accountant will have to deal with planned and estimated or future data. Furthermore, much of this data will be not be found in the historical data bank from which the accountant prepares financial statements. The management accountant may be required to do analysis requiring data of an economic nature.

MANAGEMENT ACCOUNTING AND DECISION-MAKING

In management accounting, decisionmaking may be simply defend as choosing a course of action from among alternatives. If there are no alternatives, then no decision is required. A basis assumption is that the best decision is the one that involves the most revenue or the least amount of cost. The task of management with the help of the management accountant is to find the best alternative.

The process of making decisions is generally considered to involve the following steps:

1. Identify the various alternatives for a given type of decision.
2. Obtain the necessary data necessary to evaluate the various alternatives.
3. Analyse and determine the consequences of each alternative.
4. Select the alternative that appears to best achieve the desired goals or objectives.
5. Implement the chosen alternative.
6. At an appropriate time, evaluate the results of the decisions against standards or other desired results.

From the descriptive model of the basic features and assumptions of the management accounting perspective of business, it is easy to recognise that decisionmaking is the focal point of management accounting. How businessmen make decisions has been intensively studied. In management accounting, it is useful to classify decisions as:

1. Strategic and tactical
2. Shortrun and longrun

Strategic and Tactical Decisions

In management accounting, the objective is not necessarily to make the best decision but to make a good decision. Because of complex interacting relationships, it is very difficult, even if possible, to determine the best decision. Management decisionmaking is highly subjective.

Whether a decision is good or acceptable depends on the goals and objectives of management. Consequently, a prerequisite to decisionmaking is that management have set the organisation's goals and objectives.

In setting goals and objectives, it is useful to distinguish between strategic and tactical decisions. Strategic decisions are broadbased, qualitative type of decisions which include or reflect goals and objectives. Strategic decisions are based on the subjective thinking of management concerning goals and objectives.

Tactical decisions are quantitative executable decisions which result directly from the strategic decisions. The distinction between strategic and tactical is important in management accounting because the techniques of management accounting pertain primarily to tactical decisions. Management accounting does not typically provide techniques for assisting in making strategic decisions.

Examples of strategic decisions and tactical decisions from a management accounting point of view include.

Once a strategic decision has been made, then a specific management tool can be used to aid in making the tactical decision.

The classification of decisions as strategic and tactical logically results in thinking about decisions as qualitative and quantitative. In management accounting, the approach to decisionmaking is basically quantitative. In a technical sense, management accounting consists of mathematical techniques or decision models that assist management in making quantitative type decisions.

Short run Versus Long-run Decision-making

The decisionmaking process is complicated somewhat by the fact that the horizon for making decisions may be for the shortrun or longrun. The choice between the shortrun or the longrun is particularly critical concerning the setting of profitability objectives. Profitability objectives which management might choose to maximise include:

1. Net income
2. Sales
3. Return on total assets
4. Return on total equity
5. Earnings per share

The decisionmaking process is, consequently, affected by the profitability objective and the choice of the longrun versus the short run. If the objective is to maximise sales, then the method of financing a new plant is not immediately important. However, if the objective is to maximise shortrun net income, then management might decide to issue stock rather than bonds to avoid interest expense. In the long run, the company's profit might be greater because of preventive maintenance or research and development.

Although the interests of management and the organisation may be presumed to coincide, the possibility of making decisions for the shortrun may cause a conflict in interests. An individual manager planning to make a career or job change might have a tendency to make decisions that maximise profitability in the shortrun. The motivation for pursuing shortrun profits may be to create a favorable resume.

The tools in management accounting such as CVP analysis, variance analysis, budgeting, and incremental analysis are not designed to deal with long range objectives and decision. Consequently, the results obtained from using management accounting tools should be interpreted as benefits for the shortrun, and not necessarily the longrun. Hopefully, decisions which clearly benefit the shortrun will also benefit the longrun.

Management Accounting Decision Models

Management accounting consists of a set of tools that have been proven to be useful in making decisions involving revenue and cost data. Even though many of the techniques appear to be simplistic in nature, they have proven to be of consider able value.

The techniques which are also listed in all based on mathematical equations or mathematical relationships. All of the techniques may be regarded as mathematical decision making models. For example, the foundation of CVP analysis is the equation: $I = P(Q) - V(Q) - F$.

The approach described above concerning the use of financial statements as a check list to identify decisionmaking areas may also be used to identify the appropriate management accounting technique. For every item on financial statements, there is one or more appropriate management accounting technique.

The following illustrates the association of management accounting tools with specific financial statement items.

1. Comprehensive business budgeting
2. Flexible budgeting and variance analysis
3. Variance analysis
4. Capital budgeting
5. Incremental analysis
   a) Keep or replace
   b) Additional volume of business
   c) Credit analysis
   d) Demand analysis
   e) Sales people compensation analysis
   f) Capacity analysis
6. Costvolume profit analysis
7. Cost behaviour analysis
8. Return on investment analysis
9. Economic order quantity analysis

10. Safety stock/lead time analysis
11. Segmental reporting analysis

Decision-making and Required Information

The assumption that management will use management accounting tools in making decisions places a burden on the management accountant. Each tool requires special information. The management accountant will be asked to provide the specialised information needed.

Comprehensive Management Accounting Decision Model

As the above discussion should make clear, decisionmaking is a complex network of interrelated decision variables. Management can face an overwhelming task if it tries to identify every variable and minute decision relationship. One approach to dealing with complexity is the development of models, both mathematical and descriptive for the purpose of simulating only the relevant or more important variables.

The decisionmaking process discussed in this chapter leads to the conclusion from a management accounting perspective that there is a connecting link between the following:

1. Financial statement items
2. Strategic and tactical decisions
3. Management accounting techniques
4. Decisionmaking information

The relationships among these elements may be summarised. These relationship as discussed may be used to develop a comprehensive management accounting decision model for a manufacturing business.

REFERENCES

Petty, Keown, Scott, and Martin, *Basic Financial Management*, 6th edition, Prentice Hall, 1993.

Schall and Haley, *Introduction to Financial Management*, 5th edition. McGraw-hill, 1988.

Yee, Kenton K., "Aggregation, Dividend Irrelevancy, and Earnings-Value Relations", *Contemporary Accounting Research* 22 (2): 453–480, 2000.

2

Theory of Cost Behaviour

Management accounting contains a number of decisionmaking tools that require the conversion of all operating costs and expenses into fixed and variable components. The responsibility for providing this cost behaviour information falls squarely upon the shoulders of the management accountant

The identification and measurement of fixed and variable costs is somewhat complicated by the fact that some costs are fixed or variable at the discretion of management, while other costs are not. In order to exercise this control, management also needs a solid understanding of the nature of cost behaviour.

In management accounting, the classification and measurement of fixed and variable cost is based on a body of knowledge that involves a number of assumptions. In many cases, the usefulness of fixed and variable cost data depends on the validity of these assumptions. In order to avoid poor operating results and faulty decisionmaking that is likely to occur when false cost assumptions are made, the ability to recognise and measure cost behaviour is essential.

Management Accounting Theory

The most volatile variable in any business is volume; that is, units produced or units sold. A change in volume has an immediate impact on variable costs. Variable costs are those costs that increase or decrease with corresponding changes in volume. However, the exact relationship between total variable cost and volume in practice is not always easy to describe or measure.

In management accounting theory, the relationship between volume and total variable cost is presented as a continuous linear function; that is, a straight line when plotted on a graph. In economic theory, the relationship is assumed to be curvilinear. The assumption of a curvilinear relationship is probably more realistic; however, there are special reasons why the relationship is assumed linear. At this point, you should keep in mind that all management accounting models requiring fixed and variable cost data assume that the relationship between total cost and volume is direct and proportionate; that is, on a graph the relationship is seen as a straight-line.

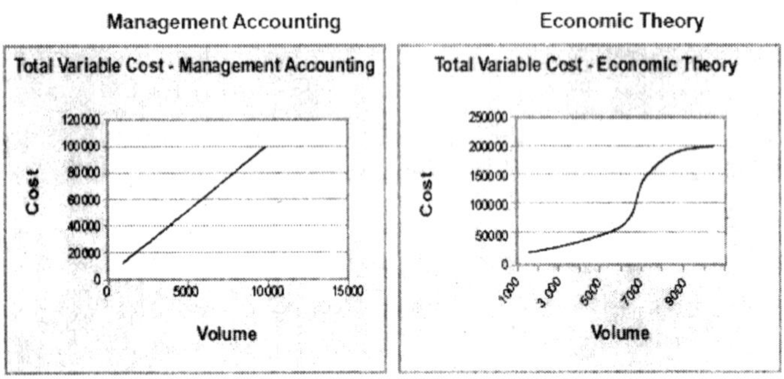

Figure 1

Variable costs are those costs that increase or decrease in direct proportion to changes in activity or volume. Variable costs are caused by activity. In other words, at zero activity there would be no variable costs. Some typical examples of variable costs and expenses directly resulting from either production or sales activity would include the following:

Table 1.

TabManufacturing Variable Costs	*Selling Variable Expenses*
Material used	Commissions
Direct labor	Supplies
Manufacturing overhead	Salesmen travel expense
Utilities for machines	Packaging
Supplies	Travel

The ability to identify and measure variable costs from historical cost data is often important. The measurement of variable cost is enhanced by an understanding of why some costs are variable in nature. Variable costs increase or decrease with activity because there is a fixed relationship between a single unit of output and certain physical and cost factors. For example, assume that a furniture manufacturer makes a table consisting of four 30" legs and a plywood top measuring 3'x 5'. Each leg costs $2 and the plywood top can be purchased for $4.00. Therefore, due to the material design specifications of the table, the material cost of each table manufactured is $12(4 legs x $2 + $4 for top). Assuming production increments of 100, at different levels of production total material cost would be:

Table 2.

Production	*Cost per Unit*	*Total Material Cost*
100	$12	$1,200
200	$12	$2,400
300	$12	$3,600
400	$12	$4,800

Notice that the increase in total cost is directly proportionate to the increase in volume. For example, an increase from 200 to 400 units (a 100% increase) would result in a corresponding 100% increase in total cost. The physical material specifcations of the table design create a fixed relationship between a unit of product (the table) and the amount of material used. As unusual as it may sound, it is this fixed relationship that causes the direct variability of cost. For other types of variable costs such as direct labor, there are similar fixed relationships.

PRESENTING COST BEHAVIOUR

The concept of variable cost is obviously important to both accountants and management. Communication of cost behaviour from the accountant to management is also critically important. The presentation of cost behaviour may be done in three ways: tabular, mathematical, and graphical.

Tabular presentation: A common method is to present cost behaviour in the form of a table. The advantage of this method is that the variable cost at set intervals of activity can be seen without first doing any math. However, some computations are necessary when cost is needed at an activity level for which a special column does not exist.

Mathematical Presentation: Because in management accounting the relationship between variable cost and volume is assumed, linear total variable cost may be defend by the following equation:

$$TVC = V(Q) \tag{1}$$

Where:

V = variable cost rate and Q = quantity. Mathematically, TVC represents the dependent variable and Q or quantity represents the independent variable. Mathematically speaking, V may be called the constant of variation.

Let V = \$12 and Q = 1,000 Then TVC = 12(1,000) = \$12,000

Given a rate of \$12 per unit and at a volume of 1,000, total variable cost is \$12,000.

Total variable cost is completely determined by the variable cost rate and the level of activity. Given a specified value for V, total variable cost for any level of activity can be easily computed.

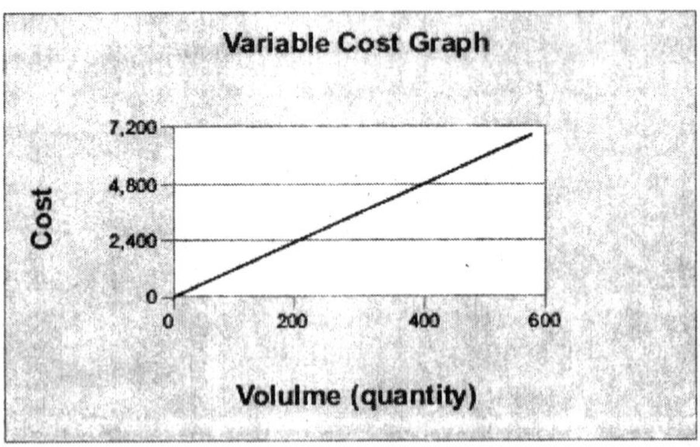

Figure 2

The key to understanding variable cost behaviour is a knowledge of *V*, the variable cost rate. *V* represents the average variable cost rate. The major assumption underlying the equation, $TVC = V(Q)$, is that regardless of the level of activity the average variable cost rate will remain the same. From this assumption results the linear relationship between volume and total variable costs.

Graphical Presentation: The behaviour of variable cost can be illustrated graphically. As true of all mathematical equations, by assigning different values to *Q*, the independent variable, the resulting dependent values can be plotted on a graph.

In Figure 3, the relationship between volume and variable cost is shown in tabular form. In many cases, management prefers to see costs is this fashion. However, the graphical portrayal is more effective in demonstrating the theoretical nature of variable costs from a management accounting viewpoint. The increase in cost resulting from increases in volume can easily be visualized. It is interesting to note that *V*, the variable cost rate, from a mathematical viewpoint measures the slope of the total variable cost line. The greater the value of *V* the steeper the slope. The affect on slope of the line for different values of *V* is illustrated in Figure 3. As the rate increases, the slope also become steeper.

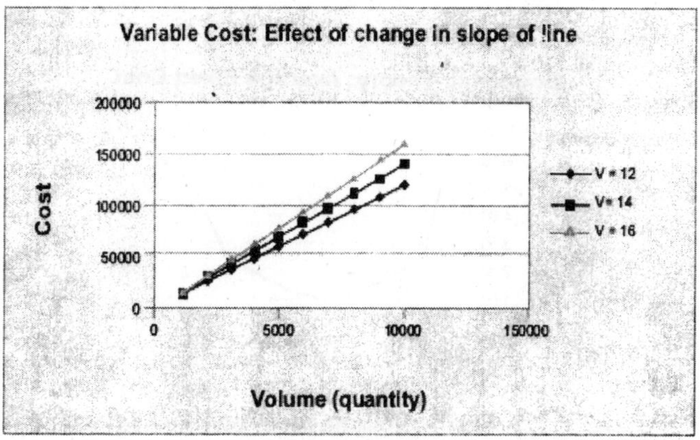

Figure 3

As explained previously, V may be interpreted as the average variable cost rate. One method of computing V is to divide the total variable cost by the related level of activity; that is, $AVC = TVC / Q$. Graphically, average variable cost may be illustrated as shown in Figure 4.

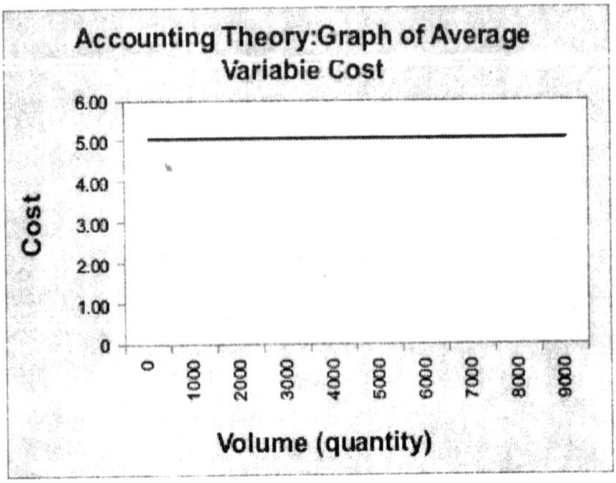

Figure 4A

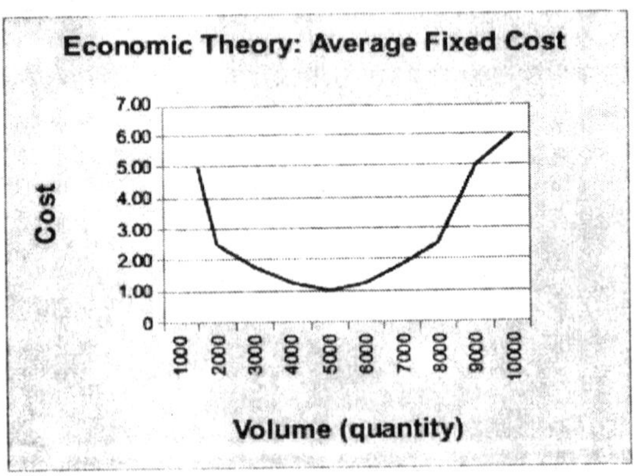

Figure 4B

Graph A visually illustrates an important management accounting assumption concerning variable cost: changes in volume have no effect on the average variable cost rate. In contrast, the average variable cost curve in economic theory is presented as a U-shaped curve as illustrated in Figure 4B.

Variable Cost Rate Components: Variable costs can be discussed at two levels: the aggregate and micro levels. At the aggregate level, *V* represents the sum of the individual variable costs rates. Variable costs/expenses are commonly classified as material, labor, overhead, selling, and administrative. Consequently, from a micro or analytical viewpoint, *V* is the aggregate of these individual rates. Mathematically, the average variable cost rate or *V* may be defend as:

$$V = V^{m} + V^{l} + V^{o} + V^{s} + V^{a}$$

Where:

V^m variable material cost rate

v^l variable labor cost rate

v^o variable overhead rate

v^s variable selling expense rate

v^a variable administrative rate

In theory the variable cost rate, or *V*, also may be computed from historical data by dividing the total variable cost by the related level of activity; that is, from a macro point of view $V = TVC / Q$. However, in practice the computation of *V* in this manner is not always easy. Very seldom is the total variable cost known without considerable analysis of cost data at a subclassifcation or micro level. The computation of *V* is, therefore, likely to be preceded by an analysis of variable cost in terms of material, labor, manufacturing overhead, selling, and administrative costs. After measurement of the individual rates, the aggregate rate is simply the sum of the individual variable cost rates.

Illustration of Using Cost Behaviour

The management of K. L. Widget Company is considering closing out a plant that has been operating at a loss. Management is tentatively planning to increase advertising and certain other fixed expenses that should increase sales to $300,000 or 15,000 units. The selling price of the Widget is currently $20.00. Fixed expenses including the proposed increases is $110,000.

Variable costs have been determined to be:

Material (V^m)	$5
Labor (V^l)	$3
Variable M/O (V^o)	$1
Selling (V^s)	$3
Administrative (V^a)	$1

Managerial Decisions and Variable Costs

An important point that needs understanding is that some costs are not inherently fixed or variable but become one or the other by management exercising its decision-making powers. Management has the discretionary power to make some costs either variable or fixed. For example, sales people compensation can be either fixed or variable. If management decides to reward sales people on the basis of a commission, then sales people's compensation is variable. If the basis for rewarding sales effort is a salary, then sales people's compensation is a fixed expense. If factory workers are paid a wage rate, then factory workers' compensation is variable. The decision to pay workers a salary would make the factory labor compensation a fixed cost in the short- run.

Some expenditures are unavoidably variable. For example, the direct use of material will always be a variable cost. However, this per unit cost of material is to a large extent controllable by the decision-making powers of management. The total material variable cost may be defend by the equation:

$$TVMC = V^m(Q) \qquad (2)$$

In this equation V^m represents the variable material cost rate. V^m is the amount of material cost incurred per unit of product manufactured. The variable material rate, V^m; however, is the result of two factors: units of material per unit of product and the cost per unit of material. For example, if a product requires 6 units of material and the material cost per unit is $2, then the material variable cost rate would be $12. V^m, then, may be defned by the following equation:

$$V^m = U^m \times C^m$$

Where:

U^m = number of units of material and C^m = cost per unit of material.

As this example illustrates, the number of units and the cost per unit are, within limits, controllable by management. For example, in the manufacture of furniture the variable cost rate for material could be decreased by the decision to use less material.

Management might use 1/2 inch wood rather than 3/4 inch. Also management could lower the variable cost rate by deciding to purchase from another seller of material whose price is lower or management might decide to use a lower quality material such as particle board.

As will be explained later, the average variable cost can be computed from historical data, however, you should remember that at any given moment management can change the variable cost rate by making decisions directly affecting the physical and cost factors that determined the variable cost rate.

Another example of an cost that is unavoidably variable is direct labor when the method of compensation is a wage rate. The equation for direct labor is:

$$TVLC = V^L(Q) \tag{3}$$

In this equation, V^L represents the variable labor cost rate. It is the dollar amount of labor incurred each time one unit of product is manufactured. As in the case of material, V^L is the result of two factors– labor hours per product and the wage rate. For example, if a product requires two hours of labor and the wage rate is $10 per hour, then the variable direct labor rate would be $20. V^L then may be defend by the following equation:

$$V^L = H^L \times R^L$$

Where:

H^L denotes the standard hours per product and R^L the wage rate. The important principle to remember is that for most types of variable costs, the factors that determine the variable cost rates can be identified. Furthermore, in all cases these fixed factors, within limits, can be changed by explicit decisions on the part of management. In addition, management's ability to affect the magnitude of the variable cost rates through decisionmaking is also revealed. For example, management may be able to reduce the variable cost rate for material by finding a supplier willing to sell the same grade of material at a lower price.

Variable Cost Behaviour and Linearity

In management accounting, the relationship between activity and total variable cost is assumed to be linear. There are several reasons for this assumption.

First, mathematical equations involving curvilinear relationships can be quite complex. Furthermore, fitting cost data to nonlinear equations may be difficult. Although the use of nonlinear equations may be preferable, the use of linear equations which are much easier to use has been found to be useful.

Also, in many cases, actual cost behaviour for a significant portion of the activity range tends to be linear. The use of standard measurements and automated equipment in many cases results in a uniform rate of output. Within a relevant range of activity, the cost per unit of output is the same. Consequently, the use of linear relationships in management accounting is justified only in what is called the "relevant range of activity." If the cost per unit of output sharply changes outside of this range of activity.

Management Accounting Theory of Fixed Costs

In order to be used, many management accounting decision-making models explicitly require that all costs be classified as either fixed or variable. On the surface, it would appear that the measurement and use of fixed costs is fairly simple matter. After variable costs have been measured, the remaining costs may be treated as fixed. However, the very nature of fixed costs presents conceptual problems that far exceeds those pertaining to variable costs.

While direct material and direct labor are variable in nature, manufacturing overhead may be both variable and fixed. The accounting for fixed costs is at the same time a problem of accounting for manufacturing overhead. An understanding of fixed manufacturing overhead also requires an understanding of the concepts underlying the setting of fixed overhead rates. Because of the complexity of accounting for fixed manufacturing costs, two theories exist, absorption costing and direct costing. These two approaches treat fixed manufacturing overhead quite differently.

Fixed costs provide capacity to manufacture or to sell. When actual activity is less than capacity available, a major problem exist. Theoretically, the portion of unused capacity cost should be measured as idle capacity cost and not treated as a production cost. In practice, many firms do not measure idle capacity cost. The consequence is that the per unit cost of goods manufactured varies significantly with the percentage of capacity utilized. For example, assume that the fixed cost of the K. L. Widget Manufacturing Company is $10,000, and that the firm has the capacity to manufacture 10,000 units. When the firm manufactures 1,000 units, the cost per unit is $10. However, when only 500 units are manufactured the cost per unit is $20 and when volume is 10,000 the cost is $1 per unit

A second serious problem exists concerning the measurement of fixed costs. The term "fixed" costs implies that changes in volume have no effect on the costs classified as such. Certain management accounting models previously identified in this book are based on the assumption that the costs identified as fixed hold constant over a range of activity. However, the assumption that these costs remain constant from zero activity to the limit of capacity is not always true.

In reality, costs defend as fixed seldom hold constant over the entire range of activity. Only in very small businesses with limited changes in activity would some fixed costs not vary. In most businesses, and in large businesses in particular, fixed costs classified as fixed in management accounting are actually step cost. When significant increases in activity occur, additional staff, equipment, and other resources involving fixed costs must be acquired.

A graphical illustration of fixed and step cost is shown in Figure 5 (A and B).

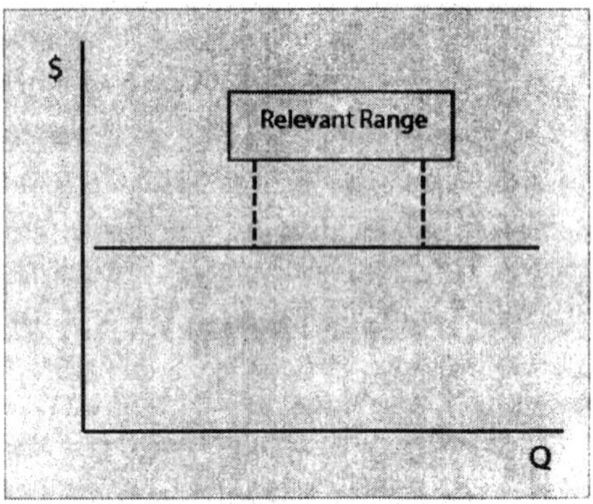

Figure 5A. Fixed

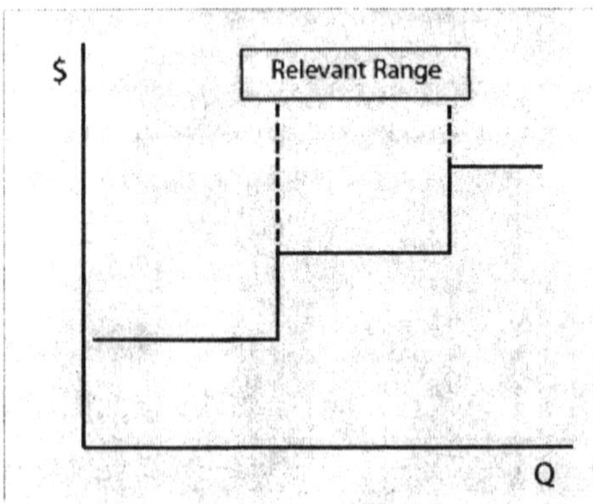

Figure 5B. Step

Despite the more realistic portrayal in Figure 5B, fixed costs are usually illustrated as shown in Figure 5A. To justify the assumption of non variation of fixed costs, the concept of the relevant range is used. As long as activity remains within the relevant range, no harm is done by portraying step costs as fixed over the entire range of activity. The relevant range may be defend as that range of activity in which actual sales or production are likely to occur. Outside of this range, fixed costs on the lower end of volume are smaller and outside of the high end of the relevant range fixed costs are higher. However, the magnitude of these costs outside the relevant range is not likely to be known; and even if known, they are irrelevant.

Another interesting aspect of fixed costs is that as soon as fixed costs exist, a business automatically has a break even point. Conceptually, no business can report net income until all fixed costs have been covered.

Fixed costs are those cost that do not change with increases or decreases in volume, that is, sales or production. In the short run, fixed costs such as rent and salaries remain the same regardless of the level of activity. Fixed costs, unlike variable costs which relate to activity, are time-related costs. For example, rent is always for a period of time such as a month or year. Likewise salaries also relate to a period of time such as a month or year. Consequently, fixed costs are commonly called period charges because these costs expire in the same time period in which they are incurred.

While variable costs are incurred directly as activity takes place, fixed costs are incurred in anticipation of providing services for an estimated level of activity, and, consequently, the expenditure is contractually made or committed prior to actual activity. Fixed cost expenditures are determined prior to the period of activity for a defend quantity of service potential. Building rent, for example, refects the right to use a defned amount of foor space. The lease of equipment provides the right to a defned number of operating hours per period. Fixed cost expenditures are then capacity costs. An understanding of fixed costs requires an understanding of the different facets of capacity. Fixed costs, therefore, make a range of production activity possible.

The term capacity in the singular is somewhat misleading. Rather than use the term "capacity", a more accurate statement would be that fixed costs provide the "capacities" to produce. Each type of fixed cost provides a different capacity service and, unless management has exercised exceptional care in planning, the capacity related to each cost might not be in balance. Imbalance in capacities created by fixed costs can create bottlenecks or constraints in both production and sales.

Fixed costs are those expenditures that are not caused by activity but rather make activity or production possible. Fixed cost provide both the ability or capacity to manufacture and also determine the limits to production. For example, without the services provided by buildings, equipment, and supervision production could not take place. Expenditures for fixed costs represent the acquisition of the various capacities necessary for actual activity to take place.

The K. L. Widget Company has 15 machines capable of producing a total of 15,000 units per quarter. One production supervisor is required for every 5 machines. Currently two supervisors are each paid a $10,000 salary. Five machines are not in use because of a lack of a supervisor. The building which the company rents has enough space to hold 20 machines. Consequently, the company has a machine capacity of 15,000 units while it has supervision capacity of 10,000 units. The building space capacity is adequate to manufacture 20,000 units.

This example illustrates that different types of fixed costs provide different types of production services each of which provides a different capacity level. In this example, there are three capacities: machine, supervision, and space. A major concern of management is to have a balance or equality among the different ranges of capacity services. Also, in this example, each type of fixed cost provide different output limits. Actual production is limited to the lower of the three levels. Furthermore, production cannot exceed 10,000 units, even though machine and space capacity is larger. A major responsibility of management is to make those fixed cost decisions that create a balance among the different types of capacity services.

In contrast to variable costs, fixed costs expire with the passing of time. Fixed costs are expenditures that contractually provide services for a defned period of time. At the end of the contract period, the services are no longer available without a new contract or time commitment of resources by management.

For example, the decision to rent ten automobiles for a year provides management with transportation services for a year. If one auto has the potential to be driven 200 miles a day, then ten autos for a year provide a capacity of 730,000 miles (200 x 365 x 10). At the end of the year, the year's purchase of transportation has fully expired.

The unused portion of miles driven cannot be transferred to the next year. The rent expenditure for autos is the same whether or not the potential services are used. The passing of each day proportionately reduces the service potential regardless of whether activity is ongoing.

Inherent in the nature of fixed cost is the potential for idle capacity. Consequently, from a management accounting viewpoint, the measurement of idle capacity is important. The cost of idle capacity cannot be transferred to another period in the manner in which unused material can be stored and used in a later period. The constant relationship between fixed costs and capacity or volume can be explained and illustrated from three points of view: tabular, mathematical, and graphical.

Tabular Presentation: The presentation of fixed costs in a table at different levels of activity is basically unnecessary for the reason that regardless of the level of activity the cost is the same. However, for illustrative purposes, a simple table of fixed costs will be presented for three types of fixed costs common in all manufacturing businesses:

Mathematical Presentation: Fixed costs may be defned mathematically in terms of total costs and in terms of average cost. On a total cost basis, volume or quantity, Q, is not a determining factor; however, for average cost quantity or Q is the important factor in the equation. Total fixed cost may be mathematically defned:

$$TFC = F \qquad (4)$$

Where:

TFC represents total fixed cost and F is the amount or magnitude of fixed costs for a given period of time such as a quarter or a year.

The interpretation of this equation is that regardless of the level of activity, the amount of fixed cost is totally independent of actual quantity. The importance of defining fixed cost mathematically as presented in the above equation will be appreciated in a later section when fixed and variable cost are combined in a total cost equation.

For some decisions such as price, a knowledge of cost per unit or average cost is very important. Mathematically, average fixed cost may be defned as follows:

$$AFC = F/Q \tag{5}$$

Where: *AFC* represent average fixed cost and *Q* is the current level of activity; that is, units manufactured or units sold. In the following section, the importance of average fixed cost will be discussed and illustrated.

Graphical Presentation - The behaviour of both total fixed cost and average fixed cost can be effectively illustrated graphically. In the following illustration, *TFC* and *AFC* are dependent variables while quantity or *Q* is the independent variable concerning the computation of average fixed cost. Consequently, values assigned to *Q* for *TFC* and *AFC* can be plotted graphically. To illustrate, assume that fixed cost is $10,000 and activity increases in increments of 100. The following graphs may be drawn:

These graphs effectively display the relationship of volume to total costs. In the case of total fixed costs, there is no effect or change. However, regarding average fixed cost, the opposite is true. As quantity increases, the average fixed costs becomes less. The effect of different levels of quantity on average fixed cost is extremely important and requires an in-depth understanding. Without a complete understanding of the impact of different capacity levels on average fixed costs, poor decisions e.g., the pricing decision, could have severe proftability consequences.

Fixed Cost Components: As the case for variable costs, fixed costs can be analyzed at two levels: the aggregate level and the micro level. At the aggregate level, *F* represents the sum of all the individual fixed costs. Fixed costs can be divided into subclassifcation levels: labor, manufacturing overhead, selling, and administrative. From a micro or analytical viewpoint, *F* is the aggregate of these individual rates. Mathematically, then *F* may be defned as:

$$F = F^{l} + F^{o} + F^{s} + F^{a} \tag{6}$$

Where:

F^L - fixed labor cost

F^s - fixed selling expenses

F^o - fixed overhead costs

F^a - fixed administrative expenses

In practice, the amount of total fixed cost, *F*, will simply be the sum of the individual fixed cost elements.

Management Control of Fixed Costs: An important point that must be understood by both management and management accountants is that fixed costs are subject to a high degree of control. The management accountant as well as management must understand the consequences of making a cost fixed or variable. In order to understand the consequences of decisions that convert variable costs to fixed costs, a more detailed discussion of capacity is required.

To illustrate the importance of the decision to make a cost either fixed or variable, the following example is presented.

The Acme Retail Company is a new retail company. Ten sales people are required to sell the product. The sales forecast indicates that average sales per sales person should be $200,000. Management is contemplating a 10% commission versus a salary of $20,000. How should sales people be compensated?

This is not an easy decision. There are important cost and psychological factors involved. A commission is likely to motivate sales people, but at the same time for an individual inexperienced sales person, the inability to attain sufficient sales may result in discouragement and thus quitting. Sales people content with a salary of $20,000 may never be tempted to quit, but because of the lack of motivation may never reach their quota. If sales due to a recession or competition decreases, then the sales people's compensation remains the same. With a commission, a decrease in sales would be accompanied with a proportionate decrease in compensation. A fixed salary would increase the risk of operating at a loss, but in times of prosperity and easy sales, compensation of sales people on a salary basis might maximize net income. In practice, management often compromises by paying sales people a combination of salary and commission.

As another example, management might be able to control the nature of costs by changing the type of equipment. Current production equipment that now requires a high degree of direct labor might be replace with automated equipment that requires considerable less direct labor and more indirect labor. For example, in many companies computerized tooling and machining equipment have replaced direct labor. The effect on cost behaviour has been a shift from a variable cost to a fixed cost.

Control over Capacity Limits: As true of variable costs, fixed costs are also subject to the decision-making powers of management. Fixed costs and their related capacities provide some difficult choices concerning the amount of capacity that is available at any given time. The greater the expenditure the greater the capacity. For example, the lease on a medium size computer might be \$500 per month, but for a larger computer the cost might be \$1,500. The capacity of the larger machine might be five times greater. However, now only the smaller machine is needed. Would management be better off to invest in the larger machine in anticipation of growth? For the short run, profits might be less, but in the long run profits might be greater, if the machine with the greater capacity is purchased.

Definition of Capacity: A major task of management is to manage the level of expenditures for fixed cost; that is, to make decisions determining the capacity to manufacture and to sell. Therefore, a major question is: what is capacity? This concept is without question the most important concept related to fixed cost. Unfortunately, the concept is elusive and very difficult to define quantitatively. In cost accounting, various degrees of capacity are recognized and defned: theoretical, practical, normal, and expected actual. In a general sense, capacity refers to the maximum number of units that can be manufactured in a given time period. However, this concept of capacity is a flexible quantity when such factors as overtime, employee training, second shifts, speed of equipment, holidays, and vacations are taken into account.

In management accounting, capacity is a strictly a short-run notion that imposes limits on sales and production capacity. Consequently, any increase in the spending for fixed manufacturing costs will normally increase capacity. For example, the leasing of additional equipment or the hiring of an additional production supervisor will increase capacity. In this sense, the short run is that length of time in which expenditures cannot be immediately increased.

Other costs such as rent are inherently time-oriented and, consequently, fixed in nature. The production services provided do not easily, if at all, divide into small discrete units. Material, for example, is easily divided and associated with individual units; however, the services of a manufacturing plant, is not easily unitized and allocated to individual units of finished product. The major problem created by fixed costs is that for costing and pricing purposes fixed costs must be converted to a per unit basis. Various methods of unitizing fixed costs have been developed including various allocation and overhead rate methodologies. The following table indicates some possible bases for allocation of various types of fixed costs.

Table 3

Cost Item	*Service Provided*	*Basis of Allocation*
Building rent	Shelter, protection	Space
Equipment	Processing of material	Direct labor hours
Indirect labor	Supervisor	Number of workers
Insurance	Financial protection	Value of equipment
Computer Cost	Processing time	CPU time
Staff	E.g., secretarial services	Hours of service
Utilities	Lighting	Floor space
Preventive maintenance	Efficiency and safety	Value of equipment

TOTAL FIXED AND VARIABLE COSTS

Based on the above discussions, we have arrived at a point where we can now talk about total fixed and variable costs. For the moment, we will assume that in a given operating period production equals sales. Therefore, the problems associated with inventory increasing or decreasing from period to period can be avoided. Given this assumption, we can now define total costs by the following equation:

$$TC = F + V(Q) \tag{7}$$

Where:

TC	total cost
V	variable cost rate
Q	quantity
F	fixed cost

Given that we know *V*, the variable cost rate and *F*, the amount of total fixed cost, we are able to compute total cost at any level of activity. For example, if we assume that $V = \$10.00$ and $F = \$100{,}000$, then total fixed cost at different assumed levels of activity would be as shown in the following table. The change in costs is due to the increase in the variable costs. The change in activity had no affect on total fixed cost. If fixed costs change, it is because of the change in some other factor than volume, for example, an increase in monthly rent of equipment.

Table 4

Volume	*V*	*TVC*	*F*	*TC*
10,000	$10.00	$100,000	$100.000	$200,000
20,000	$10.00	$200,000	$100.000	$300,000
30.000	$10.00	$300,000	$100.000	$400.000
40.000	$10.00	$400,000	$100,000	$500,000

Total costs can sometimes be better understood when presented graphically as shown in Figure 6 and Figure 7.

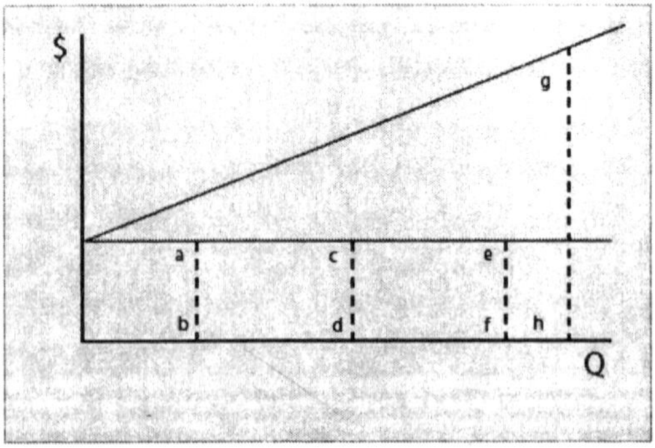

Figure 6. Total Variable and Fixed Cost

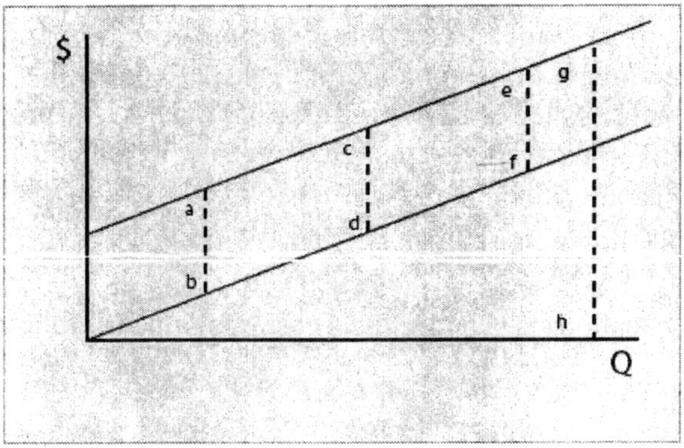

Figure 7. Total Fixed and Variable Cost

In Figure 6, fixed cost is shown first and the distances a - b, c - d, and e - f are the same at their respective volume. In this graph, the fixed nature of fixed costs is easily grasped. Line g - h represents total fixed and variable cost.

Total cost may also be defned as follow:

$$TC = V(Q) + F \tag{8}$$

In this equation, we start with total variable cost and add to this amount total fixed cost. It might seem trivial whether we define total cost using equation 7 or equation 8. However, the two equations are quite different when it comes to showing total cost graphically.

Figure 6 is easier to understand because the top line of the fixed cost is horizontal. However, it is not the line that is fixed in amount but rather the distance from the horizontal line as shown in Figure 6 to the base line that is fixed. As shown in Figure 7, the lines a - b, c d and equal in length, and are also the same length as the same lines in Figure 6. Line g - h in Figure 7 represents total cost and is the same as line g - h in Figure6.

It would seem that it is irrelevant which graph is used to portray fixed and variable costs. Figure 6 which shows the top line of total fixed cost as a horizontal line might be to be the preferred method. However, in fact, this is not the case. The preferred method is to graphically show fixed and variable cost as shown in Figure7.

Average Total Cost

The use of averages to communicate information and greater understanding is quite common in business, economics, and also government issued statistics. Relationships are often easier to understand when averages are used. For example, rather than say that disposable net income in the USA is $600,000,000,000, it is easy to understand if one were to say that the average disposable income per person in the USA is $20,000 per person.

In equation (5), average fixed cost was defned as follows:

$$AFC = F/Q$$

It is also possible to defne average variable cost as follows:

$$AVC = V(Q)/Q = V \qquad (9)$$

Consequently, average total cost now may be defned mathematically as follows:

$$AVC = V + F/Q$$

To illustrate, assume the following data:

$$V = \$10{,}000 \; F = \$200{,}000$$

Now at volumes of 10,000, 20,000, 30,000, and 40,000 we get the following results.

Table 5

Volume	*Variable Cost Rate*	*Average Fixed Cost*	*Average Total Cost*
10,000	$10.00	$20.00	$30.00
20,000	$10.00	$10.00	$20.00
30,000	$10.00	$6.67	$16.67
40,000	$10.00	$5.00	$15.00

The above analysis reveals a very important business principle. The cost of a product per unit is highly dependent on volume when the fixed cost in a business represents a major portion of the total cost. As volume (production) increases, the total cost per unit of output decreases and as the volume decreases the total cost per unit of output increases. In modern business where fixed costs tend to be very high relative to variable costs, the key to getting a low production cost per unit is to have a high volume of production and sales. Many products in our modern economy are available to consumers as a whole only because of mass production.

Since the middle of the 19th century, in large businesses the fixed costs of production have become dominant while the variable costs associated with materials and labor have decreased significantly in total amounts. This shift in costs where fixed costs are significantly greater percentage wise means that the break even point in these businesses have become much greater. Consequently, a high volume of sales and production is required first to break even and secondly, required to make a reasonable profit. The benefit to customers is that at high volumes the cost per unit becomes relatively low. Therefore, because of this fact, it is absolutely critical that management has a good understanding of average fixed and average variable cost.

Like total fixed and variable cost, average fixed and variable cost may be presented graphically.

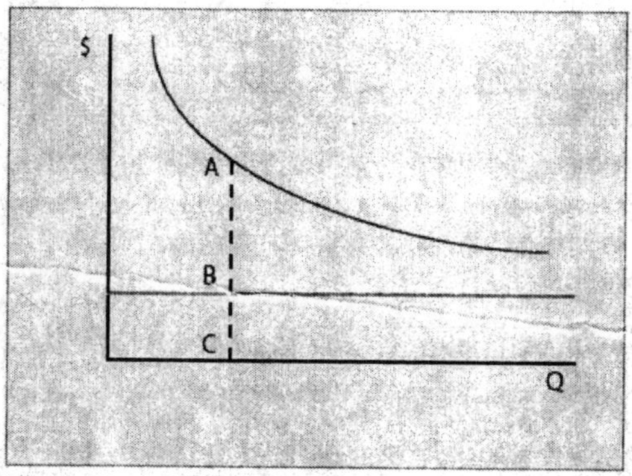

Figure 8.

In the above graph (Graph A), line B - C represents average variable cost and line A - B represents average fixed cost. Line A - C then represents total average cost. This graph portrays effectively that as volume increases the total average cost of the product decreases. The consequence of operating at less than full capacity is a much higher per unit cost of the product.

As with total fixed and variable cost, it is possible to present a graph where average fixed cost is shown first and average variable cost is shown as an addition to average fixed cost.

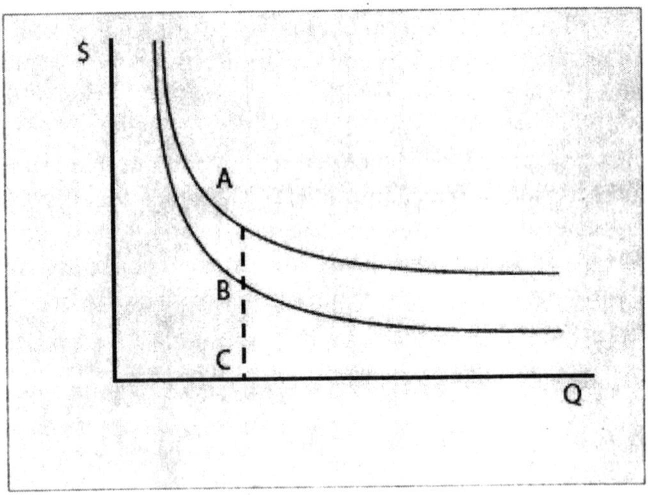

Figure 9.

In Figure 9, graph B, we again show average fixed and variable cost. As before, line A - C represents total average cost. However, now line B - C represents average fixed cost whereas in graph A line B - C represents average variable cost. Similarly, in Figure 9 now line A - B represents average variable cost.

Strange as it may sound, it is correct to say that in terms of average costs, it is the variable costs that are constant and the fixed costs that are variable. Increases in volume have no effect on the average variable cost, but do decrease the average fixed cost with each successive increase in volume.

REFERENCES

Ross, Stephen A., "The Capital Asset Pricing Model (CAPM), Short-sale Restrictions and Related Issues," *Journal of Finance*, 32 (177), 1977.

______________, Westerfield, and Jordan, *Fundamentals of Corporate Finance*, Irwin, 1991.

Seitz, Neil E. and Mitch Ellison, *Capital Budgeting and Long-term Financing Decisions*, TX: Dryden Press, 1995.

Tobin, James, *Liquidity preference as behavior towards risk*, The Review of Economic Studies, 25, 1958.

3

Classification of Manufacturing Costs

Management accounting, as previously explained, consists primarily of planning, performance evaluation, and decisionmaking models useful to management in making better decisions. In every case, these tools require cost and revenue information. A basic assumption of management accounting is that it is the responsibility of the management accountant to provide the needed cost and revenue information.

In management accounting, as in financial accounting, it may be said that a major building block in the conceptual foundation is cost. Both the financial and management accountant must have a sound understanding of the varied and complex ramifications of cost. From a financial accounting viewpoint, a faulty understanding of cost may cause financial statements to be incorrectly prepared.

There are two broad aspect of the term cost that needs to be understood: cost classification and cost behaviour. Cost classification refers to the separation of costs into categories for proper preparation of financial statements or for use in decision making models. Cost behaviour refers to the effect that volume has on total expenses or costs.

Cost Classification

In accounting, the term cost refers to the expenditure or sacrifice made to acquire something of value. In financial accounting, all transactions are recorded in terms of historical cost; that is, the money expended or to be expended at the date of the transaction. The monetary value associated with an asset acquired is said to be its cost. Cost is the sacrifice made in resources to acquire another resource. Cost is measured in monetary units which in the United States is the dollar.

Depending on the type of activity and the passage of time, the cost of an asset in accounting can be classified in several ways. Proper financial reporting and correct decisionmaking require an understanding of the different ways in which costs can be classified.

For purposes of management accounting, there are three important dual classifications of cost that require some understanding: Expired and unexpired, manufacturing and non manufacturing, and fixed and variable. These three classifications are somewhat interrelated, particularly concerning financial statements.

Expired and Unexpired Costs

Expired costs or expenses are the used up value of assets. Expired costs are always shown on the income statement as deductions from revenue. Expired costs may be thought of as that portion of the asset value benefiting current operations. It is helpful to think of expired costs as former assets values.

Manufacturing Costs/Expenses

Technically, there is a difference between a manufacturing cost and a manufacturing expense. The term manufacturing costs usually refers to material used, direct labor incurred, and overhead incurred in a manufacturing business. Material used, direct labor, and manufacturing overhead at the time incurred are not expenses; rather they incurred costs. In the manufacturing process, material, labor, and overhead do not expire; rather through manufacturing activity they become transformed from one type of utility to another.

In a manufacturing business, the accountant will debit work in process for materials used, direct labor incurred, and manufacturing overhead. Since work in process is an asset account, it would not be logical to regard material used, direct labor, and manufacturing overhead as expenses.

Manufacturing costs, however, do eventually become manufacturing expenses Material used, direct labor incurred, and manufacturing overhead are first recorded in inventory accounts and then become an expense when finished goods are sold. In a manufacturing business, only the cost of goods sold account can properly be called a manufacturing expense. In order to understand the transformation of manufacturing costs into manufacturing expenses, you should fully understand the flow of cost as taught in cost accounting.

The term, variable cost, then primarily refers to the manufacturing costs that are refected in the inventory accounts: materials, work in process, and finished goods. The term, variable expenses, refers to cost of goods sold and to other variable non manufacturing expenses such as sales people's commissions. Some writers use the term variable costs to include variable expenses. The technical difference is ignored because the theory underlying the use of variable expenses is the same as for variable costs.

There is one instance in which manufacturing costs and manufacturing expenses are the same in amount. When sales equal production, that is, all units manufactured are sold, then manufacturing costs and the manufacturing expense are equal. Under these conditions, all manufacturing costs including fixed manufacturing overhead incurred will be included in cost of goods sold.

In terms of financial statements, manufacturing costs appear on the cost of goods manufactured statement while manufacturing expenses are shown on the income statement. However, the amount of manufacturing costs are not necessarily reported on the income statement in the period incurred.

Manufacturing and Non Manufacturing Costs

The distinction between manufacturing and non manufacturing costs is important because this dual classification is refected in different types of financial statements for the manufacturing business: the income statement and the cost of goods manufactured statement. The cost of goods manufactured statement shows all the current period manufacturing costs while the income statement shows all the current non manufacturing expenses.

Manufacturing costs may be simply defend as materials used, direct labor incurred, and manufacturing overhead incurred. These are the costs that are found on the cost of goods manufactured statement. Non manufacturing costs are those expenses commonly called selling and administrative. These are the expenditures incurred in the current period directly for the benefit of generating revenue. Non manufacturing expenses should not be included in the cost of inventory. The term is somewhat misleading because the "cost" part of the term implies unexpired costs when it fact it has reference to expenses. Since "non manufacturing costs" are, in fact, expired costs, then technically a better term would be "non manufacturing expenses."

After some costs have been classified as manufacturing, they are normally further classified as direct and indirect. Materials used in the manufacturing process are either used directly or indirectly. Direct material is material that becomes part of the finished product and, therefore, significantly adds to the weight or size of the product. If the final product, for example, is a wooden chair, then the wood used to make the legs, seat, and back is a direct use of material. Also material issued but not becoming a part of the final product and used for manufacturing objects such as saw horses or shelves to store paint or other incidental materials would be regarded as an indirect use of material.

In a similar manner, factory labor is normally classified as either direct or indirect. Consequently, two types of labor are recognised: direct factory labor and indirect factory labor. Direct factory labor is the cost of labor incurred while work is done on the product itself. Normally, in one way or another, direct labor affects the physical appearance of the product. Janitorial services, repair and maintenance service, supervision of direct workers, and computer support are examples of labor incurred that would be regarded as indirect.

The significance of classifying material and labor as an indirect cost is this: indirect material and indirect factory labor are recorded as manufacturing overhead and, therefore, becomes a part of the cost of the final product through the use of overhead rates.

Although the classification of costs as manufacturing and non manufacturing is very important in preparing financial statements, this distinction is not essential from a decisionmaking viewpoint. The important point is that the tools of management accounting are equally important in both categories of cost. Important decisions in both areas can benefit from the use of management accounting tools.

Fixed and Variable Cost

The most volatile variable in a business is considered to be volume. A fundamental fact of all businesses is that some costs change with changes in volume. The costs or expenses that change with volume are called variable while those that do not change with changes in activity are called fixed. The classification of costs as fixed and variable is by far the most useful and helpful classification of costs in management accounting.

Some decisions such as a decrease in price or an increase in advertising can have an immediate impact on volume. In most instances, management will want to test decisions before execution. In management accounting, a number of planning, evaluating, and decisionmaking models have been developed to account for the effect that a change in volume has on total costs. The decisionmaking models in this text that require fixed and variable costs inputs are: cost volume profit, direct costing, fexible budgeting, variance analysis, and profit planning. Other tools such as incremental analysis and present value models may benefit from a classification and measurement of costs as fixed and variable.

The detailed study of fixed and variable costs in management accounting is commonly called the study of cost behaviour. Since cost behaviour, or the study of fixed and variable costs, is so fundamental to many management accounting tools, it represents the first area of management accounting that must be studied in depth.

References

Carmichael, Shenna, *Business Ethics: The New Bottom Line*, London: Demos, 1995.

Emery and Finnerty, *Principles of Finance with Corporate Applications*, West, 1991.

Eun, Cheol S. and Bruce G. Resnick, *International Financial Management*, New York: Irwin McGraw-Hill, 1998.

4

Cost Accounting

Management accounting is very closely linked to cost accounting; so closely, in fact, that it is difficult to say where cost accounting ends and where management accounting begins. Cost accounting simply aims to measure the performance of departments, goods and services. However, management accounting is much, much more and involves:

1 *The provision or information for management*: Indeed, the role of the management accountant could well be described as that of an 'information manager'. The information generated should be designed to assist management, to control business operations and to help management with decision-making. In fulfilling this role the management accounting department/section must consult with the users of the information, i.e. management, to assess its needs in terms of precisely what information is required and when, etc. The aim is, to provide management with a flow of relevant information, e.g. reports, statements, spreadsheets, etc. as and when required. A frequent flow of information (weekly or monthly) should enable management to respond to emerging problems/situations as soon as possible. The early detection of problems means earlier solutions & early action.

2. *Advising management*: A key part of management accounting is to advise management about the economic consequences and implications of its (proposed) decisions and alternative course of action.

3. *Forecasting, planning and control*: A lot of management accounting is concerned with the future and predetermined

systems such as budgetary control and standard costing. Such systems investigate the differences (i.e. variances) which arise as a result of actual performance being different from planned performance in terms of budgets or standards. In addition, the management accountant should also be involved in strategic planning, e.g. the setting of objectives and the formulation of policy. The forecasting process will involve accounting for uncertainty (risk) via statistical techniques, such as probability, etc.

4. *Communications*: If the management accounting system is to be really effective it is essential that it goes hand in hand with a good, sound, reliable and efficient communication system. Such a system should communicate clearly by providing information in a form, which the user, i.e. managers and their subordinates, can easily understand (reports, statements, tabulations, graphs and charts). However, great care should be taken to ensure that managers do not suffer from 'information overload', i.e. having too much information much of which they could well do without.

5. *Systems*: The management accounting department/section will also be actively involved with the design of cost control systems and financial reporting systems.

6. *Flexibility*: Management accounting should be flexible enough to respond quickly to changes in the environment in which the company/organisation operates. Where necessary information/ systems should be amended/modified. Thus, there is a need for the management accounting section/ department to be involved with the monitoring of the environment on a continuing basis.

7. *An appreciation of other business functions*: Those who provide management accounting information need to understand the role played by the other business functions. In addition to communicating effectively with other business functions, they also need to secure their cooperation and coordination, e.g. the budget preparation process relies on the existence of good communications, cooperation and coordination.

8. *Staff Education*: The management accounting department/ section needs to ensure that all the users of the information it provides, e.g. managers and their subordinates, are educated about the techniques used, their purpose and their benefits, etc.

9. *Gate keeping*: The management accounting department/ section sits at a very important information junction (Figure 1.). This gate keeping position places the management accounting section in a position of power; it has access to (can send information to and from) management and subordinates, and communicates with and receives a certain amount of information from the external environment. Its power arises because it can control the flow of information upwards to management—or downwards to subordinates.

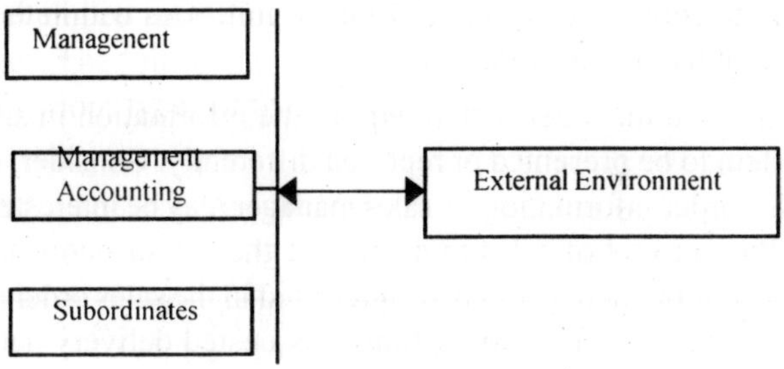

Figure 1.

10. *Limitations*: Although management accounting can, and does, provide a lot of useful information, it must be stressed that management accounting is not an exact science. A vast amount of the information generated depends upon subjective judgment, e.g. the assessment of qualitative factors or assumptions about the business environment. Management accounting is not the be all and end all of decision-making, it is just one of the tools which can help management to make more informed decisions.
11. *Being the servant*: Finally, having established that management accounting is a tool, it must be emphasized that it is there to serve the needs of management.

Accounting systems take economic events and transitions that have occurred and process the data in those transactions into information that is helpful to managers and other users, such as sales representatives and production supervisors. Processing any economic transaction entails collecting, categorising, summarising, and analysing. For example, costs are collected by cost categories (materials, labour, and shipping); summarised to determine total costs by month, quarter, or year; and analysed to evaluate how, costs have changed relative to revenues, say, from one period to the next.

Accounting systems provide information such as financial statements and performance reports. Managers use accounting information

(a) to administer each of the activity or functional areas for which they are responsible and

(b) to coordinate those activities or functions within the framework of the organisation as a whole.

Individual managers often require the information in an accounting system to be presented or reported differently. Consider, for example, sales order information. A sales manager may be interested in the total dollar amount of sales to determine the commissions to be paid. A distribution manager may be interested in the sales order quantities by geographic region and customer-requested delivery dates to ensure timely deliveries. A manufacturing manager may be interested in the quantities of various products and their" desired delivery dates to schedule production. An ideal database-sometimes called a data warehouse or inform -consists of small, detailed bits of information that can be' used for multiple purposes.

Management accounting and financial accounting have different goals. Management accounting measures and reports financial and non-financial information that helps managers make decisions to fulfil the goals of an organisation. Managers use management accounting information to choose, communicate, and implement strategy. They also use management accounting information to coordinate product design, production, and marketing decisions. Management accounting focuses on internal reporting.

Financial accounting focuses on reposing to external parties. It measures and records business transactions and provides financial statements that are based on generally accepted accounting principles (GAAP). Managers are responsible for the financial statements issued to investors, government regulators, and other parties outside the organisation. Executive compensation is often directly affected by the numbers in these financial statements. It is not difficult to see that managers are interested in both management accounting and financial accounting.

Cost accounting provides information for management accounting and financial accounting. Cost accounting measures and reports financial and no financial information relating to the cost of acquiring or utilising resources in an organisation. Cost accounting includes those parts of both management accounting and financial accounting in which cost information is collected or analysed. The internal reporting-external reporting distinction just mentioned is only one of several significant differences between-management accounting and financial accounting.

Other distinctions include management accounting's emphasis on the future-that's bud-geting-and management accounting's emphasis on influencing the behaviour of managers and employees. Another distinction is that management accounting is not nearly as restricted by GAAP as is financial accounting. For example, managers may charge interest on owners' capital to help judge a division's performance, even though such a charge is not allowable under GAAP.

Reports such as balance sheets, income statements, and statements of cash flow are common to both management accounting and financial accounting. Most companies adhere to, or only mildly depart from, GAAP for their basic internal financial statements. Why? Because accrual accounting provides a uniform way to measure an organisation's financial performance for internal and external purposes. However, management accounting is more wide-ranging than financial accounting's emphasis on financial statements.

Management accounting embraces more extensively such topics as the development and implementation of strategies and policies, budgeting, special studies and forecasts, influence on employee behaviour, and nonfinancial as well as financial information.

Cost Management and Accounting Systems

The term cost management is widely used in businesses today. Unfortunately, there is no uniform definition. We use cost management to describe the approaches and activities of managers in short-run and long run planning and control decisions that increase value for customers and lower costs of products and services. For example, managers make decisions regarding the amount and kind of material being used, changes of plant processes, and changes in product designs.

Information from accounting systems helps managers make such decisions, but the information and the accounting systems themselves are not cost management.

Cost management has a broad focus. For example, it includes but is not confined to-the continuous reduction of costs. The planning and control of costs is usually inextricably linked with revenue and profit planning. For instance, to enhance revenues and profits, managers often deliberately incur additional costs for advertising and product modifications. Cost management is not practiced in isolation. It's an integral part of general management strategies and their implementation.

Management Accounting and Financial Accounting

The 12 principal differences between management and financial accounting are described here.

1. *Necessity:* Financial accounting must be done. Enough effort must be expended to collect data in acceptable form and with an acceptable degree of accuracy to meet the requirements of the Financial Accounting Standards Board (FASB) and other outside parties, whether or not the management regards this information as useful. Management accounting, by contrast, is entirely optional, no outside agencies specify what must be done or indeed that anything need be done. Because it is optional, there is no point in collecting a piece of management accounting information unless its value to management's believed to exceed the cost of collecting it.
2. *Purpose:* The purpose of financial accounting is to produce financial statements for outside users. When the statements have been produced, this purpose has been accomplished. Management accounting information, on the other hand, is only a- means to an end, the end being the planning, implementing, and controlling functions of management.

3. *Users:* The users of financial accounting information (other than management itself) are essentially a "faceless" group. The managements of most companies' do not personally know many of the shareholders, creditors, or others who use the information in the financial statements. Moreover, the information needs of most of these external users must be presumed; most external users do not individually request the information they would like to receive. By contrast, the users of management accounting information are known managers plus the people who help these managers analyse the information. Internal users information needs are relatively well known because the controller's office solicits these needs in designing or revising the management accounting system.
4. *Underlying Structure:* Financial accounting is built around one fundamental equation: Assets= Liabilities + Owners' Equity. In management accounting, there are three types of accounting, each with its own set of principles.
5. *Source of Principles:* Financial accounting information must be reported in accordance with generally accepted accounting principles (GAAP). Outside users need assurance that the financial statements are prepared in accordance with a mutually understood set of ground rules; otherwise, they cannot understand what the numbers mean. GAAP provide these common ground rules. An organisation's management, by contrast, can employ whatever accounting rules it finds most useful for its own purposes. Thus, in management accounting, there may be information on unfilled sales orders, even though these are not financial accounting transactions; fixed assets may be stated at current values rather than historical cost; certain production overhead costs may be omitted from inventories; or revenues may be recorded before they are realised-even though each of these concepts is inconsistent with GAAP. Rather than asking whether it conforms to GAAP, the basic question in management accounting is the pragmatic one: Is the information useful?
6. *Time Orientation:* Financial accounting records and reports the financial history of an organisation. Entries are made in the accounts only after transactions have occurred. Although

financial accounting information is used as a basis, for making future plans, the information itself is historical. Management accounting includes, in its formal structure, numbers that represent estimates and plans for the future as well as information about the past. The objective of financial accounting is to "tell it like it was," not like it will be.

7. *Information Content:* The financial statements that are the end product of financial accounting include primarily monetary information. Management accounting reports deal with no monetary as well as monetary information. These reports show quantities of material as well as its monetary cost, number of employees and hours worked as well as labour costs, units of products sold as well as rupee amounts of revenue, and so on.

8. *Information Precision:* Management needs information rapidly and is often willing to sacrifice some precision in order to gain speed in reporting. Thus, in management accounting approximations are often as useful as, or even more useful than, numbers that are more precise. Although financial accounting cannot be absolutely precise either, the approximations used in management accounting are broader than those in financial accounting.

9. *Report Frequency:* Corporations issue detailed, financial statements only annually and less detailed interim reports quarterly by contrast, fairly detailed management accounting reports are issued monthly in most larger organisations; and reports on certain activities may be prepared weekly, daily, orin a few instances in real time.

10. *Report Timeliness:* Because of the needs for precision and a review by outside auditors, plus the time requirements of type setting, financial accounting reports are distributed several weeks after the close of the ending December 31 generally are not received by shareholders until March or April. By contrast, because management accounting reports may contain information on which management needs to take prompt action, these reports are usually issued within a few days of the end of a month.

11 *Report Entity:* Financial statements describe the organisation as a whole. Although companies that do business in several industries are required to report revenues and income for each industry, these are large segments of the whole enterprise. Management accounting, by contrast focuses, mainly on relatively small parts of the entity that is, on individual products, individual activities, or individual divisions, departments and other responsibility centres. The necessity for dividing the total costs of an organisation among these individual parts creates important problems in management accounting that do not exist in financial accounting.

12. *Liability Potential:* Although it happens infrequently, a company may be sued by its shareholders or creditors for allegedly reporting misleading financial information in its annual report. By contrast, as previously stated, management accounting reports need not be in accord with GAAP and are not public documents. Although a manager may be held liable for some inappropriate action and management accounting information conceivably may have played some role in has or her taking that action, it is the action itself, not the management accounting documents, that gives rise to the liability.

SURVEYS OF COMPANY PRACTICE

"A Day in the Life" of a Management Accountant

The following table, based on a survey of CMAs, shows the percentage of respondents who named a particular work activity as in the top five work activity in terms of time devoted to the activity.

Activity	Percentage
Accounting system and financial reporting	62%
Managing the accounting function	42%
Internal consulting	42%
Short-term budgeting	37%
Long-term strategic planning	25%
Financial and economic analysis	24%
Computer system and operations	21%
Process improvement	20%

Performance evaluation	17%
Tax compliance	14%
Accounting policy	13%
Project accounting	11%
Consolidations	11%

In terms of importance, management accountants ranked the abilities and skills needed to succeed as follows:

1. Communication skills
2. Ability to work on a team
3. Analytical/problem solving skill
4. Solid understanding of accounting
5. Understanding of how a business functions
6. Computer skills

What changes in work activities are projected in the future for management accountants?

Projected to become more important are.

— Internal consulting

— Process improvement

— Long-term strategic planning

— Performing financial and accounting analysis

— Computer system and operation

Projected to become less important are

— Accounting systems and financial reporting

— Consolidation

— Managing the accounting/finance function

— Accounting policy

— Short term budgeting

— Project accounting

The increasing use of information technology in the future was seen from the survey as helping management accountants spend a lower percentage of their time on data collection and financial statement preparation and a higher percentage on financial analysis.

The survey indicates a clear shift away from activities we traditionally think of as the core of the controller's responsibilities-managing the function, ensuring business controls, and planning and reporting- toward activities we think of as business partnering-strategic planning, business leadership, analysing and interpreting information, decision making, process improvements, and performance evaluation.

INSTALLATION OF MANAGEMENT ACCOUNTING

Value of Management accounting Systems

The design of a management accounting system should be guided by the challenges facing managers. The customer focus theme is particularly critical. The other three themes-value-chain and supply-chain analysis, key success factors, and continuous improvement and benchmarking-are geared to improving customer focus and customer satisfaction. Management accounting helps manager's focus on these four themes.

1. *Customer focus:* The number of organisations aiming to be "customer- driven" is large and increasing. For example, Asea Brown Boveri (ABB)-a global manufacturer of industrial products-gives high priority to customer focus: Customer Focus is a guiding principle the way we do business. It is an attitude about everything we do that prompts us to constantly ask ourselves: "How can I add value for the customer?" Our commitment to Customer Focus has been reinforced by the measurable impacts it has had on employee morale and the bottom line The challenge facing managers is to continue investing sufficient resources in customer satisfaction such that customers who provide a company the most profits are attracted and retained. It is for this reason that airline companies pay special attention to their most frequent travellers. The management accounting system must also track whether the internal business functions are adding value to customers.
2. *Value-chain and supply-chain analysis:* Value chain refers to the sequence of business functions in which usefulness is added to the products or services of a company. The term value refers to the

increase in the usefulness of the product or service and, as result its value to the customer. We illustrate these business functions using the example of SONY Corporation's television division.

— *Research and development:* Generating and experimenting with ideas related to new products, services, or processes. At SONY, this function includes research on alternative ways of television signal transmission (analog, digital, high definition) and on the clarity of different shapes of television screens

— *Design of products- services, or processes:* Detailed planning and engineering of products, services, or processes. Design at Sony includes determining the number of component parts in a television set and the effect of alternative product designs on manufacturing costs.

— *Production Acquiring* coordinating, and assembling resources to produce a product or deliver a service. Production of a SONY television set includes the acquisition and assembly of the electronic parts, the cabinet, and the packaging used for shipping

— *Marketing:* Promoting and selling products or services to customers or prospective customers. SONY markets its televisions through trade shows, advertisements in newspapers and magazines, and on the Internet.

— *Distribution:* Delivering products or services to customers. Distributions for SONY includes shipping to retail outlets, catalogue vendors, direct sales via the Internet, and other channels through which customers purchase televisions.

— *Customer service:* Providing after-sale support to customers. SONY provides customer service on its televisions in the form of customer-help telephone lines, support on the Internet, and warranty repair work.

Each function is essential to SONY satisfying its customers and keeping them satisfied (and even delighted) over time. Companies gain (in terms of cost, quality, and the speed with which new products are developed) if two or more of the individual business functions of the value chain work concurrently as a team.

The term supply chain describes the flow of goods, services, and information from the initial sources of materials and services to the delivery of products to consumers, regardless of whether those activities occur in the same organisation or in other organisations. Consider the soft drinks, Coke and Pepsi. Many companies play a role in bringing these products to consumers.

Cost management emphasizes integrating and coordinating activities across all companies in the supply chain, as well as across each business function in an individual company's value chain. For example, both Coca-Cola Company and Pepsi Bottling Croup contract with their suppliers (such as glass and can companies and sugar manufacturers)

3. *Key success factors:* Customers are demanding that companies use the value chain and supply chain to deliver ever-improving levels of performance regarding several (or even all) of the following:
   - *Cost and efficiency:* Companies face continuous pressure to reduce the cost of the products or services they sell. Understanding the tasks or activities (such as setting up machines or distributing products) that cause costs to arise useful for calculating and managing the cost of products. To set cost-reduction targets, managers start by scanning the market to determine prices that customers are willing to pay for products or services. From this "target price," managers subtract the operating income they want to earn to arrive at the target cost. Managers strive to achieve the target cost by eliminating some activities (such as rework) and by reducing the costs of performing activities. They do so across all value-chain functions and over the entire life cycle of the product-from its initial R&D to when customer service and support for the product are no longer offered.
   - *Quality:* Customers expect high levels of quality. Total quality management (TQM) is a philosophy in which management improves operations throughout the value chain to deliver products and services that exceed customer expectations. TQM encompasses designing the product or service to meet the needs and wants of customers, as well as

making products with zero (or minimal) defects and waste. Management accountants evaluate the costs and revenue benefits of TQM initiatives.

— *Time:* Time has many components. New-product development time is the time to develop and bring new products to market. The increasing pace of technological innovation has led to shorter product life cycles and the need for companies to bring new products to market more rapidly.

4. *Continuous improvement and benchmarking:* Continuous improvement by competitors creates a never ending search for higher levels of performance to satisfy customers. Some phrases that typify this theme are "We are running harder just to stand still" and "If you're not going forward, you're going backward." Customer-response time describes the speed at which an organisation responds to customer requests. To increase customer satisfaction, organisations must complete activities faster and meet promised delivery dates reliably. Delays or bottlenecks occur when the work to be performed exceeds the available capacity. To increase output, managers need to increase the capacity of the bottleneck operation. The management accountant's role is to quantify the cost and benefits of relieving the bottleneck constraints.

Innovation: A constant flow of innovative products or services is the basis for ongoing company success. The management accountant helps managers evaluate alternative investment decisions and R&D decisions. Management accountants help managers track performance on the chosen key success factors vis-a.-vis the performance of competitors on the same factors. Tracking what is happening in other companies alerts managers to changes in what their own customers are observing and evaluating. To compete, many companies are concentrating on improving different aspects of their own operations. Keep in mind, though, that different industries will focus on improving different operating factors. Airline companies, such as Southwest Airlines, seek to improve the percentage of their flights that arrive on time. Internet companies, such as 1 eBay, seek to improve the percentage of each 24-hour period that customers can access their online systems without delay.

At times a company may have to make more fundamental changes in its operations and restructure its process to achieve improvements in cost, quality, timeliness or service. Management accountants provide the financial and nonfinancial information that helps mangers make decisions about re-engineering and continuous improvement.

Designing Management Accounting

The system should fit with other organisational characteristics, including goals and objectives, nature of the goods and services produced, organisation structure, and the level of sophistication that managers have in using management accounting information. Thus, all of the considerations mention below may not necessarily apply to a given organisation.

1. *Accounting Database*: Accounting information does not just magically materialise when it is needed. The raw data must be "captured" from various source document. These documents include vendor invoices, employee time cards and other personnel-related records, customer billing and payment records, and so forth. These raw data constitute the organisation's operating information, which is recorded using double-entry record keeping procedures in the organisation's accounts. The complete set of these accounts, called the chart of accounts, determines the structure of the organisation's accounting database.
2. Level of detail A major design issue in management accounting is how' detailed the chart of accounts should be. For financial accounting purposes, not much detail is required. For example, solely for financial accounting purposes all sales could be credited to a single Sales Revenue account and debited: either to Casll or Accounts Receivable. However, this would make it difficult to perform an analysis of sales by product line, profit centre sales district, or individual customer..
3. *Cost Accounting System*: an organisation faces many choices when designing its cost accounting system. Those choices include job costing versus standard costs, volume measures and several other choices many organisations activities are

sufficiently diverse that several accounting system must be designed for a given organisation. However, there should be one integrated accounting database underlying the several systems, because each system in essence simply aggregates account building blocks in a different way

4. *Management control system:* Whereas the availability of detailed accounting database information may be crucial to support full cost and differential accounting analyses, behavioural consideration are at least as important as responsibility accounting information in the management control process.

In the management control process, behavioural considerations are at least as important as accounting considerations. Thus, a conceptually sound management control system design will not be effective if manager feel that their superiors are using responsibility accounting information in an arbitrary or unfair way.

Installation of Management Accounting System

A system is an established set of procedure for then purpose of achieving specified objectives at minimum cost. It forms basis for future operations. A lot of difficulty can be avoided if a system is introduced carefully. The approach should be to develop the system that ties up with the existing practices. The executives responsible for the introduction of the system should intimately familiarise themselves with the plant, process and special problems relating to the organisation. The installation of a costing system can be discussed below:

— Basic consideration: the following consideration are relevant in the introduction of a costing system:

  a. It should be simple and practical

  b. It should be tailor made to the requirement of the organisation

  c. The cost of installation should justify the result

  d. The system should not sacrifice the utility by introducing meticulous and unnecessary details.

e. Textbook approach should be avoided. Sometimes, practical considerations may require adoption of what are theoretically known as " second best".

f. A carefully phased programme should be prepared for the introduction of the system. Network analysis may be careful in the context.

g. Active co-operation and participation of executives from different departments will promise best system.

h. The structure of costing system will be influenced by data-input and data-output of different department.

i. General attitude of management towards cost control.

j. Information requirement of management.

2. *Preliminary step:* special attention should be directed to collected information about the various aspects of the organisation. This information will provide a base for the steps to be taken for introduction of effective costing system. Following points should attract special attention in collecting the information about the organisation:

   a. Size of the firm and nature of business.

   b. Number of products to be manufactured or the extent of services being rendered.

   c. Complexities of manufactured and other operations.

   d. Organisational structure

   e. Various objectives, responsibilities and job description

   f. Analysis of material

   g. Routing of operations and flow charts

   h. Scheduling of operations.

   i. Ascertainment of standard time and methods by time study and motion study.

3. *Formal steps:* the introduction of actual system will involve the following points:

   a. Coding and classification.

   b. Establishing of cost centres.

c. Guidelines for separation of fixed and variable costs.

d. Guidelines for allocation of indirect costs.

e. Introduction of formats

f. Specification of different reports and their periodicity

g. Cost accounts manual

h. Guidelines for post installation appraisal of costing system.

The procedure of installation of management accounting system may vary from organisation to organisation depending upon the various factors like size of the organisation, type of product, technology used, etc.

Management Accountant's Role

Managers implement strategy by translating it into actions. Managers do this using planning systems and control systems designed to help the collective decisions throughout the organisation. Planning comprises;

(a) selecting organisation goals, predicting results under various alternative ways of achieving those goals, deciding how to attain the desired goals and

(b) communicating the goals and how to attain them to the entire organisation, One common planning tool is a budget.

A budget is the quantitative expression of a proposed plan of action by management and is an aid to coordinating what needs to be done to implement that plan. The information used to project budgeted amounts includes past financial and non-financial information routinely recorded in accounting systems. The budget expresses the strategy by describing the sales plans; the costs and investments that would be needed to achieve sales goals, the anticipated cash flows, and the potential financing needs. The process of preparing a budget forces coordination and communication across the business functions of a company, as well as with the company's suppliers and customers. Control comprises (a) taking actions that implement the planning decisions and (b) deciding how to evaluate performance and what feedback to provide that will help future decision-making.

Individuals pay attention to how they are measured. They tend to favour those measures that make their performance look best. Performance measures tell managers how well they and the subunits they are managing are doing. Linking rewards to performance helps to motivate managers. These rewards are both intrinsic and extrinsic. A budget gets serves as much as a control tool as a planning tool.

Feed Back

Planning and control are linked by feedback: Feedback involves managers examining past performance (the control function) and systematically exploring alternative ways to make better informed decisions and, plans in the future. Feedback can lead to changes in goals, changes in the ways decision alternatives are identified, and changes in the range of information collected when making predictions. Management accountants play an active role in linking control to future planning. A Plan must be Flexible enough so that Managers can Seize Sudden opportunities unforeseen at the time the plan is formulated. In no case should" control mean that managers cling to a plan when unfolding events indicate that actions not encompassed by that plan would offer better results for the company.

Problem-Solving and Scorekeeping

Directing roles

Management accountants contribute to the company's decisions about strategy, planning, and control, by problem solving, scorekeeping, and attention directing.

1. *Problem solving:* Comparative analysis for decision making of the several alternatives available, which is the best?
2. *Scorekeeping:* Accumulating data and reporting results to all levels of management describing how the organisation is doing. Examples of scorekeeping are the recording of actual revenues and purchases relative to budgeted amounts.
3. *Attention directing:* Helping managers focus on opportunities and problems. Attention directing means getting managers to focus on all opportunities that would add value to the company and not to focus only on cost reduction opportunities.

Different decisions place different emphasis on these three roles. For strategic decisions and planning decisions, the problem solving role is most prominent. For control decisions (which include both actions to implement planning decisions and decisions about performance evaluation 0, the scorekeeping and attention keeping and attention directing roles are most prominent because they provide feedback to managers.

Feedback from scorekeeping and attention directing often leads to revise planning decisions and some times make new strategic decisions. Information that prompts a planning decision is frequently re-analysed and supplemented by the management accountant in the problem-solving role. The ongoing interaction among strategic decisions, planning decisions, and control decisions means that management accountants often are simultaneously doing problem solving, scorekeeping and attention directing activities. Management accounting information must be relevant and timely to be useful to managers.

Management accounting is successful when it provides information to managers that improve their strategic, planning and control decisions. The relationship between managers and management accounting goes both ways, managers who support their management accountants allocate the resources they need to de their jobs. With these resources, management accountants are able to provide better support to the managers enabling them to take right decision. The survey of company practice indicates the increasingly important role management accountants are playing in helping in helping managers develop and implement strategy. It also describes the abilities and skills needed to be a successful management accountant in the future.

Management Accounting as a Career

The many types and levels of accounting personnel found in the typical organisation mean that there are broad opportunities waiting those who master the accounting discipline. When accounting is mentioned, most people think first of independent auditors who reassure the public about the reliability of the financial information supplied by company managers. These external auditors are called certified public accountants in the United States and Chartered Accountants in many other English-speaking nations. In the United States, an accountant earns the designation of Certified Public Accountant (CPA) and in India Chartered Accountant or Cost Accountant by a combination of education, qualifying experience. The major U.S. professional association in the private sector that regulates the quality of outside auditors is the American Institute of Certified Public Accountants (AICPA).

Top Management Position Training

In addition to preparing you for a position in an accounting department, studying accounting-and working as a management accountant-can prepare you for the very highest levels of management. Accounting deals with all facets of an organisation, no matter how complex, so it provides an excellent opportunity to gain broad knowledge. Accounting must embrace all management functions, including purchasing, manufacturing, wholesaling, retailing, and a variety of marketing and transportation activities. Senior accountants or controllers in a corporation are sometimes picked as production or marketing executives. Why? Because they may have impressed other executives as having acquired general management skills. A number of surveys have indicated that more chief executive officers began their careers in an accounting position than in any other area, including marketing, production, and engineering.

According to Business Week, management accountants are now getting involved with the operating side of the company, where they give advice and influence production, marketing, and investment decisions as well as corporate planning. Moreover, many controllers who have not made it to the top have won ready access to top management.... Probably the main reason the controller is getting the ear of top management these days is that he or she is virtually the only person familiar with all the working parts of the company. The growing interest in management accounting also stems from its ability to help managers adapt to change. The one constant in the- world of business is change.

Today's economic decisions differ from those of 10 years ago. As decisions change, demands for information change. Accountants must adapt their systems to the changes in management practices and technology. A system that produces valuable information in one setting may be valueless in another. Accountants have not always been responsive to the need to change. A decade ago many managers complained about the irrelevance of accounting information. Why? Because their decision environment had changed but accounting systems had not. However, most progressive companies have now changed their accounting systems to recognise the realities of today's complex, technical, and global business environment.

Instead of being irrelevant, accountants in such companies are adding more value than ever. For example, Management Accounting reported on a Champion International Corporation paper mill that made major changes in its accounting system. By working with managers to produce the information considered relevant for their decisions, accountants were regarded as "business partners." Previously, managers had considered accountants to be a "financial police department." Instead of merely pointing out problems, the accountants became part of the solution.

Current Trends

Three major factors are causing changes in management accounting today:

1. Shift from a manufacturing-based to a service-based economy
2. Increased global competition
3. Advances in technology

Each of these factors will affect your study of management accounting. The service sector now accounts for almost 80% of the employment in the United States. Service industries are becoming increasingly competitive and their use of accounting information is growing. Global competition has increased in recent years as many international barriers to trade, such as tariffs and duties, have been lowered. In addition, there has been a worldwide trend toward deregulation.

The result has been a shift in the balance of economic power in the world. Nowhere has this been more evident than in the United States. To regain their competitive edge, many U.S. companies are redesigning their accounting systems to provide more accurate and timely information about the cost of activities, products, or services. To be competitive, managers must understand the effects of their decisions on costs, and accountants must help managers predict such effects. By far the most dominant influence on management accounting over the past decade has been technological change. This change has affected both the production and the use of accounting information.

The increasing capabilities and decreasing cost of computers, especially personal computers (PCs), has changed how accountants gather, store, manipulate, and report data. Most accounting systems, even small ones, are automated. In addition, computers enable managers to access data directly and to generate their own reports and analyses in many cases. By using spreadsheet software and graphics packages, managers can use accounting information directly in their decision process. Thus, all managers need a better understanding of accounting information now than they may have needed in the past. In addition, accountants need to create database that can be readily under stood by managers.

RESPONSIBILITY ACCOUNTING

Responsibility Accounting is a system under which managers are given decision-making authority and responsibility for each activity occurring within a specific area of the company. Under this system managers are made responsible for the activities of segments. These segments may be called departments or divisions. Eric Kohier defines Responsibility Accounting as "a method of accounting in which costs are identified with persons assumed to be capable of controlling them, rather than with products or functions. It differs from activity accounting, in that it does not in itself require an organisational grouping by activities and sub-activities or provide a systematic criterion of system design."

Charles T. Homgreen defines "Responsibility Accounting is a system of accounting that recognises various responsibility centres throughout the organisation and reflects the plans and actions of each of these centres by assigning particular revenues and costs to the one having the pertinent responsibility. It is also called profitability accounting and activity accounting. Institute of Cost and Works

Accountants of India defines Responsibility Accounting as a system of management accounting under which accountability is established according to the responsibility delegated to various levels of management and management information and reporting system instituted to give adequate feedback in terms of the delegated responsibility. Under this system, divisions or units of an organisation under a specified authority in a person are developed as responsibility centres and evaluated individually for their performance.

David Fanning defines Responsibility Accounting as a system or mechanism for controlling the wider freedom of action 'that executives—decision centre manager in other words—are given by senior management and for holding those executives responsible for the consequences of their decisions.' Robert Anthony defines Responsibility Accounting as "that type of management accounting that collects and reports both planned and actual accounting information in terms of responsibility centres."

Responsibility Accounting focused main attention on responsibility centres. The managers of different activity centres are responsible for controlling the costs of their centres. Information about costs incurred for different activities is supplied to the persons in charge of various centres. The performance is constantly compared to the standards set and this process is very useful in exercising cost controls. Responsibility Accounting is different from cost accounting in the sense that the former lays emphasis on cost control whereas the latter lays emphasis on cost ascertainment.

Responsibility Accounting is a system, which makes everyone conscious and responsible: for the job that is entrusted to him by his supervisor, i.e. a control by delegating and locating responsibility for cost. Each supervisory area in the organisation is charged only with the cost for which it is responsible or over which it has control. Not only the costs but also the revenues are assigned. That is why it is defined as "a system of accounting that recognises various responsibility centres throughout the organisation and that reflects plans and actions of each of these centres, by assigning particular revenues and cost to one having pertinent responsibility. This system defines the specific responsibility of the departmental supervisor as well as functional managers, which should be performed.

Practically it is the management that has to chalk out the plan and control the activities relating to the responsibility centre. It follows the basic principle like any other control system, such as Standard Costing or Budget. The only difference is that the fixation of responsibility lies in the hands of individuals or departments.

The following inferences can be made from the above definitions:

1. Responsibility Accounting stresses on communication of information in general and accounting information in particular to various decisional centres.
2. Responsibility Accounting lays greater emphasis on persons (human resources management)
3. Responsibility Accounting is tailored to the organisational structure so that the process of communication of information follows principles of organisation.
4. It is an accounting system, which collects and report both planned and actual accounting data in terms of sub-units, which are recognised as responsibility centres.

Responsibility Accounting is used as a control device. Following steps are necessary to effect control through the Responsibility Accounting:

1. The organisation is divided into various responsibility centres. Each responsibility centre is put under the charge of a responsibility manager.
2. The targets or budgets of each responsibility centre are set in consultation with the manager of responsibility centre, so that he may be able to give full information about his department. The manager of responsibility centre should know as what is expected of him—each centre should have a clear set of goals. The responsibility and authority of each centre should be well defined.
3. Managers are charged with the items and responsibility, over which they can exercise a significant degree of direct control.
4. Goals defined for each area of responsibility should be attainable with efficient and effective performance.
5. The actual performance is communicated to the managers concerned. If it falls short of the standards, the variances are conveyed to the top management. The names of persons

responsible for the variances are also conveyed so that responsibility may be fixed.

6. The performance reports for each centre should be prepared highlighting the variances and items requiring management's attention. The corrective measures are suggested or taken and communicated to the concerned managers of the centres.

The purpose of all these steps is to assign responsibility to different individuals so that their performance is improved and costs are controlled. The personal factor in Responsibility Accounting is most important. The management may prepare the best plan or the budget and put up before its staff, but its success depends upon the initiative and the will of the workers to execute it. The essence of Responsibility Accounting is to communicate the right information to the right person at the right time. Responsibility Accounting provides a means of control, it cannot control. Control is a personalised affair. The people do control, not the reports. Responsibility Accounting will certainly act as a control device and it will help in improving the overall performance of the business.

Role of Responsibility Centres

A responsibility centre is a set of activities assigned to a manager, a group of managers, or other employees. A set of machines and machining tasks, for example, may be a responsibility centre for a production supervisor. The full production department may be a responsibility centre for the department head. Finally, the entire organisation may be a responsibility centre for the president. In some organisations, management responsibility is shared by groups of employees to create wide "ownership" of management decisions, allow creative decision making, and prevent one person's concern (or lack of concern) for risks of failure to dominate decisions.

An effective management control system gives each lower-level manager responsibility for a group of activities and objectives and then monitors and reports on (1) the results of the activities and (2) the manager's influence on those results. Such a system has innate appeal for most top managers because it helps them delegate decision-making and frees them to plan and control. Lower-level managers appreciate the autonomy of decision-making they inherit. Thus system designers apply responsibility accounting to identify what parts of the organisation have primary responsibility for each objective, develop performance measures and targets to achieve, and design reports of these measures by organisation subunit or responsibility centre.

Responsibility centres usually have multiple objectives that the management control system monitors. Responsibility Accounting focuses attention on responsibility centres. A responsibility centre is a sub-unit of an organisation under the supervision of a manager who has the responsibility for the activities of that responsibility centre. Each sub-unit has certain activities to perform and its manager is assigned the responsibility and/or authority to carry out those activities.

Responsibility centre is the segment of business with reference to which information will be communicated to pin point responsibilities. In the words of Anthony and Races, "A responsibility centre is like an engine in that it has inputs, which are physical quantities of material, hours of various types of labour, and a variety of services; it works with these resources usually; working capital and fixed assets are also required. As a result of this work, it produces output, which are classified either as goods, if they are tangible or as services, if they are intangible. These goods or services go either to other responsibility centre; within the company or to customers in the outside world."

Responsibility centres, for planning and control purposes, are classified into the following cases:

Expense Centre: An expense centre or a cost centre, is a responsibility centre in which inputs, but not outputs, are measured in monetary terms. A cost centre is a responsibility centre in which a manager is accountable for costs only. Its financial responsibilities are to control and report costs only. An entire department may be considered a single cost centre, or a department may contain several cost centres. For example, although one manager may supervise an assembly department, it may contain several assembly lines and regard each assembly line as a separate cost centre. Likewise, within each line, separate machines or test equipment may be regarded as separate cost centres.

Responsibility Accounting is based on financial information relating to input (costs) and outputs (revenues). In an expense centre of responsibility, the accounting system records only the cost incurred in /

by the centre or unit, but revenues earned (output) are excluded. In case of certain responsibility centres, it is neither possible nor necessary to measure the output in terms of monetary units. Most of the service departments come in this category. For example, it is almost impossible to measure the monetary value of the finance or the account department's contribution to the company. The accounting system, therefore, records the cost incurred in respect of these centres but not the revenue incurred. The performance of the responsibility centre managers is evaluated by comparing the costs incurred with the budgeted costs. Management focuses its attention on cost variances for control purposes.

Revenue Centre: A revenue centre is a segment of the organisation, which is primarily responsible for generating sales revenue. A revenue centre manager does not possess control over cost, investment in assets, but usually has control over some of the expenses of the marketing department. The performance of a revenue centre is evaluated by comparing the actual revenue with budgeted revenue. The marketing manager of a product line is an example of revenue centre.

Profit Centre: A responsibility centre is called a profit centre when the manager is held responsible for both costs (inputs) and revenues (outputs) and thus for profit. Despite the name, a profit centre can exist in nonprofits organisations (though it might not be referred to as such) when a responsibility centre receives revenues for its services. A profit centre is a big segment of activity for which both revenues and costs are accumulated: A centre whose performance is measured in terms of both—the expense it incurs and revenue it earns, is termed as a profit centre. The output of a responsibility centre may either be meant for internal consumption or for outside customers.

In the latter case, the revenue is realised when the sales are made. That is, when the output is meant for outsiders, then the revenue will be measured from the price charged from customers. If the output is meant for other responsibility centre, then management takes a decision whether to treat the centre as profit centre or not. In fact, any responsibility centre can be turned into a profit centre by determining a selling price for its outputs. For instance, in case of a process industry, the output of one process may be transferred to another process at a profit by taking into account the market price. Such transfers will give some profit to that responsibility centre. Although such transfers do not increase the Company's assets, they help in management control process.

Investment Centre: An investment centre goes a step further than a profit centre does. Its success is measured not only by its income but also by relating that income to its invested capital, as in a ratio of income to the value of the capital employed. In practice, the term investment centre is not widely used. Instead, the term profit centre is used indiscriminately to describe centres that are always assigned responsibility for revenues and expenses, but may or may not be assigned responsibility for the capital investment.

It is defined as a responsibility centre in which inputs are measured in terms of cost / expenses and outputs are measured in terms of revenues and in which assets employed are also measured. A responsibility centre is called an investment centre, when its manager is responsible for costs and revenues as well as for the investment in assets used by his centre. He is responsible for maintaining a satisfactory return on investment e. asset employed in his responsibility centre. The investment centre manager has control over revenues, expenses and the amounts invested in the centre's assets. The manager of an investment centre is required to earn a satisfactory return. Thus, return on investment (ROI) is used as the performance evaluation criterion in an investment centre. He also formulates the credit policy, which has a direct influence on debt collection, and the inventory policy, which determines the investment in inventory.

The Vice President (Investments) of a mutual funds company may be in charge of an Investment Centre. In the Investment Centre, the manager in charge is held responsible for the proper utilisation of assets. He is expected to earn a satisfactory return on the assets employed in his responsibility centre. Measurement of assets employed poses many problems. It becomes difficult to determine the amount of assets employed in a particular responsibility centre. Some of the assets are in the physical possession of the responsibility centre while for some assets it may depend upon other responsibility centres or the Head Office of the company. This particularly true of cash or heavy plant and equipment. Whether such assets should be included in the figure of assets employed of the responsibility centre and if included, at how much value, is a difficult question. On account of these difficulties, investment centres are generally used only for relatively large units, which have independent divisions, both manufacturing and marketing, for their individual products.

Advantages

Management uses Responsibility Accounting as a control device. The aim of Responsibility Accounting is to help management in achieving organisational goals. It is an invaluable support to modern management. It contributes to the firm's management by providing relevant information on a continuous basis. The following are some of the advantages of Responsibility Accounting:

1. It introduces sound system of control—a system of closer control.
2. Each and every individual in the organisation is assigned some responsibility and they are accountable for their work.
3. Everybody knows what is expected of him. Nobody can shift responsibility to anybody else if something goes wrong.
4. It is effective tool of cost control and cost reduction applied with budgetary control and standard costing.
5. It facilitates the management to set realistic plans and budgets.
6. It is not only a control device but also facilitates decentralisation of decision-making.
7. It measures the performance of individuals in an objective manner.
8. It fosters a sense of cost-consciousness among managers and their subordinates.
9. It helps the management to make an effective delegation of authority and required responsibility as well.
10. Under the system of Responsibility Accounting, detailed information is collected about costs and revenues, on a continuous basis and the data is helpful in planning for future costs and revenues.
11. Timely corrective action can be taken and better control over costs can be achieved.

Cost Centres and Responsibility Centres

A cost centre is "a location, person or item of equipment (or group of these) for which costs may be ascertained and used for purposes of cost control". Thus, cost centre is used as a means of assembling items of cost, so that they can be assigned to goods and services. In the case of cost centre, emphasis is more on products, jobs or processes whose costs are to be ascertained. Thus here the emphasis is not on the persons who may be managing a level or product or process. Responsibility centres, on the other hand, are established on the basis of responsibility delegated to responsible personnel of the organisation with a view to identify costs which can be controlled by each one of them. However, cost centres sometimes may be used as responsibility centres too. In that case cost reports are prepared both cost wise-wise and responsibility—centre- wise.

Developments and performance measures

Because most responsibility centres have multiple objectives, only some of these objectives are expressed in financial terms, such as operations budgets, profit targets, or required return on investment, depending on the financial classification of the centre. Other objectives, which are to be achieved concurrently, are non-financial in nature. For example, many companies list environmental stewardship and social responsibility as key objectives. The well-designed management control system functions alike for both financial and non-financial objectives to develop and report measures of performance.

Good performance measures will:

1. Relate to the goals of the organisation
2. Balance long-term and short-term concerns
3. Reflect the management of key results and activities
4. Be affected by actions of managers and employees
5. Be readily understood by employees
6. Be used in evaluating and rewarding managers and employees
7. Be reasonably objective and easily measured
8. Be used consistently and regularly

Both financial and non-financial performance measures are important. Sometimes accountants and managers focus too much on financial measures such as profit or cost variances because they are readily available from the accounting system. Managers, however, can improve operational control by also considering non-financial measures of performance. Such measures may be more timely and more closely affected by employees at lower levels of the organisation, where the product is made or the service is rendered.

Non-financial measures are often easier to quantify and understand. Hence, employees can be easily motivated toward achieving performance goals. For example, AT&T Universal Card Services, which was awarded the prestigious Baldrige National Quality Award (presented by the U.S. Department of Commerce), uses 18 performance measures for its customer inquiries process. These measures include average speed of answer, abandon rate, and application processing time (three days compared to the industry average of 34 days).

Often the effects of poor non-financial performance (quality, productivity, and customer satisfaction) do not show up in the financial measures until considerable ground has been lost. Financial measures often are lagging indicators that arrive too late to help prevent problems and ensure the organisation's health. What is needed are leading indicators. As a result, many companies now stress management of the activities that drive venues and costs rather than waiting to explain the revenues or costs themselves after the activities have occurred. Superior financial performance usually follows from superior nonfinancial performance.

Balanced Scorecard

There are several approaches to performance reporting. Each approach attempts to link organisational strategy to actions of managers and employees. One popular approach to performance reporting is the balanced scorecard. A balanced scorecard is a performance measurement and reporting system that strikes a balance between financial and operating measures, links performance to rewards, and gives explicit recognition to the diversity of organisational goals.

Companies such as Champion International, AT&T, Allstate, and Apple Computer use the balanced scorecard to focus management's attention on items subject to action on a month-by-month and day-to-day basis. One advantage of the balanced scorecard approach is that line managers can see the relationship between non-financial measures, which they often can relate more easily to their own actions, and the financial measures that relate to organisational goals. Another advantage of the balanced scorecard is its focus on performance measures from each of the following four components of the successful organisation. This enhances the learning process because managers learn the results of their actions and how these actions are linked to the organisational goals.

VALUE ADDED ACCOUNTING

The concept of value added is considerably old. It originated in the USA. Treasury in the 18th Century and periodically accountants have deliberated upon whether the concept should be incorporated in financial accounting practice. But actually, the value added statement has come to be seen with greater frequency in Europe and more particularly in Britain. The discussion paper "Corporate Report" published in1975 by the then Accounting Standard Steering committee (now known as Accounting Standards Board) of the U.K. advocated the publication of value added statement along with the conventional annual corporate report.

In 1977, the Department of Trade, U.K.published 'The Future of Company Report' which stated that all substantially large British companies should include a value added (V.A.) statement in their annual reports. Also a few companies in the Netherlands include V.A. information in their annual reports, but the disclosures often fall short of being a full V.A. statement and also the method of arriving at V.A. is grossly non-standardised. In India Britannia Industries Limited and some other prepare value added statement as supplementary financial statement in its annual report.

Value Added (V.A.): VA is the wealth a reporting entity has been able to create through the collective effort of capital, management and employees. In economic terms, value added is the market price of the output of an enterprise less the price of the goods and services acquired by transfer from other firms. VA can provide a useful measure in gauging performance and activity of the reporting entity.

Gross Value Added (GVA): GVA is arrived at by deducting from sales revenue the cost of all materials and services, which were brought in from outside suppliers. We know that the retained profit of a company for a given accounting year is derived as below:

$$R = S - B - Dep - W - I - T - Div \quad (1)$$

Where R= Retained profit, S= Sales revenue, B= Bought in cost of materials and services, Dep= annual depreciation charge, W= Annual wage cost, I= Interest payable for the year T= Annual Corporate tax and Div = Total dividend payable for the year. Rearranging the equation (1) we get GVA as below:

$$S - B = R + Dep + W + I + T + Div \quad (2)$$

Each side of equation (2) represents GVA. However this is a very simple definition of GVA. In practice GVA includes many other things. Besides sales revenue, any direct income, investment income and extraordinary incomes or expenses are also included in calculation of GVA. Including these items in the above equation No.2, we get

$$(S + Di) - B + Inv + EI = R + Dep + W + T + I + Div \quad (3)$$

Where Di = Direct incomes, Inv = Investment incomes, EI= Extraordinary items.

The above equation can be shown by way of the following statement.

Gross Value added of a manufacturing company

Sales		X
Add: Royalties and other direct income		X
Less: Materials and Services used		X
Value added by trading activities		X
Add: Investment Income	X	
Add/Less: Extraordinary items	X	X

Gross Value Added		X
Applied as follows :		
To employees as salaries, wages etc.	X	
To government as taxes, duties, etc.	X	
To Financiers as interest on Borrowing	X	
To Shareholders as dividends	X	
To retained earnings including depreciation	X	

Net Value Added (NVA): NVA can be defined as GVA less depreciation. Rearranging the equation (1) we can get NVA as below:

$$S - B - Dep = R + W + I + T + Div.$$

Reporting Value Added

The 'Corporate Report' of the U.K. advised the British companies to report Gross value Added (GVA). The 'Report' did not consider the possibility of the alternative Net Value Added (NVA). As a result the majority of British companies prefer to set forth their VA statement as a report on GVA, so that depreciation is an application of VA rather than a cost to be deducted in calculating VA In India also GVA is more popular among reporting companies than NVA The reasons for reporting GVA are as follows:

GVA can be derived more objectively than NVA. This is because depreciation is more Prone to subjective judgment than are bought-in costs.

a. GVA format involves reporting depreciation along with retained profit. The resultant sub-total usefully shows the portion of the year's VA, which has become available for rein vestment.

b. The practice of reporting GVA would lead to a closer correspondence between VA and national income figures.

This is because economists generally prefer gross measures of national income to net one. However, there are also valid reasons for reporting NVA. They are:

a. Wealth Creation will be overstated if no allowance made for the wearing out or loss of value of fixed assets, which occurs as new assets are created.

b. NVA is a firmer base for calculating productivity bonus than is Gather productivity of a company may increase because of additional investments in modernisation of plant and machinery. Consequently, the value added component may improve significantly. The employees of the company will naturally claim and be given some share of additional VA as productivity bonus. But if the share is based on GVA then no recognition is given to the need for an increased depreciation charge.

c. The concept of matching demands that depreciation be deducted along with bought in costs to derive NVA GVA is inconsistent, for costs would be charged under the bought heading if the item has a life of under one year. But if the item has a longer life it would be treated as a depreciable fixed assets and its cost would never appear as a charge while arriving at GVA.

From the above discourse it can be said that it is better to report on NVA rather than on GVA.

Influence of VA Statement

The advantages claimed for the VA statement are considerable. The main thrust of financial accounting development in the recent decades has been in the area of 'how' we measure income rather than 'whose' income we measure. The common belief the traditional accountants that net income or profit is the reward of the proprietors had been considered as a very narrow definition of income In fact, proponents of the proprietary theory argued that the proprietor is the centre of interest. The assets were assumed to be owned by the proprietor and the liabilities were the proprietor's obligations.

The notion of proprietorship was accepted and practiced so long as the nature of business did not experience revolutionary changes. The proprietary theory did hold good for a sole proprietorship or a partnership kind of business. But with the emergence of corporate entities and the legal recognition of the existence of business entity separate from the personal affairs and other interests of the owners led to the rejection of the proprietary theory and formulation of other theories like entity theory, enterprise theory and fund theory. The entity theory has its main application in the corporate form of business enterprise.

The entity theory is based on the basic accounting equation and it suggests that the net income of the reporting entity is generally expressed in terms of the net change in the stockholders' equity. It represents the residual change in equity position after deducting all outsiders' claims. The enterprise theory is a broader concept than the entity theory. For entity theory, the reporting entity is considered to be a separate economic unit operating primarily for the benefit of the equity shareholders, whereas in the enterprise theory, the reporting entity is a social institution, operating for the benefit of many interested groups. The most relevant concept of income in this broad social responsibility concept of the enterprise is the value added concept. Therefore, the origin of concept of value added lies in the enterprise theory. Proponents of VA argue that there are advantages in defining income in such a way as to include the rewards of a much wider group than just the shareholders.

Advantages of the VA Statement

1. Reporting on VA improves the attitude of employees towards their employing companies this is because the VA statement reflects a broader view of the company's objectives and responsibilities.
2. VA statement makes it easier for the company to introduce a productivity linked bonus scheme for employees based on VA. The employees may be given productivity bonus on the basis of VA/Payroll ration.
3. VA based ratios are useful diagnostic and predictive tools. Trends in VA ratios, comparisons with other companies and international comparisons may be useful. In India, the VA statement of Britannia Industries Limited for the two years 1992-93 and 1993-94 showed that almost 50% of the value addition is applied in payment of various taxes and duties. The employees and shareholders get almost and constant share of value added of 35% and 5% respectively. The value added as a percentage of sales revenue has increased from 23.8% to 25.6% over the two years period. However, it may be noted that the VA ratios can be made more useful if the ratios are based on inflation adjusted VA data.

4. VA provides a very good measure of the size and importance of a company. To use sales figures or capital employed figures as a basis for company rankings can cause distortion. This is because sales may be inflated by large bought in expenses or a capital intensive company with a few employees may appear to be more important that a highly skilled labour intensive company.
5. VA statement links a company's financial accounts to national income. A company's VA indicates the company's contribution to national income.
6. Finally VA statement is built on the basic conceptual foundations, which are currently accepted in balance sheets and income statements. Concepts such as going concern, matching, consistency and substance over form are equally applicable to the VA statement.

REFERENCES

Lowenstein, Roger, *When Genius Failed: The Rise and Fall of Long-Term Capital Management*, Random House, 2000.

Marlow, Michael L., *Public Finance Theory and Practice*, Dryden Press, 1997.

Martin, Justin, *The Man Behind Money*, Perseus Book Group, 2000.

_______________, Petty, Keown, and Scott, *Basic Financial Management*, 5th edition, Prentice Hall, 1991.

Nagle, Thomas T. and Reed K. Holden, *The Strategy and Tactics of Pricing: A Guide to Profitable Decision Making*, NJ: Pearson, 1994.

Nash, Robert C. and Joseph F. Sinkey, Jr., "On Competition, Risk, and the Hidden Assets in the Market for Bank Credit Cards," *Journal of Banking and Finance*, pp. 89-112, (January 1997), January 1997.

Petty, Keown, Scott, and Martin, *Basic Financial Management*, 6th edition, Prentice Hall, 1993.

5

Financial Statements

Accounting plays a critical role in decision-making. Accounting provides the results of an executed set of decisions and makes possible the continuous success of a business or improvement in operations. Secondly, accounting provides much of the necessary information needed in making good decisions. Thirdly, the management accountant provides a knowledge of basic decision-making tools that helps find the best alternative in decision-making.

It is the accountant's knowledge about preparing financial statements and his or her abilities to analyse and interpret financial statements that makes the controllership function in a business so valuable to management.

A primary objective of a business is to increase the assets from operations. By operations is meant all the revenue and expense transactions of a business for a defend period of time. Since the excess of revenue over expenses increases the equity of a business, it is often said that the primary objective is to increase stockholders' wealth, assuming the business is a corporation. In other terms, the decisions that management makes concerning the operations of the business are of paramount importance. Management has the responsibility to make the kinds of decisions that generates net income.

Revenues are the inflow of assets caused by the operations of the business. The term revenue necessarily implies increases in assets. If a transaction does not cause an increase in an asset, then that transaction is not a revenue transaction.

Expenses are the outflow of assets from the operations of the business. Expenses are caused by activities necessary to generate revenue. When revenues exceeds expenses as is the goal, the difference is called net income. If a transaction does not cause a decrease in an asset, then that transactions is not an expense.

Technically, the asset outflow associated with salaries is not cash. Payments are made to workers and other employees because they create something of value. In more technical terms an expense is the expired value of an asset. A janitor is paid to clean foors. However, when the clean foor becomes dirty again, then the value of the clean foor asset has expired. Because many assets have a very short life, the accountant often simply records the expense even though the value of the assets at the time of recording has not yet expired.

Often the acquisition of an asset is not paid for immediately and the amount then owed is called a liability. Liabilities are debts or obligations to pay at some future date and are a common form of financing in a business. There are three primary sources of assets in a business: (1) revenues (2) liabilities (3) capital.

In one sense, the purpose of management is to make asset, liabilities, capital, revenue, and expense decisions. Since the income statement shows revenues, expenses and net income and the balance sheet shows assets, liabilities, and capital, we can say that the purpose of management is to manage assets, liabilities, capital, revenue, and expenses.

Because of the importance of sound operations and financial condition, it is critically important for both management and accountants to have a sold understanding of financial statements. While accountants prepare financial statements, it is management that creates financial statements through the decisions it makes.

The four financial statements of critical value in this text are as follows:

1. Balance sheet
2. Income statement
3. Cost of goods manufactured statement
4. Statement of cash flow

Financial statements are based on well defend accounting concepts and standards, some of which are fairly technical and require some concentrated study to learn and use. The following is a list of accounting terminology and concepts important in understanding financial statements for a manufacturing business.

Hopefully, you have learned these terms in a previous accounting course and only some review of these terms is needed.

In addition to terminology, there are some accounting concepts and conventions of a broader nature that involve theory and even, in some cases, considerable differences of opinion.

Accounting Financial Statement Relationships

In addition to important financial statement terminology, there are a number of manufacturing financial statement relationships critical to understanding and using financial statements. These relationships may be summarised as simple mathematical equations. The most important of these relationships are the following:

Cost of Goods Manufactured Statement

Material used = materials (beginning) + material purchases - materials inventory (ending)

Cost of goods manufactured = materials used + factory labor + manufacturing overhead + work in process (beginning) - work in process (ending)

Income statement

Cost of goods sold = finished goods (beginning) + cost of goods manufactured - finished goods (ending)

Finished goods (beginning) plus cost of goods manufactured is often called goods available for sale.

Net income = sales - cost of goods sold - operating expenses

The difference between sales and cost of goods sold is often reported as gross profit.

Balance Sheet

Assets = liabilities + stockholders' equity
Assets = current assets + fixed assets + other assets
Liabilities = current liabilities + long-term liabilities
Stockholders' equity = common stock + premium/discount on common stock + retained earnings

Statement of Cash Flow

Change in cash = sources and uses from operations + sources and uses from financing activities + sources and uses from investing activities.

While the above equations may seem a bit complex and imposing, these relationships still, nevertheless, form the foundation of financial statements for a manufacturing company. Since it is critical that managerial decision-makers understand and use financial statement information, it is essential that the serious student of management understand these basic financial statement relationships.

ANALYSING FINANCIAL STATEMENTS

Understanding financial statements is only the first step in using them. The second step is to analyse them in order to discover any existing or potential problem areas of profit performance or financial conditions that needs corrective action. Several tools exist that may be used including the following:

1. Comparative statements
2. Financial statement ratios

The use of ratios is a commonly used method to determine conditions that might be a current or future problem. The current ratio can be computed to determine if current assets are sufficient to make payments of current liabilities. The debt/equity ratio is a good indicator of whether the company is too heavily burdened with debt. The computation of the return on investment ratio is an excellent benchmark for determining whether net income is satisfactory or unsatisfactory. Numerous other ratios may be computed and most elementary accounting textbooks do an excellent job of discussing the more important ratios.

A Model of Decision-Making

Also, financial statements may be used as a guide to identifying what financial statements elements are directly affected by a specific decision. This approach is not commonly used, but because it is helpful in understanding how decisions affect the various items of financial statements, it is discussed here now in some detail. It is management's primary responsibility to manage each element of a given financial statement. Financial statements, in one sense, are a check list of what management is to manage.

To clarify the above statements, the following financial statements of the V. K. Gadget Company are presented in terms of decisions and required information.

These financial statement models presented in terms of decisions and required information rather than actual values clearly indicate an important point. It is management rather than accountants that actually creates financial statements. The financial well being of the company's operations is clearly the full responsibility of management.

Accounting Policies and Procedures

While the operating and financial success of a company falls squarely on the shoulders of management, there is still considerable latitude on the part of accountants in preparing financial statements. Any accounting system involves rules, standards, and procedures that can vary from company to company. In the V. K. Gadget Company, the following procedures and methods have been adopted.

Management Accounting Systems

In addition to understanding and utilising financial statements and financial accounting tools, it is important that both accountants and management have a good understanding of management accounting concepts and tools. One of the most effective tools is comprehensive business budgeting. The objective of comprehensive budgeting is to prepare a set of financial statements in advance. The end result of the budgeting process is a planned set of financial statements. Whether or not this system should be used is a decision that you would make, assuming you are a participant in the simulation, and serving in the role of new management. In addition to the comprehensive budget, other computerised management accounting tools are available for use. These tools include:

1. Business budgeting
2. Cost behaviour
3. Cost-volume-proft analysis
4. Capital budgeting analysis
5. Credit analysis
6. Demand sensitivity analysis
7. Direct costing analysis
8. Incremental analysis
9. Inventory management analysis
10. Keep or replace analysis
11. Performance evaluation
12. Return on investment
13. Sales people compensation analysis
14. Segmental contribution reporting
15. Wage rate analysis

If your instructor has adopted this simulation in connection with this text book, then hopefully your participation in *The Management/ Accounting Simulation* will give you an experience that will solidly persuade you that in any business the accounting department is a vital function in the process of decisions being made and executed.

Merchandising and Manufacturing Businesses

In order to understand financial statements for a manufacturing business, as a student you first need a good understanding of financial statements for a merchandising business. In general, merchandising and manufacturing statements are the same, In fact, in terms of basic components they are identical.

The major difference is in the need to know how to compute cost of goods manufactured as seen in the following comparison.

The Cost of Goods Manufactured Statement

The major difference here is obviously in the need to know how to compute cost of goods manufactured. A second difference is that in a manufacturing business inventory that is sold is called finished goods rather than being called merchandise inventory and cost of goods manufactured has replaced merchandise purchases. Rather than purchasing goods from another company, the company manufactures what it sells.

The purpose of the cost of goods manufactured statement is to compute the cost of goods completed or finished in a given time period. The cost of goods manufactured is the cost of goods finished this period. Cost of goods manufactured consists of three basic cost elements: (1) materials, (2) factory labor, and (3) manufacturing overhead. Materials used is a computation.

There are two types of inventory systems that may be used in a manufacturing business: (1) periodic and (2) perpetual. If a periodic inventory system is used, then it is necessary to compute materials used. If perpetual inventory is used, the inventory system keeps an accurate perpetual record of materials used and, consequently, it is not necessary to compute materials used.

Balance Sheets: Merchandising and Manufacturing Compared

The balance sheet of a manufacturing business in terms of basic elements is identical to the balance sheet of a merchandising business. The only difference is in one area, the current asset section. Instead of one inventory account, the manufacturing business has three inventory accounts.

Manufacturing Business Transactions

The manufacturing business has a number of unique transactions not found in a merchandising business. These transactions as a whole all fall into the manufacturing costs category. Basically, there are three types of manufacturing transactions:

1. Material
2. Factory labour

3. Manufacturing overhead

The most common of these three types of transactions are the following:

1. Purchase of raw materials
2. Freight on material purchased
3. Material returns and allowances
4. Incurrence of direct factory labour
5. Incurrence of manufacturing overhead

Examples of manufacturing overhead incurred include:

1. Indirect factory labour and indirect material
2. Factory utilities
3. Repairs and maintenance on factory equipment
4. Factory insurance
5. Depreciation on factory equipment

Examples of how to record material, factory labor, and manufacturing overhead transactions are now presented. These transactions are refected in the adjusted trial balance on the next page.

Manufacturing End-of-Period Journal Entries

Additional information:

Materials inventory (ending)	$ 8,000
Work in Process (ending)	$12,000
Finished goods (ending)	$11,000

In addition to these normal reoccurring periodic transactions, there are unique manufacturing end-of-period entries that must be made.

End-of-period entries must be made to record:

1. Transfer of materials inventory balance to cost of goods manufactured
2. Transfer of beginning material purchases to cost of goods manufactured
3. Transfer of materials freight-in to cost of goods manufactured
4. Transfer of manufacturing overhead incurred to cost of goods manufactured

5. Recording of ending balance of material inventory
6. Transfer of cost of goods manufactured account to cost of goods sold account
7. Transfer of finished goods account balance to cost of goods sold account
8. Recording of ending finished goods inventory

Based on this adjusted trial balance, the end-of-period entries for manufacturing costs.

While the mechanics of preparing financial statements are important to the accountant, they are not that important to management. It is important that management understands financial statements in order to use information and relationships on the financial statements to make better decisions.

The Accounting Cycle for a Manufacturing Business

The accounting cycle for a manufacturing business is basically the same as the accounting cycle for a merchandising businesses. The major difference concerns how certain end-of-period journal entries are made for the manufacturing transactions. As illustrated above, a cost of goods manufactured account was used in the recording process. This particular account does not necessarily have to be used; however, if not used, some other account such as work-in-process has to be used for the same purpose. The accounting cycle may be summarised as follows:

Step 1 Make journal entries for regular during-the-period transactions including the transactions for manufacturing costs and post to the accounts in the general ledger.

Step 2 At the end of the operating period, prepare a trial balance.

Step 3 Make adjusting entries and post to the general ledger.

Step 4 Prepare an adjusted trial balance.

Step 5 Prepare financial statements.

Step 6 Make end-of-the-period journal entries:

a. Make entries to transfer appropriate manufacturing costs to the cost of goods manufactured account.

b. Make regular closing entries for revenue and expense accounts.

Step 7 Prepare a post closing trial balance.

Please note that the above steps assume that making journal entries and posting are part of the same step.

DIRECT COSTING FINANCIAL STATEMENTS

Accounting has evolved slowly over many centuries. The first important complete treatise on the principles of accounting and bookkeeping was a book by Pacoli in the 1490s. The development of accounting principles and procedures are still continuing to evolve. In the early 1900s, many controversial issues were debated and some were resolved. In the 1950s and 1960s here in the USA, the lack of standardisation in accounting was of primary concern.

One of controversial areas debated extensively in the 1930s and 1940s was the treatment of manufacturing overhead in the costing of inventory and cost of goods sold. The controversy was commonly labeled absorption costing versus direct costing. To understand the issues involved, a good understanding of the principles of cost accounting is helpful.

In direct costing, fixed manufacturing overhead is treated as an operating expense. Absorption costing regards fixed manufacturing overhead as a manufacturing cost properly included in inventory and cost of goods sold. Because of the difference in the treatment of fixed manufacturing overhead, a substantial difference in the measurement of net income can result.

Accounting for Manufacturing Overhead

Manufacturing overhead is one of the three major manufacturing costs. For the most part, materials and labor are considered direct costs and can be easily associated with a specific product or job. However, manufacturing overhead tends to be more intangible and difficult to trace to a product or job. For example, utility cost such as power and light is necessary to the production process, but it is not easily assignable to a product, job, or department. The main solution to distributing overhead cost has been the use of overhead rates. Rates are typically determined by dividing estimated overhead cost by some estimated measure of activity. Activity bases for overhead typically used are direct labor hours, direct labor cost, machine hours, and units of product. The conventional theory is that direct labor which is easily capable of being measured correlates directly with the amount of overhead being incurred.

However, accountants quickly realised that manufacturing overhead varies in nature in that some overhead tends to be fixed and some tends to be variable. Variable cost was recognised to be caused by activity and to vary directly with changes in activity. If production doubled, for example, the variable overhead likewise doubled. However, fixed manufacturing as the term "fixed" implies remained the same regardless of the level of activity. A theory of accounting for fixed manufacturing overhead developed which stated that fixed overhead provides the capacity to produce and that the bases for application of fixed manufacturing overhead should be some estimate of capacity. Consequently, in cost accounting theory four levels of capacity were developed: expected actual, normal, practical, and theoretical. Overhead rates for fixed manufacturing overhead were developed by dividing estimated fixed manufacturing overhead by some estimated capacity level.

The methods developed for overhead, particularly fixed manufacturing overhead, at times can have a profound effect on net income. The choice of a capacity base and the method of application can cause significant variations in net income. Among cost accountants, it became quickly recognised that net income was not only a product of sales but also of the accounting for overhead.

To illustrate, assume fixed manufacturing overhead is $1,000,000 and the company is debating whether to make 50,000 units or 100,000 units of product. The estimated fixed manufacturing overhead cost per unit of product would, therefore, be either $10.00 or $20.00. If the company were to actually manufacture 50,000 units of product, then income would be less because cost of goods sold would be $10 per product greater. If management is only concerned about short-term maximisation of net income, then the obvious decision would be to make 100,000 units. If the excess inventory is never sold or has to be sold at a big price decrease, then in the long-term the potential inventory loss could easily more than offset any short-term benefit of over producing.

The traditional method of accounting for overhead just described is called absorption costing. The term absorption implies that fixed manufacturing is absorbed into the cost of inventory and cost of goods sold by means of using manufacturing overhead rates. Absorption costing as pointed out by advocates of direct costing has an inherent and potentially serious faw in that it is possible to manipulate net income by deliberately manufacturing more units than is required to meet the needs of the production budget. In a company with only variable manufacturing overhead, the deliberate act of increasing production in excess of sales can not cause net income to become larger.

Some accounting theorists in the 1930s and 1940s began suggesting an alternative method of applying fixed overhead to inventory. Fixed manufacturing overhead, it was argued, was not caused by the act of producing and, therefore, could not properly be called a production cost. Since fxed manufacturing overhead tends to remain the same from period to period, treating it as a periodic charge on the income statement is more appropriate. The proposed solution to the problem of absorption costing was called direct costing and in some cases variable costing.

Absorption Costing Versus Direct Costing

While the main difference between absorption costing and direct costing lies in the treatment of fxed manufacturing overhead, there are consequences that makes the two methods different in other respects:

Basis Features of Absorption Costing. Absorption costing which is traditional cost accounting may be summarised as follows:

1. Both fxed and variable overhead are applied to inventory
2. Manufacturing overhead is usually applied by means of a predetermined overhead rate.
3. The use of a predetermined overhead rate generally will result in manufacturing overhead being over-applied or under-applied.
4. Under-applied overhead is generally charged to cost of goods sold or shown on the income statement as a separate line item.

5. The actual level of production then has an impact on net income. The greater the level of production relative to sales the less is under-applied overhead and the greater is net income.
6. The cost of inventory properly includes both fxed and variable manufacturing overhead.
7. Manufacturing overhead, except for under-applied overhead, therefore,becomes an expense only when the goods manufactured are sold.
8. Under absorption costing, net income is a function of both production and sales.

The advocates of absorption costing, by far the majority viewpoint, argue strenuously that fxed manufacturing cost is a necessary production cost because it makes production possible and, therefore, must be include in determining the cost of inventory.

Basis Features of Direct Costing - The basic points of direct costing or variable costing as it is often called may be summarised as follows:

1. Fixed manufacturing overhead is not considered to be a production cost properly included in the cost of inventory.
2. Fixed manufacturing overhead is regarded as a periodic charge, an operating expense. Regardless of the level of activity, it remains the same in a given time period.
3. Fixed manufacturing is not caused by production. Even at sero level of activity, the cost would still remain.
4. An overhead rate is only needed for variable overhead.
5. Because it is a cost of each accounting period and remains the same independent of production activity, it should be treated as an expense on the income statement.
6. The treatment of fxed manufacturing overhead as a periodic charge eliminates the distortion to net income caused by fuctuations in production relative to sales.
7. The cost of inventory should only consist of variable manufacturing costs. Variable overhead should be included in inventory, but not fxed manufacturing overhead.

Fixed manufacturing overhead does not fow through inventory but rather is a direct charge against revenue on the income statement. When both cost fow diagrams are compared, the only difference between direct costing and absorption become quite obvious.

Production Units and Sales Units

In order to fully understand the difference consequences of using absorption costing as opposed to using direct costing, the effect of production being more or less than units sold needs to be clearly understood. Some important relationships are the following:

1. When production units equals sales units, there is no difference in net income between absorption costing and direct costing.
2. When production is greater than units sold, absorption costing will show greater net income than direct costing.
3. When production is less than units sold, absorption costing will show less net income than direct costing.
4. Under direct costing, assuming sales is constant from period to period, net income will be the same regardless of the level of production.
5. Under absorption costing, even assuming sales is constant from period to period, net income will vary directly with changes in production.

Production Changes on Net Income

A number of important observations can be made from a careful examination of the income statements for both direct costing and absorption costing.

1. As production increased by 10 units while sales remained constant, net income under absorption costing increased by $100. In case IV, net income decreased because production was less than sales. An increase in production of 10 units causes a $100 decrease in under-applied overhead.

2. Under direct costing, net income remained the same at in all four cases at $1,050. In direct costing the differences between production and sales had no effect on net income.
3. In absorption costing, the manufacturing cost per unit is $20 while under direct costing it is $10.
4. Ending inventory is greater under absorption costing than direct costing by $10 per unit, the amount of the fxed overhead rate. In absorption costing, fxed overhead is included in the cost of inventory whereas in direct costing it is excluded.
5. The direct costing income statement above was based on cost-volume-profit principles and clearly delineated all variable and fxed expenses. As a matter of practice when direct costing is used, a separation of fxed and variable cost is made and contribution margin is shown. However, even under absorption costing, variable and fxed costs may be shown.

Mathematical Equations for Direct Costing Absorption Costing

The principles of cost-volume-proft analysis have been presented mathematically. The cost-volume-proft net income equation was presented as follows:

$$I = P(Q^s) - V^d(Q^s) - (F^m + F^{ga} + F^s)$$

$$V^d = V^m + V^l + V^o + V^s + V^{ga}$$

V^d - Variable cost rate in direct costing

This equation is, in fact, the equation for the direct costing viewpoint. In order to easily compute break even point and target income point, it is necessary to adopt a direct costing approach to income measurement. The basic assumption of cost-volume-profit analysis is that during the period of analysis production units equals sales units. A similar equation for absorption may be created; however, because fxed overhead is considered to be a production cost and because there is the possibility of a variation in production units and sales units, the equation is considerably more complex.

Important Concepts in Direct Costing and Absorption Costing

The study of absorption costing and direct costing is rich in accounting concepts.

The study of absorption costing versus direct costing should be based on an understanding of the following concepts:

1. Absorption costing
2. Direct costing
3. Capacity
4. Inventory changes
5. Quantity sold
6. Planned quantity
7. Variable costs (direct)
8. Fixed expenses
9. Manufacturing costs
10. Quantity manufactured
11. Fixed overhead rate
12. Variable overhead rate
13. Period charges
14. Cost of inventory
15. Under-over-applied overhead
16. Contribution margin
17. Fixed manufacturing cost

Since direct costing is not an acceptable method for external reporting to stockholders and other external parties, the question of its value must be raised. When used it must be done only internally and for some perceived beneft to management in their role as decision makers. Advocates of direct costing believe (1) that direct costing eliminates misleading fuctuations in net income caused by using absorption costing and (2) eliminates the tendency on the part of some management to deliberately over produce to gain only a temporary boost in net income.

Effect of Direct Costing on Inventory Cost

The main argument against direct costing is that it understates the value of ending inventory. It is true that direct costing creates a smaller inventory value. Proponents of absorption costing argue that fxed manufacturing overhead is a true production cost because it makes production possible. That is, the product can be manufactured without any paid labor or any need to buy raw materials. Furthermore, to complete this extreme example the following is assumed.

Based on this information income statements for periods 1 and 2 would show the following

For the period 1, two completely different net income pictures are painted. Absorption costing shows income to be zero and ending inventory to be $1,000. Direct costing shows the business operating at a loss of $1,000 and that the ending inventory has a zero cost.

Direct costing shows net income to be $500 and under absorption costing a net loss of $500 is reported. Absorption costing shows the loss to be greater when the company had sales. As long as it is manufacturing at capacity under absorption costing, the company will not show a loss. Proponents of direct costing would point out this does not seem to be reasonable. They would argue that a zero value assigned to inventory is unrealistic. Both absorption costing and direct costing show that for the two periods combined the company lost $500.

Analysis of Financial Statement

A countless number of financial market participants will use and analyse financial statement information, particularly bankers, other lenders, suppliers, investors, and even some of the firm's customers. Often firms make their financial data available to the public to show workers and investors how well the company is doing. For private firms, statement analysis and industry comparisons are done for internal use.

Successful financial analysis and planning require an understanding of a company's external and internal environments. External factors that affect a firm's profitability may be issues such as inflation, interest rates, exchange rates, and government policy. The firm's internal environment includes items that can be affected by management, such as organisational structure, employee motivation and productivity, cost control, and the company's plant and operations. Pricing decisions are also influenced by the state of the economy, actions by competitors, and the firm's production costs. The joint impact of the external and internal environment on a firm should be reflected in its financial statements. These statements are a good way to assess the success or failure of the company's strategies and operations.

Using Financial Statements

Different groups use financial statements for different purposes. Banks use financial statements to determine if they should loan money to a firm. Stock brokers use financial statements to determine if the stock of the company is going to be profitable and if the stock is a good buy.

The information found on the financial statements is valuable to the company's managers, to stock and bond analysts, bank loan officers, and competitors. However, the way that investors view the results that come from analysing financial statements often depends upon the current state of the economy. That's because as economic growth begins, increased sales will generate cash to pay interest, leaving high levels of profits. Of course, the same debt ratios at the end of a period of economic growth, with a recession growing near, may make investors turn away.

Keep in mind that many individuals and organisations analyse financial statements. A company that seeks credit, either from a supplier or a bank, is usually required to submit financial statements for examination.

1) Describe how financial statements are used by a variety of different groups to discover information about a firm.
2) Identify the external factors that affect a business's profitably.
3) What are the internal factors that have an effect on the firm's profitably?
4) How investors view the analysis of financial statements is affected by what current aspect?

Ratio Analysis

In this section we discuss ratio analysis as a means by which to gain insight into a firm's strengths and weaknesses. Ratio analysis is a financial technique that involves dividing various financial statement numbers into one another.

Ratios are computed by dividing one amount on the financial statements into another. They are percentages that are easily obtained by entering the numbers from financial data into a calculator. The ratios can then be examined to determine trends and reasons for changes in the financial statement from month to month.

Ratios are used to produce the commonsize financial statements that made it possible for us to compare Walgreens, Microsoft, and ExxonMobil despite the differences in their sizes and business activities. numbers. A firm with $10 billion in sales can be easily compared to a firm with $1 billion or $200 million in sales.

Three basic categories of ratio analysis are used.

1) Trend or timeseries analysis uses ratios to evaluate a firm's performance over time.
2) Crosssection analysis uses ratios to compare different companies at the same point in time.
3) Industrycomparative analysis is used to compare a firm's ratios against average ratios for other companies in the same industry.

Comparing a firm's ratios to average industry ratios requires a degree of caution. That's because some sources of industry data report the average for each ratio; others report the median; others report the interquartile range for each ratio, which is the range for the middle 50% of ratio values reported by firms in the industry

The analyst must also be aware that industry ratios may be narrowly focused on a specific industry, but the operations of large firms such as GE, ExxonMobil, and IBM often cross many industry boundaries. Also, accounting standards often differ among firms in an industry. This can create confusion, particularly when some firms in the industry adopt new accounting standards set forth by the Financial Accounting Standards Board before others. Adopting standards early can affect a firm's ratios by making them appear unusually high or low compared to the industry average.

Care also must be taken when comparing different types of firms in the same industry. In one industry there may be a mixture of very large and very small firms.

Analysts and sources of public information on ratios may compute ratios differently. Some may use after-tax earnings, some pre-tax earnings; others may assume *debt* refers only to long-term debt while others include all liabilities as debt.

Sometimes how a ratio is interpreted depends on who has requested it—that is, whether a ratio appears favorable or unfavorable depends on the perspective Interpreting Ratios

If a short-term creditor such as a bank loan officer wants to see a high degree of liquidity, the analyst would be somewhat less concerned with a firm's profitability than if the user was an equity holder who would rather see less liquidity and more profitability. of the user. Therefore, the analyst must keep in mind the viewpoint of the user in evaluating and interpreting the information contained in financial ratios.

1. Define ratio analysis and explain what it is used for.
2. Explain why ratios are used for financial analysis.
3. List and briefly explain the three basic categories of ratio analysis.
4. Why must caution be used in comparing ratios of different companies?

Types of Financial Ratios

Many types of ratios can be calculated from financial statement data or stock market information. However, it is common practice to group ratios into five basic categories:

1. Liquidity ratios
2. Asset-management ratios
3. Financial-leverage ratios
4. Profitability ratios
5. Market-value ratios

The first four categories are based on information taken from a firm's income statements and balance sheets. The fifth category relates stock market information to financial statement items.

Liquidity Ratios

Liquidity refers to how quickly a firm can turn its assets into cash. A firm, for example, that has only cash assets is completely liquid. On the opposite extreme would be a firm whose only assets are real estate. Because real estate sales can take months, or even years, and may even take a loss on the transaction, the firm is illiquid. If a firm cannot pay its financial obligations, it will go bankrupt.

The less liquid the firm, the greater the risk of insolvency or default. Because debt obligations are paid with cash, the firm's cash flows ultimately determine solvency.

We can estimate the firm's liquidity position by examining specific balance sheet items. Liquidity ratios indicate the ability to meet short-term obligations to creditors as they mature or come due.

This form of liquidity analysis focuses on the relationship between current assets and current liabilities, and the speed with which receivables and inventory turn into cash during normal business operations. This means that the immediate source of cash funds for paying bills must be cash on hand, proceeds from the sale of marketable securities, or the collection of accounts receivable. Additional liquidity also comes from inventory that can be sold and thus converted into cash either directly through cash sales or indirectly through credit sales. The dollar amount of a firm's net working capital is sometimes used as a measure of liquidity.

The net working capital of a firm is its current assets minus current liabilities. However, two popular ratios are also used to gauge a firm's liquidity position.

The current ratio is a measure of a company's ability to pay off its short-term debt as it comes due. The current ratio is computed by dividing the current assets by the current liabilities.

A low current ratio may indicate that a company faces difficulty in paying its bills. A high value for the current ratio, however, does not necessarily imply greater liquidity. Excessive amounts of inventory, accounts receivable, or idle cash balances could contribute to a high current ratio.

The balance sheet shows a large increase in Walgreens's cash account in 2003, and both accounts receivables and inventory rose. At first glance, analysts may think Walgreens has slow-paying accounts or sales slowdowns.

The quick ratio, or acid-test ratio, is computed by dividing the sum of cash, marketable securities, and accounts receivable by the current liabilities.

In general, a ratio of 1.0 indicates a reasonably liquid position in that an immediate liquidation of marketable securities at their current values and the collection of all accounts receivable, plus cash on hand, would be adequate to cover the firm's current liabilities. However, as this ratio declines, the firm must increasingly rely on converting inventories to sales in order to meet current liabilities as they come due. Walgreens's quick ratios for 2003 and 2002 are

According to the financial statement data, Walgreens's quick ratio is well below 1.0. As we will soon see, this is not a major cause for concern in the retail drug-store industry. When assessing the firm's liquidity position, financial managers also are interested in how trade credit from suppliers, which we call *accounts payable,* is being used and paid for.

1. The average payment period is computed by dividing the year-end accounts payable amount by the firm's average cost of goods sold per day We calculate the average daily cost of goods sold by dividing the income statement's cost of goods sold amount by 365 days in a year. The average payment period is calculated

The industry's current and quick ratios rose slightly while the average payment period fell over the 1997-2003 period. Walgreens's current and quick ratios are above those of the industry in 1997 and 1998, but their relative positions reversed in 2000. Between 2000 and 2003, Walgreens's liquidity ratios recovered and moved closer to those of the industry

Walgreens's average payment period remained constant, about 32 days, during this period.

Asset-Management Ratios

Asset-management ratios indicate the extent to which assets are used to support sales. These are sometimes referred to as *activity* or *utilisation ratios,* and each ratio in this category relates financial performance on the income statement with items on the balance sheet. Once again.

The total-assets-turnover ratio is computed by dividing net sales by the company's total assets.

This ratio indicates how efficiently the firm is utilising its assets to produce revenues or sales. It is a measure of the dollars of sales generated by $1 of the firm's assets. The size of the ratio is significantly influenced by characteristics of the industry within which the firm operates.

Capital-intensive electric utilities might have asset turnover ratios as low as 0.33, indicating that they require $3 of investment in assets in order to produce $1 in revenues. In contrast, retail food chains with asset turnovers as high as 10 would require a $0.10 investment in assets to produce $1 in sales.

Asset utilisation was consistent between 2002 and 2003, with each $1 in assets supporting slightly less than $3 in sales.

The fixed-assets-turnover ratio is computed by dividing net sales by the fixed assets and indicates the extent to which long-term assets are being used to produce sales.

Similar to the interpretation given to the total asset turnover, the fixed assets turnover represents the dollars of sales generated by each dollar of fixed assets. Investment in plant and equipment is usually quite expensive. Consequently unused or idle capacity is very costly and often represents a major factor in a firm's poor operating performance. On the other hand, a high fixed-assets-turnover ratio is not necessarily a favorable sign. It may come about because of efficient use of assets or it may come about because of the firm's use of obsolete equipment with reduced book values because of the effects of accumulated depreciation.

Walgreens's fixed assets turnover increased from 6.25 to 6.58 between 2002 and 2003, indicating that sales increased more rapidly than fixed assets. In percentage terms, net fixed assets increased 7.6% compared to 13.3% for sales. In light of an increase in the fixed asset turnover, it may be surprising that total asset turnover fell slightly from 2002 to 2003. This is an indication that Walgreens used its working capital less efficiently.

The average collection period is calculated by taking the year-end accounts receivable divided by the average net sales per day.

This indicates the average number of days that sales are outstanding. In other words, it reports the number of days it takes, on average, to collect credit sales. The average collection period measures the days of financing that a company extends to its customers.

Another measure that can be used to provide this same information is the receivables turnover.

The receivables turnover is computed by dividing annual sales, preferably credit sales, by the year-end accounts receivable.

If the receivables turnover is six, this means the average collection period is about 2 months. If the turnover is four times, the firm has an average collection period of about 3 months. Walgreens's average collection periods for 2003 and 2002 were.

Walgreens's average collection period fell slightly from 2002 to 2003. Comparing the average collection and payment periods, Walgreens is in a positive situation, as it collects from its customers about 20 days faster than it pays its suppliers.

When comparing these figures to an industry average, an unusually low number of days required to collect sales may indicate that the company uses a rigid internal credit policy that might result in lost sales. On the other hand, a very high average collection period may indicate that the firm has too lax a credit

The ratios computed on accounts receivable and accounts payable give an analyst a good sense of how well a company is operating. Policy and may be in danger of experiencing a larger number of credit accounts that cannot be collected. Remember that these ratios are only guides, and it is important to monitor trends over time in addition to comparing a company's ratio numbers to the industry averages.

The inventory-turnover ratio is computed by dividing the cost of goods sold by the year-end inventory. Here we are seeking to determine how efficiently the amount of inventory is being managed. With inventory management, it is prudent to have an adequate amount to avoid running out of products while avoiding the accumulation of too many products that may necessitate extra financing.

Cost of goods sold is often used to compute this ratio instead of sales in order to remove the impact of profit margins on inventory turnover. Profit margins can vary over time, making it more difficult to interpret the relationship between volume and inventory.

Walgreens's annual inventory turnover decreased slightly from 5.70 in 2002 to 5.56 in 2003.

Inventory management also requires a delicate balance between having too low an inventory turnover, which increases the likelihood of holding obsolete inventory, and too high an inventory turnover, which could lead to stock-outs and lost sales.

When a firm is growing rapidly the use of year-end data may distort the comparison of ratios over time. To avoid such possi-ble distortions, analysts can use the average inventory to calculate inventory turnovers for comparison purposes. Likewise, average data for other balance sheet accounts should be used when rapid growth or contraction is taking place for a specific firm.

Financial-Leverage Ratios

To assess the extent to which borrowed money or debt is used to finance assets, analysts use financial-leverage ratios.

Financial-leverage ratios indicate the extent to which borrowed or debt funds are used to finance assets.

These ratios are also a good way to assess the ability of the firm to meet its debt payment obligations.

The total-debt-to-total-assets ratio is computed by dividing the total debt or total liabilities of the business by its total assets. This ratio shows the portion of the total assets financed by all creditors and debtors. Taking the relevant information from the Walgreens balance sheet the computation is done as follows:

Walgreens's total debt ratio has not changed, meaning that the firm's debt load grew at approximately the same rate as its asset base. Additional debt funds may be more costly in terms of the rate of interest that will have to be paid. Lenders will want higher expected returns to compensate for their risk of lending to a firm that has a high proportion of debt to assets.

It is also possible to have too low a ratio of total debt to total assets. This can be quite costly to a corporation. Since interest expenses are deductible for income tax purposes, the government in effect pays a portion of the debt-financing costs.

Sometimes a debt ratio is calculated to show the total debt in relation to the dollars the owners have put in the firm. This is referred to as the *total-debt-to-equity ratio.*

The total-debt-to-equity ratio shows a firm's total debt in relation to the total dollar amount owners have invested in the firm. Walgreens's ratio for 2003 was 0.59 and 0.59 in 2002. This means for every dollar of equity, the firm has borrowed about 59 cents.

The equity multiplier ratio provides another way of looking at the firm's debt burden. The equity multiplier ratio is calculated by dividing total assets by the firm's total equity.

Similar to the total-debt-to-total-assets ratio, the equity multiplier was unchanged between 2002 and 2003. Since Walgreens does not have long-term debt outstanding, these modest changes in the debt ratios occur because of changes in short-term debt or Walgreens's other liabilities, such as pension fund or health care benefits for workers.

At first glance, this last ratio appears to have little to do with leverage; it is simply the total assets divided by stockholders' equity. However, recall the concept behind the balance sheet. The concept is simple. In order to acquire assets, a firm must pay for them with either debt or with the owner's capital. Therefore the following equation must hold true: Assets = Liabilities + Equity. This is also known as the *accounting identity.* This formula shows that more assets relative to equity suggest greater use of debt.

This is simply one plus the debt-to-equity ratio. Clearly, more reliance on debt results in a larger equity multiplier. While the equity multiplier does not add to the information derived from the other debt ratios, it is useful when financial analysis is conducted using certain financial models.

In addition to calculating debt ratios, the financial manager should be interested in the firm's ability to meet or service its interest and principal repayment obligations on the borrowed funds. This is accomplished through the calculation of interest coverage and fixed-charge-coverage ratios.

The interest coverage, or times-interest-earned ratio, is calculated by dividing the firm's operating income or earnings before interest and taxes (EBIT) by the annual interest expense.

Walgreens's interest coverage ratios are not defined for 2002 and 2003 since interest-paying notes payable and long-term debt are both zero on the firm's balance sheet in 2002 and 2003.

The interest coverage figure indicates the extent to which the operating income or EBIT level could decline before the ability to pay interest obligations would be impeded. This would mean that Walgreens's operating income could drop to 20%, or one-fifth of its current level, and interest payments still could be met.

The fixed-charge-coverage ratio indicates the ability of a firm to meet its contractual obligations for interest, leases, and debt principal repayments out of its operating income.

Rental or lease payments are deductible on the income statement prior to the payment of income taxes just as is the case with interest expenses. In contrast, a sinking fund payment is a repayment of debt and thus is not a deductible expense for income tax purposes. However, to be consistent with the other data, we must adjust the sinking fund payment to a before-tax basis.

While footnotes to Walgreens's balance sheets are not provided, examination of the footnotes in Walgreens's annual reports shows property lease payments of $1,187.0 million in 2003 and $897.9 million in 2002. Walgreens has no interest-bearing liabilities, and it has no sinking fund obligations. We compute the fixed-charge-coverage ratio as follows: First, the numerator in the ratio must reflect earnings before interest, lease payments, and taxes, which we determine by adding the lease payment amount to the operating income or EBIT amount. Second, the denominator needs to show all relevant expenses on a before-tax basis.

This is a marked difference from the interest coverage ratio. Information in Walgreens's annual report to shareholders tells us that the firm usually leases its store space rather than purchasing it.

The graphs of Walgreens's financial-leverage ratios industry debt ratios declining slightly during the 1997-2003 time period. The deterioration in the industry's interest coverage, from about 9 in 1998 to about 3 in 2000, was a concern. Since then, however, the industry's interest coverage ratio recovered.

In contrast to the retail drug store industry, Walgreens' debt ratio declined slightly while its interest-coverage ratio was either at extremely high levels or was undefined because of the absence of interest-bearing debt.

From looking at Walgreens, we can come to three important conclusions. First, not all liabilities are contractual debt. Walgreens has a debt-to-assets ratio of about 40% but has no interest-bearing short-term or long-term on its balance sheet. Second, not all liabilities require interest to be paid. Again, Walgreens has a debt ratio of 40% but virtually no interest payments. Third, to get a truer perspective of a company's financial situation, all contractual fixed charges, including interest, lease payments, and sinking fund payments, should be examined. Walgreens's sky-high interest coverage ratio is brought back to earth when fixed charges are considered and a fixed charge-coverage ratio is computed.

Profitability Ratios

To determine a firm's ability to generate returns on its sales, assets, and equity, analysts use profitability ratios. *Profitability ratios* indicate the firm's ability to generate returns on its sales, assets, and equity.

Two basic profit margin ratios are important to the financial manager, the operating profit margin and the net profit margin. *The operating profit margin* is calculated on the firm's earnings before interest and taxes divided by net sales.

This ratio indicates the firm's ability to control operating expenses relative to sales.

These results indicate that Walgreens was able to slightly improve its operating profitability from 2002 to 2003. Whether it was because of higher selling prices or lower costs, operating profit (EBIT) rose about 13.8% on a sales increase of about 13.3%.

The net profit margin, a widely used measure of a company's profitability, is calculated as the firm's net income after taxes divided by net sales.

In addition to considering operating expenses, this ratio also indicates the ability to earn a return after meeting interest and tax obligations. Walgreens's net profit margin shows a slight improvement in 2003 over 2002:

Three basic rates-of-return measures on assets and equity are important to the financial manager. *The operating return on assets* is computed as the earnings before interest and taxes divided by total assets.

Notice that this ratio focuses on the firm's operating performance and ignores how the firm is financed and taxed. Relevant data for Walgreens must be taken from both the balance sheets and the income statement:

The net return on total assets, commonly referred to as the *return on total assets,* is measured as the firm's net income divided by total assets.

Here we measure the return on investment in assets after a firm has covered its operating expenses, interest costs, and tax obligations. Walgreens's return on total assets remained constant in 2002 and 2003:

Since Walgreens leases many of its stores, this not only reduces its financing needs but also reduces its level of fixed and total assets.

A final profitability ratio is the return on equity.

The return on equity measures the return that shareholders earned on their equity invested in the firm.

The return on equity is measured as the firm's net income divided by stock-holders' equity. This ratio reflects the fact that a portion of a firm's total assets Cost Efficiency

Walgreens is more cost-efficient and generates more profit from its asset and equity base than the retail drugstore industry as a whole are financed with borrowed funds. As with the return on assets, Walgreens's return on equity remained virtually the same from 2002 to 2003.

Market-Value Ratios

Market-value ratios indicate the willingness of investors to value a firm in the marketplace relative to financial statement values.

A firm's profitability, risk, quality of management, and many other factors are reflected in its stock and security prices by the efficient financial markets.

We know that stock prices seem to reflect much of the known information about a company and are fairly good indicators of a company's true value.

The price/earnings ratio, or P/E ratio, is simply the market price of the firm's common stock divided by its annual earnings per share.

Sometimes called the *earnings multiple,* the P/E ratio shows how much investors are willing to pay for each dollar of the firm's earnings per share. Though earnings per share cannot reflect the value of the firm's patents or assets, human resources, culture, quality of management, or its risk, stock prices can and do reflect all these factors.

Comparing a firm's P/E relative to that of the stock market as a whole, or the firm's competitors, indicates the market's perceptions of the true value of the company. *The price-to-book-value ratio* measures the market's value of the firm relative to balance sheet equity.

The book value of equity is simply the difference between the book values of assets and liabilities appearing on the balance sheet. The price-to-book-value ratio is the market price per share divided by the book value of equity per share.

The P/E ratio and price/book ratio for Walgreens and the retail drugstore industry. Just as our analysis of financial statement ratios pointed out, Walgreens's higher profitability and consistency in its ratios over time has translated into higher relative market valuations.

The market is optimistic in its valuation of Walgreens's future prospects. Both the earnings multiple and price/book ratios have fallen for Walgreens and the industry, but Walgreens's ratios continue to exceed those of the industry.

Financial managers and analysts often talk about the quality of a firm's earnings or the quality of its balance sheet. This has nothing to do with the size of a company's earnings or assets or who audited the financial statements. Quality financial statements are those that accurately reflect the firm's true economic condition. In other words, accounting methods were not used to inflate its earnings or assets to make the firm look stronger than it really is. Earnings are not affected by onetime charges. A quality balance sheet will represent inventory that is marketable, not out of fashion or technologically obsolete. It will represent limited debt, indicating the firm could easily borrow money should the need arise.

All else constant, a firm with higherquality financial statements will have higher marketvalue ratios. This occurs because the market will recognise and reward the economic reality of a firm's earnings and assets that are not temporarily bloated by accounting gimmicks.

Attempts to play accounting tricks will affect the firm's ratios. Overstating existing inventory can have the effect of making current cost of goods sold appear lower, thus inflating profits. Booking revenue in advance of true sales to customers will inflate both sales and profits. The effect of such actions will be to increase profitability and asset management ratios. Unfortunately, watching for accounting tricks or outright fraud is necessary for investors, as problems with companies in different industries such as telecommunications equipment dot-com firms and energy trading have shown in recent years.

Summing up Ratios

Here's what we've learned about Walgreens by computing their ratios and comparing them to the industry averages. The liquidity ratios show consistency over time, but the favorable gap between Walgreens and its industry-average ratios has narrowed or been reversed. This is also true of the asset-management ratios. Walgreens's historical advantages have disappeared.

Should Walgreens need to raise money quickly, it should be able to issue debt, as Walgreens's debt ratios are lower than the industry averages and its interest coverage. But a truer picture would include fixed charges such as lease payments in the analysis.

Part of Walgreens's success can be traced to good control and, until recently, superior asset-management. The receivables collection period is shorter than average as well. The combination of good cost control and efficient asset management has resulted in good profitability compared to the industry averages. The stock market has recognised Walgreens's abilities, and Walgreens's market-value ratios are above those of the industry.

1) What do liquidity ratios measure?
2) Name three liquidity ratios and describe what they tell about a firm.
3) What do asset-management ratios measure?
4) List three asset-management ratios and describe what they tell analysts about a firm.
5) What do financial-leverage ratios tell analysts about a firm?
6) What do profitability ratios measure?

Du Pont Method of Ratio Analysis

How does a supermarket generate profits? In general, supermarkets have very low profit margins. Many of its goods are sold for pennies above cost. Profits are generated by rapid turnover. The shelves are restocked daily with new items to take the place of items that were purchased.

Jewelry stores generate their profits differently. They typically have very high profit margins but low turnover. Jewelry items may sit on the shelf for months at a time until they are sold.

This indicates there are two basic methods by which a firm can generate a return on its assets. It can offer low prices and low profit margins seeking high sales volumes on commodity products, like a supermarket, or it can sell its quality or differentiated goods at high prices and rely mainly on high profit margins to generate returns on low sales, like a jewelry store.

The return on total-assets ratio can be used to examine this relationship and to determine how a given firm generates profits. It equals the product of the profit margin and total asset turnover ratio.

A supermarket's profit margin may be 1%, but its total asset turnover may be 10. This would give it a return on total assets of 1% x 10 or 10%. A jewelry store may have a 25% profit margin and have a very low asset turnover of 0.40, also giving it a return on total assets of 10%. Year-to-year variations in a firm's return on total assets can be explained by changes in its profit margin, total asset turnover, or both.

Like the return on total assets, return on equity can be broken down into component parts to tell us why the level of return changes from year to year or why two firms' returns on equity differ. The return on equity is identical to return on total assets multiplied by the equity multiplier.

Thus, a firm's return on equity may differ from one year to the next, or from a competitor's, as a result of differences in profit margin, asset turnover, or leverage. Unlike the other measures of profitability, return on equity directly reflects a firm's use of leverage or debt. If a firm uses relatively more liabilities to finance assets, the equity multiplier will rise, and, holding other factors constant, the firm's return on equity will increase.

This technique of breaking return on total assets, and return on equity into their component parts is called Du Pont analysis, named after the company that popularised it.

The Du Pont analysis is the technique of breaking down return on total assets and return on equity into their component parts.

Du Pont analysis can break return on equity and return on total assets into different components and how these components can then be broken into their constituent parts for analysis. Therefore, an indication that a firm's return on equity has increased as a result of higher turnover can lead to study of the turnover ratio, using data from several years, to determine if the increase has resulted from higher sales volume, better management of assets, or some combination of the two. Between 2000 and 2001, the main reason for the decrease in Walgreens's return on equity was a decrease in the net profit margin and asset efficiency. Between 2001-2003, Walgreens's profit margin and asset-efficiency ratios recovered, but return on equity fell as its use of leverage declined.

Long-Term Financial Planning

Financial ratios and financial statement relationships can be used to analyse firms and their competitors, but they have another more practical use for managers who use them in the company's financial planning process.

Financial planning requires foresight. Long-range plans covering several years must be prepared to project growth in sales, assets, and employees.

Return on Equity and Investing

Return on equity is an important factor for many investors when they choose stocks to buy. The return on equity is the quickest way to determine if a firm is an asset creator or cash consumer.

A manufacturing firm may need to invest in a plant and equipment to produce an inventory that will fill forecasted sales orders.

forecast is the first step, and it should take into consideration expected developments in the economy and competition from other similar businesses. The sales forecast then must be supported by plans for adequate investment in assets. After determining the size of the necessary investment, plans must be made for estimating the amount of financing needed and how to acquire it.

In addition to long-range financial plans or budgets, the financial manager should also be concerned with cash inflows and outflows associated with the business. Cash flows are often monitored on a daily basis for large firms, while small firms may make only monthly cash budgets.

Using the ratios we have just learned about goes hand in hand with successful financial planning. An established firm should conduct a financial ratio analysis of past performance to aid in developing realistic future plans. The new firm should analyse the performance characteristics of other firms in the same industry before making plans.

1) How can ratios be used to help managers do financial planning?
2) What should long-range plans project?

Cost-Volume-Profit Analysis

Cost-volume-profit analysis represents another tool used by managers for financial planning purposes.

Cost-volume-profit analysis is used by managers for financial planning to estimate the firm's operating profits at different levels of unit sales.

A variation, called *break-even analysis,* can be used to estimate how many units of product must be sold in order for the firm to "break even" or have a zero profit. *Break-even analysis* is used to estimate how many units of product must be sold in order for the firm to break even or have a zero profit.

As an example of cost-volume-profit analysis, let's assume that a Walgreens store is considering adding a new product to its stores. It will be sold for $10 per item. The variable costs will be $6. Fixed costs are expected to be $1,000 annually. Management is interested in knowing what level of operating profit will occur if unit sales are 2,000 per year.

From the format of an income statement, we know that sales revenues minus various costs gives us operating profit or earnings before interest and taxes (EBIT). Sales can be expressed as unit price multiplied by quantity sold. The costs can be expressed by variable costs and fixed costs. The variable cost per unit (VC) times the quantity sold (Q) gives us total variable cost: (VC)(Q). Total fixed costs, FC, are constant; they are called *fixed* because they do not change with increases or decreases in output.

If sales reach 2,000 units per year, the firm expects an increase in operating profit of $7,000.

Management also may want to know how many units will have to be sold in order to break even—that is, what volume needs to be reached so that the amount of total revenues equals total cost. The quantity of unit sales that solves this equation is the break-even quantity (QBE)

In 2005, the automaker General Motors failed to break even. In fact, General Motors lost $8.6 billion. The losses were due to lower market share, higher labor costs, and higher health care costs. Due to the poor performance, General Motors, was forced to lay off tens of thousands of workers world-wide and decrease benefits. General Motors hopes to break even or post a small profit in 2006.Walgreens must sell 250 units of the new product in order to break even. The break-even point occurs when total revenues equal total costs.

Since a company's sales revenues are rarely constant, the variability of sales or revenues over time indicates a basic operating business risk that must be considered when developing financial plans. In addition, changes in the amount of income shown on the income statement are affected by both changes in sales and the use of fixed versus variable costs.

References

Beaney, Shaun, *Defining corporate finance in the UK*, The Institute of Chartered Accountants, April 2005.

Bear, Larry A. and Rita Maldonado-Bear, *Free Markets, Finance, Ethics, and Law*, Upper Saddle, NJ: Prentice Hall, 1994.

Block and Hirt, *Foundations of Financial Management*, 6th edition, Richard Irwin & Co, 1992.

Brealey, Richard A., *Principles of Corporate Finance*, NY: McGraw Hill, 2000.

Campsey and Brigham, *Introduction to Financial Management*, 3rd edition, Dryden Press, 1991.

6

Process Cost Systems

JOB ORDER COST SYSTEM

The job order cost system is best suited to industries that make special orders for customers or manufacture different products in groups. Industries that may use job order cost systems include special-order printing, custom-made tailoring, furniture manufacturing, shipbuilding, aircraft building, and construction .

In some ways, the process cost and job order cost systems are similar. Both systems accumulate product costs—direct materials, direct labor, and factory overhead—and allocate these costs to the units produced. Both systems maintain perpetual inventory accounts with subsidiary ledgers for materials, work in process, and finished goods. The main difference between the two systems is the form in which the product costs are accumulated and reported.

In a job order cost system, product costs are accumulated by job and are summarised on job cost sheets. The job cost sheets provide unit cost information and can be used by management for product pricing, cost control, and inventory valuation. The process manufacturer does not manufacture according to "jobs." Thus, costs are accumulated by department. Each unit of product that passes through the department is similar. In a job order cost system, the work in process inventory at the end of the accounting period is the sum of the job cost sheets for partially completed jobs.

Physical Flows and Cost Flows

Materials costs are a large portion of the costs for most process manufacturers. Often, the materials costs can be as high as 70% of the total manufacturing costs. Thus, accounting for materials costs is very important for process operations.

Exhibit 1 illustrates the physical flow of materials for a steel processor. Direct materials in the form of scrap metal are placed into a furnace in the Melting Department. The Melting Department uses conversion costs during the melting process. The molten metal is then transferred to the Casting Department, where it is poured into an ingotment also uses conversion costs during the casting pr transferred to the finished goods inventory for shipment to customers.

Purchased materials are debited to Materials and credited to Accounts Payable. Direct materials used by the Melting Department are debited to Work in Process—Melting and credited to Materials. In addition, indirect materials and other overhead incurred are debited to department factory overhead accounts and credited to Materials and other accounts. Direct labor in the Melting Department is debited to the department's work in process account and credited to Wages Payable. Applied factory overhead is debited to Work in Process—Melting, using a predetermined overhead rate. The cost of completed production from the Melting Department is transferred to the Casting Department by debiting Work in Process—Casting and crediting Work in Process—Melting. The direct labor and applied factory overhead costs in the Casting Department are debited to Work in Process—Casting. The cost of the finished ingots is transferred out of the Casting Department by debiting Finished Goods and crediting Work in Process—Casting. The cost of ingots sold to customers is transferred out of finished goods with a debit to Cost of Goods Sold and a credit to Finished Goods.

Business on Stage

Product

In manufacturing, inputs are processed into a product with physical attributes. In business, however, a product is often thought of in terms other than just its physical attributes.

Four types of products are (1) convenience products, (2) shopping products, (3) specialty products, and (4) unsought products. To illustrate, consider the following four products:

1. Convenience product:
2. Shopping product:
3. Specialty product:
4. Unsought product:

For each of these products, the frequency of purchase, the profit per unit, and the number of retailers differ. As a result, the sales and marketing approach for each product differs.

The First-In, First-Out (Fifo) Method

In a process cost system, the accountant determines the cost transferred out and thus the amount remaining in inventory for each department. For many manufacturing processes, materials are added at the beginning of production, and the units are moved through the production processes in a first-in, first-out (fifo) flow.

Most process manufacturers have more than one department. In the illustrations that follow, McDermott Steel Inc. has two departments, Melting and Casting. Mc-Dermott melts scrap metal and then pours the molten metal into an ingot casting.

To illustrate the first-in, first-out method, we will simplify by using only the Melting Department of McDermott Steel Inc. The following data for the Melting Department are for July of the current year.

We assume that all materials used in the department are added at the beginning of the process, and conversion costs are incurred evenly throughout the melting process. The objective is to determine the cost of goods completed and the ending inventory valuation, which are represented by the question marks. We determine these amounts by using the following four steps:

1. Determine the units to be assigned costs.
2. Calculate equivalent units of production.
3. Determine the cost per equivalent unit.
4. Allocate costs to transferred and partially completed units.

Determine the Units to Be Assigned Costs

A unit can be any measure of completed production, such as tons, gallons, pounds, barrels, or cases. We use tons as the definition for units in McDermott Steel.

There are three categories of units to be assigned costs for an accounting period: (A) units in beginning inprocess inventory, (B) units started and completed during the period, and (C) units in ending inprocess inventory. Exhibit 4 illustrates these categories in the Melting Department for July. The 500ton beginning inventory (A) was completed and transferred to the Casting Department. Of the 1,000 tons introduced in July, 400 tons were left incomplete at the end of the month (C). Thus, only 600 of the 1,000 tons were actually started and completed in July (B).

Note that the total tons to be assigned costs equals the total tons accounted for by the department. The three unit categories are used in the remaining steps to determine the cost transferred to the Casting Department and the cost remaining in work in process inventory at the end of the period.

Calculate Equivalent Units of Production

Process manufacturers often have some partially processed materials remaining in production at the end of a period. In these cases, the costs of production must be allocated between the units that have been completed and transferred to the next process and those that are only partially copleted and remain within the department.

The equivalent units of production are the number of units that *could have been* completed within a given accounting period. In contrast, who units are the number of units in production during a period, whether or not competed.

Equivalent units for materials and conversion costs are usually determined separately because they are often introduced at different times or at different rates in the production process. In contrast, direct board and factory overhead are combined together as conversion costs because they are often incurred in production a the same time and rate.

Units Materials Equivale

To allocate materials costs between the completed and partially completed units, it is necessary to determine *h w* materials are added during the manufacturing process. In the case of McDermott Steel, the materials are added at the beginning of the melting process.

The direct materials for the 500 tons of July inprocess inventory were introduced in June. Thus, no materials units were added in July for the inventory in process on July 1. All of the 600 tons started and completed in July were 100% complete with respect to materials. All the materials for the July 31 inprocess inventory were introduced at the beginning of the process. Thus, 400 equivalent units of material for the July 31 inprocess inventory were added in July.

Conversion Equivalent Units

The conversion costs are usually incurred evenly throughout a process. For example, direct labor, utilities, and machine depreciation are usually used uniformly during processing. Thus, the conversion equivalent units are added in July in direct relation to the percentage of processing completed in July.

The whole units from Step 1 are multiplied by the percentage of conversion completed in July for the inprocess inventories and units started and completed.

The conversion equivalent units of the July 1 inprocess inventory are 30% of the 500 tons, or 150 equivalent units. Since 70% of the conversion had been completed on July 1, only 30% of the conversion effort for these tons was incurred in July. Thus, conversion equivalent units are 100% of these tons. The equivalent units for the July 31 inprocess inventory are 25% of the 400 tons because only 25% of the converting has been completed with respect to these tons in July.

Determine the Cost per Equivalent Unit

In Step 3, we calculate the cost per equivalent unit. The July equivalent unit totals for McDermott Steel's Melting Department are reproduced from Step 2.

The cost per equivalent unit is determined by dividing the direct materials and conversion costs incurred in July by the respective total equivalent units for direct materials and conversion costs.

Allocation of Costs

In Step 4, we multiply the equivalent unit rates by their respective equivalent units of production in order to determine the cost of transferred and partially completed units. The cost of the July 1 inprocess inventory, completed and transferred out to the Casting Department.

The July 1 inprocess inventory cost of $28,150 is carried over from June and will be transferred to Casting. The cost required to finish the July 1 inprocess inventory is $1,710, which consists of conversion costs required to complete the remaining 30% of the processing. The conversion costs required to complete the beginning inventory are added to the balance carried over from the previous month to yield a total cost of the completed July 1 inprocess inventory of $29,860.

The 600 units started and completed in July receive 100% of their direct materials and conversion costs in July. The costs associated with the units started and completed are determined by multiplying the equivalent units in Step 2 by the unit costs in Step 3.

The total cost transferred to the Casting Department is the sum of the beginning y cost from the previous period the additional costs incurred in July complete the beginning inventory and the costs incurred for the units started ompleted in July. Thus, the total cost transferred to Casting is $66,700. The units of ending inventory have not been transferred, so they must be valued at July 31.

The units in the ending inventory have received 100% of their materials in July. Thus, the materials cost incurred in July for the ending inventory is $20,000, or 400 equivalent units of materials multiplied by $50. The conversion cost incurred in July for the ending inventory is $1,140, which is 100 equivalent units of conversion for the ending inventory multiplied by $11.40.

Cost of Production Report

A cost of production report is normally prepared for each processing department at periodic intervals. The July cost of production report for McDermott Steel's Melting Department. As can be seen on the report, the two question marks from page M55 can now be determined.

The report summarises the four previous steps by providing the following production quantity and cost data:

1. The units for which the department is accountable and the disposition of those units.
2. The production costs incurred by the department and the allocation of those costs between completed and partially completed units.

The cost of production report is also used to control costs. Each department manager is responsible for the units entering production and the costs incurred in the department. Any failure to account for all costs and any significant differences in unit product costs from one month to another should be investigated.

Journal Entries for a Process Cost System

To illustrate the journal entries to record the cost flows in a process costing system, we will use the July transactions for McDermott Steel. The entries in summary form for these transactions are shown here and on the following page.

Note that the highlighted amounts in Exhibit 8 were determined from assigning the costs charged to production in the Melting Department. Likewise, the amount transferred out of the Casting Department to Finished Goods would have also been determined from a cost of production report for the Casting Department.

Cost of Production Report for Decision Making

The cost of production report is one source of information that may be used by managers to control and improve operations. A cost of production report will normally list costs in greater. This greater detail helps management isolate problems and opportunities. In addition, assume that the Blending Department had no beginning or ending work in process inventory either month. Thus, in this simple case, there is no need to determine equivalent units of production for allocating costs between completed and partially completed units. The cost of production reports for April and May in the Blending Department.

Note that the preceding reports provide more cost detail than simply reporting direct materials and conversion costs. The May results indicate that total unit costs have increased from $0.50 to $0.53, or 6% from the previous month.

Both energy and tank cleaning perunit costs have increased dramatically in May. Further investigation should focus on these costs. For example, an increasing trend in energy may indicate that the machines are losing fuel efficiency, thereby requiring the company to purchase an increasing amount of fuel.The tank cleaning costs could be investigated in a similar fashion.

In addition to unit production cost trends, managers of process manufacturers are also concerned about yield trends. Yield is the ratio of the materials output quantity to the input quantity. A yield less than one occurs when the output quantity is less than the input quantity due to materials losses during the process. Two percent or 20 pounds of sugar were lost or spilled during the packing process.

Just-in-Time Processing

The objective of many companies is to produce products with high quality, low cost, and instant availability. One approach to achieving this objective is to implement just-in-time processing. Just-in-time processing (JIT) is a philosophy that focuses on reducing time and cost and eliminating poor quality. In a traditional production process, a product moves from process to process as each function or step is completed. Each worker is assigned a specific job, which is performed repeatedly as unfinished products are received from the preceding department.

The Internet complements a just-in-time processing strategy. Ford Motor Company states that the impact of the Internet is the equivalent of "the moving assembly line of the 21st Century." This is because the Internet will connect the whole supply chain to create a fast and efficient manufacturing system. As stated by William Clay Ford, Chairman of Ford Motor, "The automobile is about to undergo the most profound and revolutionary changes it's seen since the Model T first hit the streets."

For the furniture maker in the illustration, manufacturing would begin in the Cutting Department, where the wood would be cut to design specifications. Next, the Drilling Department would perform the drilling function, after which the Sanding Department would sand the wood, the Staining Department would stain the furniture, and the Varnishing Department would apply varnish and other protective coatings.

In the traditional production process, production supervisors attempt to enter enough materials into the process to keep all the manufacturing departments operating. Some departments, however, may process materials more rapidly than others. In addition, if one department stops production because of machine breakdowns, for example, the preceding departments usually continue production in order to avoid idle time.

In a just-in-time system, processing functions are combined into work centers, sometimes called manufacturing cells. For example, the seven departments just illustrated for the furniture manufacturer might be reorganised into three work centers. Work Center One would perform the cutting, drilling, and sanding functions, Work Center Two would perform the staining and varnishing functions, and Work Center Three would perform the upholstery and assembly functions.

In the traditional production line, a worker typically performs only one function. Research has indicated that workers who perform several manufacturing functions identify better with the end product. This creates pride in the product and improves quality and productivity.

Implementing JIT may also result in reorganising service activities. Specifically, the service activities may be assigned to individual work centers, rather than to centralised service departments. For example, each work center may be assigned the responsibility for the repair and maintenance of its machinery and equipment. Accepting this responsibility creates an environment in which workers gain a better understanding of the production process and the machinery.

In a JIT system, wasted motion from moving the product and materials is reduced. The product is often placed on a movable carrier that is centrally located in the work center. After the workers in a work center have completed their activities with the product, the entire carrier and any additional materials are moved just in time to satisfy the demand or need of the next work center. Each work center is connected to other work centers through information contained on Kanbans, which is a Japanese term for cards.

The experience of Caterpillar Inc. illustrates the impact of JIT. Before implementing JIT, an average transmission would travel 10 miles through the factory and require 1,000 pieces of paper for materials, labor, and movement transactions.

References

Fabozzi, Frank J.; Sergio M. Focardi, Petter N. Kolm, *Financial Modeling of the Equity Market: From CAPM to Cointegration*, Hoboken, NJ: Wiley, 2004.

______________ , *Assessing Capital Market Through Securitization*, New Hope, PA: Frank J. Fabozzi Associates, 2001.

Flannery, Mark J., "Using Market Information in Prudential Bank Supervision: A Review of U.S. Empirical Evidence," *Journal of Money*, Credit and Banking, pp. 274-305, August 1998.

French, Warren A. and John Granrose, *Practice Business Ethics*, Upper Saddle River, NJ: Prentice Hall, 1995.

7

Cost Volume Profit Relationships

When the last of her three children went off to school, Amy began looking for a job. At this same time, her daughter asked to take dance classes. The nearest dance studio was over 20 miles away, and Amy didn't know how she would balance a new job and drive her daughter to dance class. Suddenly it hit her—why not start her own dance studio?

Amy sketched out a business plan: A local church would rent its basement for $6 per hour. The size of the basement limited the number of students she could teach, but the rent was low. Insurance for a small studio was $50 per month. Initially she would teach classes only for young kids since that was all she felt qualified to do.

Amy soon realised that the demand for dance classes far exceeded her capacity. She considered renting a bigger space that could serve 15 students per class. But her rent would also increase significantly.

However, with a bigger space Amy could offer classes for teens and adults. Teens and adults would pay a higher fee—$5 per hour—though the number of students per class would have to be smaller, probably only 8 per class. She could hire a part-time instructor at about $18 per hour to teach advanced classes. Insurance costs could increase to $100 per month.

Amy laid out a new business plan based on these estimates. If she failed, she stood to lose real money. Convinced she could make a go of it, she made the big plunge.

Her planning paid off: Within 10 years of starting her business in a church basement Amy had over 800 students, seven instructors, two administrators, and a facility with three separate studios. As the Feature Story indicates, to manage any size business you must understand how costs respond to changes in sales volume and the effect of costs and revenues on profits. A prerequisite to understanding cost-volume-profit (CVP) relationships is knowledge of how costs behave.

Cost Behaviour Analysis

Cost behaviour analysis is the study of how specific costs respond to changes in the level of business activity. As you might expect, some costs change, and others remain the same. For example, for an airline company such as Southwest or United, the longer the flight the higher the fuel costs. A knowledge of cost behaviour helps management plan operations and decide between alternative courses of action. Cost behaviour analysis applies to all types of entities, as the Feature Story about Amy's dance studio indicates.

The starting point in cost behaviour analysis is measuring the key business activities. Activity levels may be expressed in terms of sales dollars, miles driven room occupancy or dance classes taught. Many companies use more than one measurement base. A manufacturer, for example, may use direct labor hours or units of output for manufacturing costs and sales revenue or units sold for selling expenses.

For an activity level to be useful in cost behaviour analysis, changes in the level or volume of activity should be correlated with changes in costs. The activity level selected is referred to as the activity index.

With an appropriate activity index, it is possible to classify the behaviour of costs in response to changes in activity levels into three categories: variable, fixed, or mixed.

Variable Costs

Variable costs are costs that vary in total directly and proportionately with changes in the activity level. If the level increases 10 percent, total variable costs will increase 10 percent. If the level of activity decreases by 25 percent, variable costs will decrease 25 percent. A variable cost may also be defined as a cost that *remains the same per unit at every level of activity.*

To illustrate the behaviour of a variable cost, assume that Damon Company manufactures radios that contain a $10 digital clock. The activity index is the number of radios produced. As each radio is manufactured, the total cost of the clocks increases by $10. As shown in part (a) of Illustration 6-1, total cost of the clocks will be $20,000 if 2,000 radios are produced, and $100,000 when 10,000 radios are produced. As shown in part (b) of Illustration 6-1, the unit cost of $10 for the clocks is the same whether 2,000 or 10,000 radios are produced.

Companies that rely heavily on labor to manufacture a product, such as Nike or Reebok, or to provide a service, such as Hilton or Marriott, are likely to have many variable costs.

Fixed Costs

Fixed costs are costs that remain the same in total regardless of changes in the activity level. Examples include property taxes, insurance, rent, supervisory salaries, and depreciation on buildings and equipment. Because total fixed costs remain constant as activity changes, it follows that fixed costs *per unit* vary inversely with activity: As volume increases, unit cost declines, and vice versa.

To illustrate the behaviour of fixed costs, assume that Damon Company leases its productive facilities at a cost of $10,000 per month. Total fixed costs of the facilities will remain constant at every level of activity, as shown in part (a) of Illustration 6-2. But, on a per unit basis, the cost of rent will decline as activity increases, as shown in part (b) of Illustration 6-2. At 2,000 units, the unit cost is $5. When 10,000 radios are produced, the unit cost is only $1.

The trend for many manufacturers is to have more fixed costs and fewer variable costs. This trend is the result of increased use of automation and less use of employee labor. As a result, depreciation and lease charges increase, whereas direct labor costs decrease.

Management Perspective

When Thomas Moser quit teaching communications at Bates Col l lege 25 years ago, he turned to what he loved doing—furniture woodworking. Today he has over 120 employees. In a business where profit margins are seldom thicker than wood shavings, cost control is everything. Because computer-driven machines cut most of the standardised parts and joints, "we're free to be inefficient in assembly and finishing work, where the craft is most obviously expressed," says Moser. By keeping a tight lid on costs and running an efficient operation, Moser is free to spend most of his time doing what he enjoys most—designing furniture.,

Relevant Range

In Illustrations 6-1 and 6-2, straight lines were drawn throughout the entire activity index for total variable costs and total fixed costs. In essence, the assumption was made that the costs were linear.

In most business situations, a straightline relationship does not exist for variable costs throughout the entire range of possible activity. At abnormally low levels of activity, it may be impossible to be cost efficient. Smallscale operations may not allow the company to obtain quantity discounts for raw materials or to use specialised labor. In contrast, at abnormally high levels of activity, labor costs may increase sharply because of overtime pay. Also at high activity levels, materials costs may jump significantly because of excess spoilage caused by worker fatigue.

Total fixed costs also do not have a straightline relationship over the entire range of activity. Some fixed costs will not change. But it is possible for management to change other fixed costs. For example, in the Feature Story the dance studio's rent was originally variable and then became fixed at a certain amount. An example of the behaviour of total fixed costs through all potential levels of activity.

For most companies, operating at almost zero or at 100 percent capacity is the exception rather than the rule. Instead, companies often operate over a somewhat narrower range, such as 40-80 percent of capacity. The range over which a company expects to operate during a year is called the relevant range of the activity index.

As you can see, although the straightline relationship may not be completely realistic, the linear assumption produces useful data for CVP analysis as long as the level of activity remains within the relevant range.

Mixed Costs

Mixed costs are costs that contain both a variable element and a fixed element. Sometimes called semivariable costs, mixed costs change in total but not proportionately with changes in the activity level. The rental of a U-Haul truck is a good example of a mixed cost. Assume that local rental terms for a 17-foot truck, including insurance, are $50 per day plus 50 cents per mile. The graphic presentation of the rental cost for a oneday rental is as follows.

In this case, the fixed cost element is the cost of having the service available. The variable cost element is the cost of actually using the service. Another example of a mixed cost is utility costs where there is a flat service fee plus a usage charge.

For purposes of CVP analysis, mixed costs must be classified into their fixed and variable elements. How does management make the classification? One possibility is to determine the variable and fixed components each time a mixed cost is incurred. But because of time and cost constraints, this approach is rarely followed. Instead, the customary approach is to determine variable and fixed costs on an aggregate basis at the end of a period of time. Management may use any of several methods in making the determination. We will explain the high-low method here. Other methods are more appropriately explained in cost accounting courses.

High-Low Method

The high-low method uses the total costs incurred at the high and low levels of activity. The difference in costs between the high and low levels represents variable costs, since only the variable cost element can change as activity levels change.

The high and low levels of activity are 50,000 miles in April and 20,000 miles in January. The maintenance costs at these two levels are $63, 000 and $30,000, respectively. The difference in maintenance costs is $33,000 ($63,000 — $30,000) and the difference in miles is 30,000 (50,000—20,000). Therefore, for Metro Transit, variable cost per unit is $1.10, computed as follows.

$33,000 + 30,000 = $1.10

Determine the fixed cost by subtracting the total variable cost at either the high or the low activity level from the total cost at that activity level.

Maintenance costs are therefore $8,000 per month plus $1.10 per mile. For example, at 45,000 miles, estimated maintenance costs would be $8,000 fixed and $49,500 variable.

The high-low method generally produces a reasonable estimate for analysis. However, it does not produce a precise measurement of the fixed and variable elements in a mixed cost because other activity levels are ignored in the computation.

Cost-Volume-Profit Analysis

Cost-volume-profit (CVP) analysis is the study of the effects of changes in costs and volume on a company's profits. CVP analysis is important in profit planning. It also is a critical factor in such management decisions as setting selling prices, determining product mix, and maximising use of production facilities.

Basic Components

The following assumptions underlie each CVP analysis.

1. The behaviour of both costs and revenues is linear throughout the relevant range of the activity index.
2. All costs can be classified with reasonable accuracy as either variable or fixed.
3. Changes in activity are the only factors that affect costs.
4. All units produced are sold.
5. When more than one type of product is sold, the sales mix will remain constant. That is, the percentage that each product represents of total sales will stay the same. Sales mix

complicates CVP analysis because different products will have different cost relationships.

When these five assumptions are not valid, the results of CVP analysis may be inaccurate.

Cvp Income Statement

Because CVP is so important for decision making, management often wants this information reported in a CVP income statement format. The CVP income statement classifies costs as variable and fixed and computes a contribution margin. Contribution margin is the amount of revenue remaining after deducting variable costs.

A traditional income statement and a CVP income statement both report the same bottomline net income of $120,000. However a traditional income statement does not classify costs as variable and fixed, and therefore a contribution margin would not be reported. In addition, both a total and a per unit amount are often shown on a CVP income statement to facilitate CVP analysis. That is, cost includes manufacturing costs plus selling and administrative expenses.

Contribution Margin Per Unit

From Vargo Video's CVP income statement, we can see that the contribution margin is $320,000, and the contribution margin per unit is $200. The formula for contribution margin per unit and the computation for Vargo Video are Contribution margin per unit indicates that for every CD/DVD sold, Vargo will have $200 to cover fixed costs and contribute to net income. Because Vargo Video has fixed costs of $200,000, it must sell 1,000 CD/DVDs before it earns any net income. Vargo's CVP income statement, assuming a zero net income, would report the following.

It follows that for every CD/DVD sold above 1,000 units, net income is increased $200. For example, assume that Vargo sold one more CD/DVD, for a total of 1,001 CD/DVDs sold.

Contribution Margin Ratio

Some managers prefer to use a contribution margin ratio in CVP analysis. The contribution margin ratio is the contribution margin per unit divided by the unit selling price. For Vargo Video, the ratio is as follows.

The contribution margin ratio of 40 percent means that $0.40 of each sales dollar is available to apply to fixed costs and to contribute to net income. This expression of contribution margin is very helpful in determining the effect of changes in sales on net income. For example, net income will increase $40,000 if sales increase $100,000. Thus, by using the contribution margin ratio, managers can quickly determine increases in net income from any change in sales.

Break-even Analysis

A key relationship in CVP analysis is the level of activity at which total revenues equal total costs. This level of activity is called the break-even point. At this volume of sales, the company will realise no income and will suffer no loss. The process of finding the break-even point is called break-even analysis. The break-even point can be:

1. Computed from a mathematical equation.
2. Computed by using contribution margin.
3. Derived from a cost-volume-profit (CVP) graph.

The break-even point can be expressed either in sales units or sales dollars.

Mathematical Equation

A common equation used for CVP analysis is shown in Illustration.

Identifying the break-even point is a special case of CVP analysis. Because at the break-even point net income is zero, break-even occurs where total sales equal variable costs plus fixed costs.

The break-even point in units can be computed directly from the equation by using unit selling prices and unit variable costs. The computation for Vargo Video.

The Internet is wringing inefficiencies out of nearly every industry.

While commercial aircraft spend roughly 4,000 hours a year in the air, chartered aircraft spend only 500 hours flying. That means that they are sitting on the ground—not making any money—nearly 90 percent of the time. Enter flightserve.com. For about the same cost as a firstclass ticket, flightserve.com matches up executives with charter flights in small "private jets." Flightserve.com says that the average charter jet has eight seats. When all eight seats are full, the company has an 80 percent profit margin. It breaks even at an average of 3.3 full seats per flight.

Contribution Margin Technique

We know that contribution margin equals total revenues less variable costs. It follows that at the breakeven point, contribution margin must equal total fixed costs. On the basis of this relationship, we can compute the breakeven point using either the contribution margin per unit or the contribution margin ratio.

We know that the contribution margin ratio for Vargo Video is 40 percent.

Graphic Presentation

An effective way to find the breakeven point is to prepare a breakeven graph. Because this graph also shows costs, volume, and profits, it is referred to as a cost-volume-profit (CVP) graph.

As shown in the CVP graph in Illustration 6-21, sales volume is recorded along the horizontal axis. This axis should extend to the maximum level of expected sales. Both total revenues and total costs are recorded on the vertical axis.

The construction of the graph, using the data for Vargo Video, is as follows.

1. Plot the total-revenue line, starting at the zero activity level. For every CD/DVD sold, total revenue increases by \$500. For example, at 200 units, sales are \$100,000. At the upper level of activity (1,800 units), sales are \$900,000. Note that the revenue line is assumed to be linear throughout the full range of activity.
2. Plot the total fixed cost using a horizontal line. For the CD/DVDs, this line is plotted at \$200,000. The fixed cost is the same at every

level of activity.

3. Plot the total cost line. This starts at the fixed-cost line at zero activity. It increases by the variable cost at each level of activity. For each CD/DVD, variable costs are $300. Thus, at 200 units, total variable cost is $60,000, and the total cost is $260,000. On the graph, the amount of the variable cost can be derived from the difference between the total cost and fixed cost lines at each level of activity.
4. Determine the break-even point from the intersection of the total cost line and the total revenue line. The break-even point in dollars is found by drawing a horizontal line from the break-even point to the vertical axis. The break-even point in units is found by drawing a vertical line from the break-even point to the horizontal axis.

The CVP graph also shows both the net income and net loss areas. Thus, the amount of income or loss at each level of sales can be derived from the total sales and total cost lines.

A CVP graph is useful because the effects of a change in any element in the CVP analysis can be quickly seen. For example, a 10 percent increase in selling price will change the location of the total revenue line. Likewise, the effects on total costs of wage increases can be quickly observed.

Management Perspective

Computer graphics are a valuable companion to many computer software packages. Colour graphs can be instantly changed to provide visual "what if" analysis.Current technology allows for stunning graphs in a variety of different formats. In the appropriate situation, a graph can literally be worth a thousand words.

Margin of Safety

The margin of safety is another relationship that may be calculated in CVP analysis. Margin of safety is the difference between actual or expected sales and sales at the break-even point. This relationship measures the "cushion" that management has, allowing it to still break even if expected sales fail to materialise. The margin of safety may be expressed in dollars or as a ratio.

SERVICE COMPANY PERSPECTIVE

Computation of break-even and margin of safety is important for service companies as well. Consider how the promoter for the Rolling Stones' tour used the break-even point and margin of safety. For example, one outdoor show should bring 70,000 individuals for a gross of $2.45 million. The promoter guarantees $1.2 million to the Rolling Stones. In addition, 20 percent of gross, or approximately $500,000, goes to the stadium in which the performance is staged. Add another $400,000 for other expenses such as ticket takers, parking attendants, advertising, and so on. At 75 percent, the promoter breaks about even. At 50 percent, the promoter loses hundreds of thousands of dollars.

Target Net Income

Management usually sets an income objective for individual product lines. This objective is called target net income. It indicates the sales necessary to achieve a specified level of income. The sales necessary to achieve target net income can be determined from each of the approaches used to determine break-even sales.

Mathematical Equation

We know that at the break-even point no profit or loss results for the company. By instead adding an amount for target net income to the same basic equation, we obtain the following formula for determining required sales.

The sales dollars required to achieve the target net income is found by multiplying the units sold by the unit selling price.

Graphic Presentation

The CVP graph in Illustration can also be used to find the sales required to meet target net income. In the profit area of the graph, the distance between the sales line and the total cost line at any point equals net income. Required sales are found by analysing the differences between the two lines until the desired net income is found.

CVP AND CHANGES IN THE BUSINESS ENVIRONMENT

When the IBM personal computer (PC) was introduced, it sold for $2,500. Today the same type of computer sells for much less. Recently, when oil prices rose, the break-even point for airline companies such as American, Southwest, and United rose dramatically. The point should be clear: Business conditions change rapidly, and management must respond intelligently to these changes. CVP analysis can help.

Case I. A competitor is offering a 10% discount on the selling price of its CD/DVDs. Management must decide whether to offer a similar discount. Question: What effect will a 10 percent discount on selling price have on the break-even point for CD/DVDs? Answer: A 10 percent discount on selling price reduces the selling price per unit to $450. Variable costs per unit remain unchanged at $300. Thus, the contribution margin per unit is $150.

For Vargo Video, this change would require monthly sales to increase by 333 units, or $33^1/_3$ percent, in order to break even. In reaching a conclusion about offering a 10 percent discount to customers, management must determine how likely it is to achieve the increased sales. Also, management should estimate the possible loss of sales if the competitor's discount price is not matched.

Case II. To meet the threat of foreign competition, management invests in new robotic equipment that will lower the amount of direct labor required to make CD/DVDs. It is estimated that total fixed costs will increase 30 percent and that variable cost per unit will decrease 30 percent. Question: What effect will the new equipment have on the sales volume required to break even? Answer: Total fixed costs become $260,000. The variable cost per unit becomes $210.

These changes appear to be advantageous for Vargo Video. The break-even point is reduced by 10 percent, or 100 units.

Case III. Vargo's principal supplier of raw materials has just announced a price increase. The higher cost is expected to increase the variable cost of CD/DVDs by $25 per unit. Management would like to hold the line on the selling price of CD/DVDs. It plans a cost-cutting program that will save $17,500 in fixed costs per month. Vargo is currently realising monthly net income of $80,000 on sales of 1,400 CD/DVDs.

To achieve the required sales, 1,500 CD/DVDs will have to be sold, an increase of 100 units. If this does not seem to be a reasonable expectation, management will either have to make further cost reductions or accept less net income if the selling price remains unchanged.

When analysing an Internet business, the socalled "conversion rate" is closely watched. It is calculated by dividing the number of people who actually take action at an Internet site by the total number of people who visit the site. Average conversion rates are from 3 to 5 percent. A rate below 2 percent is poor, while a rate above 10 percent is great.

Conversion rates have an obvious effect on breakeven point. Suppose you spend $10,000 on your site, and you attract 5,000 visitors. If you get a 2 percent conversion rate your site costs $100 per purchase. A 4 percent conversion rate gets you down to a cost of $50 per transaction, and an 8 percent conversion rate gets you down to $25.

How can a company use CVP analysis to improve profitability? Data on what effect a price change, a fixedcost change, or a tradeoff between fixed and variable costs, would have on volume and costs.Measurement of income at new volume levels. If profitability increases under proposed change, adopt change.

References

Modigliani, F.; Miller, M., "The Cost of Capital, Corporation Finance and the Theory of Investment", *American Economic Review* 48 (3): 261–297, 1958.

Nagle, Thomas T. and Reed K. Holden, *The Strategy and Tactics of Pricing: A Guide to Profitable Decision Making*, NJ: Pearson, 1994.

Nash, Robert C. and Joseph F. Sinkey, Jr., "On Competition, Risk, and the Hidden Assets in the Market for Bank Credit Cards," *Journal of Banking and Finance*, pp. 89-112, (January 1997), January 1997.

Ongkrutaraksa, Worapot, *Financial Modeling and Analysis: A Spreadsheet Technique for Financial, Investment, and Risk Management,* 2nd Edition, Frenchs Forest: Pearson Education Australia, 2006.

8

Capital Budgeting Practices

In general, capital budgets in governments have multiple roles: as instruments of fiscal policy and to improve the net worth of government, and—particularly in the area of economic infrastructure—as vehicles for economic development. This is usually achieved through greater reliance on debt than on such conventional sources of financing as taxation. In some cases, more attention has been paid to capital budgets as a way to reduce deficits caused by an excess of recurrent expenditures versus revenues.

Notwithstanding the seeming virtues of capital budgets, opinions continue to be divided, as they have been during the past seven decades, about their utility in governments. In the developing world, however, where many governments operate on the edge of financial instability, the debate about capital budgets and their equivalents continues.

A key challenge in government budgeting is to define an appropriate balance between current and capital expenditures. Budgeting for government investment also remains not wellintegrated into the formal budget preparation process in many countries.

It is arguable whether these poor results could have been prevented by the establishment of capital budgets. Moreover, for countries that continue to depend on debt finance as a major instrument of budgetary resources, the issue arises whether capital budgets promote an improved process of decision making and an overall management culture that permits continuing attention to the government's net worth. More specifically, it is important to consider whether capital budgets provide an improved framework for allocating, using, and accounting for resources.

This chapter aims to provide an overview of the evolution of past and current budgeting practices for capital budgets. The paper will also provide a comparison between the budget practices between lowincome countries (LICs) and more advanced countries, and make a series of recommendations to ensure more efficient integration of public investment planning and budget management in LICs.[4] However, the paper will not aim to address other important and related issues such as publicprivate partnerships and other mechanisms for outsourcing the costs and risks associated with capital investment projects; the earmarking arrangements and extrabudgetary funds.

Overview of Capital Budgeting Practices

The United Nations' *System of National Accounts* (SNA) and the IMF's *Government Finance Statistics Manual 2001* (GFSM) prescribe how a government's consumption and investment activities should be separately recorded in the government budget and in accounting records and statistics.

Defining Capital

Governments around the world may define "capital" in different ways. *Capital spending is generally about physical assets with a useful life of more than one year.* But it also includes capital improvements or the rehabilitation of physical assets that enhance or extend the useful life of the asset.

Capital spending is sometimes equated with *investment* or *development spending*, where expenditures have benefits extending years into the future. Under this definition, governments may include physical assets for government use physical assets of a public good nature that also enhance private sector development and intangibles. It can be quite difficult to distinguish between investment and noninvestment expenditures, and if investment spending receives favored treatment in the annual budgeting process, nearly all spending, whether recurrent or not, will end up being classified as investment.

Every government establishes some arbitrary cutoff point to distinguish capital from current expenditures. For budgeting purposes, the relevant distinction is between capital and current expenditures. Current expenditures are purchases of assets to be consumed within one year, regardless of expenditure size. Small expenditures are regarded as current, regardless of the fact that it could be consumed over a period longer than one year.

But even given the different definitions of capital[6], it does not necessarily call for a dual budgeting system. Separate data on government consumption and investment can be maintained within a unified government budget.

This chapter is concerned mainly with public investment. However, some of the most common and serious problems with public sector capital budgeting can arise from its interface with current spending.

The Distinction Between Capital and Current Expenditure

Capital and current expenditures need, for some purposes, to be considered separately:

1) capital spending within the budget needs to be clearly identified *separately*; and
2) *capitalspecific procedures* are needed for asset procurement and for project management, and for subsequent monitoring and management and disposal of capital assets.

For other purposes, capital and current expenditures need to be considered together:

1) For planning and budgeting capital and current spending need to be considered *together*; and
2) investment proposals need to be appraised in terms of *both* capital *and* operating costs.

Contrary to general belief, the funding of a capital budget can be more than borrowing—although depending on the situation, borrowing may be the most important source of funds. In principle, taxes levied on property, although paid from current income, are considered levies on capital and included in capital receipts. In some countries, income from natural resources may be earmarked for capital projects and, therefore, included in receipts. In countries with development plans, surpluses from the current budget are yet another source of receipts.

It is normal in developed economies for the section in the ministry of finance, that is familiar with a spending unit's activities, to deal with both capital and current spending.

The annual government budget for all public spending in most developed countries is broken down into several hundred headings for approval by the parliament. Indeed parliaments often require capital expenditures to be specifically identified in the budget documentation. However, presentation and debate in the parliament and in public focuses on the expenditure programs as a whole.

However, program budgets in these countries still have capital and current components, usually with only limited freedom (if any) to vire between them. Capital and current expenditure are also distinguished in the *accounts* of spending units and in *reporting* expenditure. Specific ministry of finance approval may be needed for some large capital projects.

Golden Rules, Balanced Budgets and Limits on Borrowing

Some countries have or are developing explicit links or rules between the level of net public investment and the level of public debt. This may include "the golden rule," which specifies that increases in the stock of public debt should not exceed net public investment.

There has also been increasing interest in recent years in rules limiting the budget balance and the total level of public debt. These developments were reinforced in the European Union in the 1990s by the conditions for membership of the Monetary Union, which put limits on budget deficits and the total level of debt.

The golden rule and budget balance are specified in the German Constitution. However, a law was passed in 1967 allowing exceptions for federal and state governments where more public investment is considered justified by macroeconomic conditions. This exception has been applied many times. The Netherlands applied the golden rule between 1927 and 1958.

Control of public debt is at least as important in lowincome countries as in developed economies. However, the first priority is to develop reliable measures of public assets and, especially, liabilities. Information on capital assets and liabilities should ideally be monitored, and some countries have found it helpful to establish some form of the golden rule.

The Evolution of Capital Budgeting Practices

Budgeting for capital expenditure has evolved over the decades and its importance has increased over time. Overall, six discernible stages of changes in capital budgeting practices and systems can be identified. The first stage is the Great Depression years during which efforts were mainly focused on designing ways to ensure economic recovery. At the time, public borrowing for financing capital outlays, except for emergencies, was not favored. This socalled investment budget found extended application in other Nordic countries in following years.

The second stage took place during the late 1930s when the colonial government in India introduced a capital budget to reduce the budget deficit by shifting some items of expenditures from the current budget.

The third stage refers to the growing importance attached to capital budgets as a "vehicle" for development plans. Partly influenced by the Soviet-style planning, many low-income countries formulated comprehensive five-year plans and considered capital budgets the main impetus for economic development. Where capital budgets did not exist, a variant known as the *development budget* was introduced.

Capital Budgeting in the 1960s to 1990s

The fourth stage reflects the importance of economic policy choices on the allocation of resources in government. Quantitative appraisal techniques were applied on a wider scale during the 1960s leading to more rigorous application of investment appraisal and financial planning.

In the 1960s and 1970s, it was widely believed that government budget allocation, including investment expenditures, could be largely reduced to a "scientific" process by systems such as PPBS or even

ZBB. Spackman believed that this turned out not to be true, for three main reasons. One reason was that, for most public policies, finding the best way forward depends not only on analysis but very largely on pragmatism, political intuition and windows of political opportunity. Second, the information demands were equivalent to those required to run a centrally controlled economy. Third, the implied power structure within government was that of control in detail from the center, as opposed to delegated authority, incentive structures and local initiative.

A fifth stage saw a revival of the debate about the need for a capital budget in government, particularly in the United States. Along with the growing application of quantitative techniques during the 1960s came the view that the introduction of a capital budget could be advantageous. Having rejected the use of separate capital budgets, the commission advocated the introduction of accrual accounting in government accounts. The introduction of accrual accounting,[18] which did not make any progress in the United States until the early 1990s, would have meant the division of expenditures into current and investment outlays.

Meanwhile, however, a development cast more serious doubts on the need for capital budgets. Sweden which had made pioneering efforts in the 1930s, undertook a review of its budget system in the early 1970s. They found that excessive focus on capital budgets would need to be tempered by a recognition that the overall credibility and creditworthiness of a government depend more on its macroeconomic policy stance and less on a government's net worth. This shift in emphasis contributed to a decline in the popularity of the use of the capital budget until the late 1980s, when it came to be revived in a different form.

During this sixth stage, partly because of the experiences of Australia and New Zealand, there was a renewed push by the professional bodies and, from the late 1990s, the international financial institutions for the introduction of accrual budgeting and accounting. These ideas found a foothold in the United States, where advocates held the view that the absence of a distinction between investment outlays and ordinary or current outlays led to unintended neglect of infrastructure or accumulated assets. Ensuring proper asset maintenance required a division of outlays into current and capital outlays, as a part of day-to-day budget management.

CURRENT CAPITAL BUDGETING PRACTICES

In Developed Countries

Dual budgeting originated in European countries, but in those countries it lasted only for a short period. It was introduced in the late 1930s in order to help governments ensure that the resources they borrowed were used only for capital expenditures. After the Second World War, as governments relaxed their use of borrowed funds, budgets were integrated. The change in approach reflected several factors: massive postwar reconstruction work and increased recurrent expenditures, along with the acceptance of the Keynesian model of linking government spending and the size of the budget deficit and borrowing requirements to both fiscal and monetary determinants and the business cycle. Hence, it came to be accepted that regardless of their financing sources, government's recurrent spending and capital investment are complements in any logical combination that may be required, and that the two types of expenditures together produce results, provided the context is one of overall macro-fiscal balance.

Most OECD countries have also achieved a high degree of integration of their current and capital budgets. This has usually occurred through a process of development in their public administration and budgetary systems that has taken place over many decades. It is the result of a growing realisation by these governments that: (i) the distinction between recurrent and capital spending is often quite arbitrary or uncertain; and (ii) better resource allocation and management decisions can often be made within a single, unified framework for revenues and expenditures.

While there are now few developed countries which maintain totally separate budgets, the extent and form of budgetary integration—particularly the management of capital spending—still differs significantly in some instances. For this reason, effective integration of current and capital budgets is perhaps best measured qualitatively by the extent to which the current and investment spending decisions of the government are "well-balanced," in the sense of being logically consistent with, and mutually supportive of, a given policy framework or set of policy objectives.

A few examples of these unsatisfactory balances between current and capital spending can be highlighted, which can often be found in the education sector. More general imbalances may also develop between expenditures on administrative services of government and broader infrastructural development needs.

Although many developed administrations may not consciously seek to optimise this current/capital spending balance, they nonetheless aspire to achieve consistency and efficiency within the context of their ongoing resource allocation and budget management decisions. In fact, getting the right balance between current and capital spending across the whole range of budget interventions and activities will depend substantially on the quality of budget planning systems and capabilities.

The budget systems of countries with a high degree of integration between current and capital expenditures exhibit several key features:

1) A single annual budget law and appropriation process;
2) Clear, and unified, responsibilities for budgetary preparation and implementation within the relevant public sector institutions;
3) The existence of effective and widely employed investment appraisal techniques;
4) A unified budget presentation, with supporting classification and accounting systems; and
5) Budget planning and management techniques within individual spending agencies that encourage and enable good use of financial resources.

Most developed countries' budgetary systems incorporate some of these features. However, the full benefits of a unified budget can only be achieved where each of these conditions is present. And although each of these features is important, it is often in the last area the budget planning and management within spending agencies where the most challenging reform measures, and greatest gains, are to be found.

A medium-term Approach to Public Investment

Above-mentioned characteristics of a sound budgetary system are often strengthened by the use of a medium-term approach to public investment. Public investments are primarily meaningful in a medium- to long-term perspective. If the sole focus is only on preparing and executing the annual budget, the main reasons for pursuing investment projects will be related to short-term macro-economic effects, for instance on employment, and short-term political considerations. In such a setting, the potential long-term effects of the investments may be accorded little importance. In addition, project selection will tend to prioritise high-visibility, fast-track projects, not the projects that give the highest net benefits.

Allocation of resources to different sectors and investment projects should ideally be based on efficiency. What are the benefits compared to the costs of the projects? In a longer-term perspective, dynamic efficiency becomes more important: resource allocation should also be governed by the possibilities for improving the capacity of the sectors over time, and investment projects will play a critical role in this regard.

It is also important to pursue cost-effective delivery of individual public goods and services. In the short term, efforts to improve cost-effectiveness will tend to focus on cost minimisation, without any fundamental changes in production processes and methods.

Many of the efforts to extend the time horizon for investment planning also include the introduction of medium-term budget frameworks. There are many differences between countries in the exact nature of these MTBFs, and in their focus and level of detail. However, in general, effective MTBFs tend to share certain characteristics:

1. The ministry of finance develops a medium-term macroeconomic forecast, which forms the basis for multi-year spending ceilings by organisations or programs.
2. The line ministries develop policy-based, three-year budget estimates for their activities.
3. The ministries' budget estimates distinguish clearly between the costs of existing policies and programs, and the costs of new proposals, including investments.
4. The budget preparation process gives a formal status to the out-year estimates.

Currently, the majority of OECD countries prepare comprehensive MTBFs. Few low-income countries have been able to introduce full-fledged MTBFs so far. Experience shows that this type of reform is conceptually and practically very demanding. In particular, it has turned out to be difficult for line ministries to develop credible, multi-year budget estimates.

Several important stages of the budgetary management of public investment can be distinguished. The degree of overall success in conducting these stages of budget management of public investment would depend on the maturity of the public financial management system in the country. In the more developed countries, most of these activities are well integrated into their budgetary processes.

A viable alternative is to begin by preparing multi-year budget estimates only for public investments and for major expenditures driven by demographics and entitlements. These estimates should be based on common methodologies, and the estimates should be agreed upon by the line ministries and the ministry of finance. While this approach does not provide the stringency of a full MTBF, it does give a much better basis for effective budget deliberations than the traditional, annual approach.

Appraisal of Capital Projects

Most developed countries have had capital project appraisal processes for decades. However, there are differences of view between developed countries about some technical aspects of appraisal methodology. However, investment appraisal in government is overall considered as a mainly economic analysis of the national costs and benefits which might be generated by the proposed investment, or by alternative options. The appraisal in principle includes all costs, certainly including the costs of using the asset throughout its lifetime. It preferably should include a sensitivity analysis where costs or benefits are uncertain. It also considers items such as legislative impact or environmental impact, and any impacts on other sectors.

According to Spackman, the following requirements are crucial:

1) Well-informed and open-minded consideration of alternative options, against well-defined policy objectives;

2) Taking proper account of opportunity costs;
3) Consideration of factors which cannot be explicitly valued in money terms as well as those which can.

This contrasts with what is often understood by project appraisal in low-income countries, which is a *cost* analysis of an already well defined proposal. The capacity of some low-income countries to undertake such an analysis is often strong, whereas the capacity for *economic* analysis, to question initial proposals, is usually weak.

Capital Budgeting in Low-income Countries

For many countries, separate current and capital budgets—i.e., a "dual budget" process— have their origins in the public finance management policies and structures established by colonial administrations. These administrations distinguished clearly between the recurring operational costs involved in maintaining a narrow range of government services and the "developmental" expenditures needed from time to time to establish new facilities or new administrative functions.

Dual budgeting did not disappear, however, with the departing colonial administrations. The continued separation of current and development budgets also appealed to the new administrations in that it enabled them to separate the ongoing costs of government with ambitious new development plans and their associated financing needs. Development assistance donors have reinforced this separation over the years through their traditional preference for funding of "development" activities, while at the same time shying away from the "consumption spending" associated with current expenditures.

During the 1960s, low-income countries' nascent institutions of political and economic management tended to adopt the technical practices of the western democracies. For example, most Anglophone African countries used dual budgets, with an "above-the-line account" showing revenues and mainly "recurrent" expenditures, and a "below-the-line account" showing "extrabudgetary," interest and lending to nationalised industries and a very few local governments, where the latter implemented a central government's investment plans. Many countries in Africa, Latin America, and the Middle East adopted national development planning, which had European roots and was still being practiced in Belgium, France, and Spain. Inexperienced finance ministries could not carry out the new tasks of medium-term development planning and capital project appraisal, so planning or development or economic affairs ministries were set up for the purpose.

Frequently, finance and development ministries issued their own separate budget circulars, and the dual approach to budgeting also took root in the line ministries. Politically visible gaps in physical infrastructure, and then capital project supremacy in government budgeting, helped to create new financial power bases, leaving the finance ministries responsible for budgeting civil service salaries and the needs of some small government ministries with minimal operational expenditures. Such settings made it difficult to introduce consolidated budget presentation and classification systems. Moreover, some substantial but unforeseen recurrent costs evolved from the expansion of investment projects.

International lending institutions and the donor community at large found the new ministries more capable than weak finance ministries of conducting business in the area of capital spending, as well as so-called developmental recurrent spending. The donors' responses further institutionalised the practice of separate organisations preparing separate budgets. Though the use of public investment programs (PIP) in the 1980s, as promoted by the World Bank and other donor agencies, saw the introduction of more coordinated project selection and appraisal processes, replacing individual project appraisal, it intensified the dynamics of dual budgeting.

Both before and during the PIP era, emphasis was placed on calculating the recurrent spending that capital projects would need after their completion, but in practice finance ministers were uninformed and reluctant or financially unable to provide the necessary funds. The lack of provision for recurrent funds added to the concerns that had already been created by the organisational separation of the two budgets. But a counterargument is that the fiscal stress could have been projected before the projects were initiated. Alternatively, it might be said that other spending priorities always crowded out the claims of these projects on recurrent budgets.

A less often mentioned problem in these circumstances was double or overlapping budgeting for the same or similar recurrent activities of government. Frequently, line ministries managed to receive funds from two sources for the same cause by negotiating separately with the finance and planning ministries. They succeeded in this not only because development budgets contained substantial noninvestment and nonproject related recurrent spending, in addition to capital spending, but also because the finance ministries had no proper information, either on the recurrent cost implications of the investment projects or on the independent recurrent expenditures being financed by donors.

In several countries, dual budget preparation in terms of contents, classification, and even calendars, resulted in two different budgets being presented to parliament. Even in some countries where the timing of budget presentation has been unified, the documentation, classification, and presentation format of the two budgets has remained separate.

The main impact of a dual budgeting system on budget execution and reporting occurred through capital or recurrent projects financed by donors, which usually required governments to keep separate accounts for domestic counterpart funds and to deposit such funds along with donor funds in special bank accounts, outside the purview of central treasuries or accountants-general. These special accounts, mainly in commercial banks, were governed by flexible spending rules and often bypassed the national budget systems, undermining the objective of comprehensive government accounting, banking, and cash management coverage. This contributed to weaker reporting and delays in closing government accounts, due to the difficulty of reconciling government accounting records with government banking transactions. Although in most countries central treasury offices and accountants-general issued circulars requiring line ministries to report their transactions, in practice these reports were not complete or timely.

Special project management units were created in line ministries, dealing with the accounting and banking of the cash components of external loans and grants, as well as with government counterpart funds. Since these recurrent and capital transactions were not classified in terms of the object of expenditures, in practice the decision to itemise expenditures was entrusted to line ministries in the course of budget execution.

Since the late 1990s, new financial assistance policies and instruments such as poverty-reduction strategy papers (PRSPs), monitoring of poverty-reducing expenditures, sector-wide and budget support approaches have been changing the dynamics of donor/client relationships. Moreover, responding to urgent needs in health, education, and other sectors in poor countries, several donors have substantially increased their financing of recurrent expenditures. Public expenditure reviews (PERs), as done by the World Bank, clearly have moved toward more intra-and inter-sectoral analyses, combining both recurrent and development expenditures, and where data are available, reviewing the joint impact of both types of spending on budgetary outcomes including economic growth, poverty reduction, and asset maintenance.

Some low-income countries have merged their finance ministries with their planning or development ministries, though others are slow in doing so. In many developing and transition countries, finance ministries have traditionally been much weaker than planning ministries which have benefited from close relations with the World Bank and other aid providers. The organisational separation of planning and finance ministries has become institutionalised in culture and politics in several countries. Political concerns about eliminating a ministerial portfolio, combined with institutional revivalism between the two ministries at the institutional level, persist in many low-income countries.

Over the years, staff of planning or development ministries have tended to be better paid, and to benefit from various allowances and better professional treatment, than staff of finance ministries. Their favored position in part reflects the additional financing possibilities associated with externally financed projects. This feature might be a cause of difficulty in the integration of the two institutions.

Line ministries have a strong incentive to prepare and defend separate budgets because they can use the opportunity of donor-negotiated projects to demand further complementary financing and to expand their operations without attention to the future cost implications. These projects may include either capital projects or specific and independent recurrent activities.

Today more than ever, the integration of recurrent and development budgets in low-income countries has become a necessity:

1) government borrowing is no longer limited to capital expenditures;
2) only an integrated analysis of recurrent and development expenditures can identify those poverty-reducing expenditures that have immediate impact or an indirect impact through accelerating economic growth;
3) part of external concessional credits, and the bulk of donor grants, are used for recurrent expenditures, supplementing the government recurrent budget; and
4) even after several decades of experience, the recurrent costs of capital projects continue to be ignored, in part for lack of coordination between two separate budgets.

DEVELOPMENT OF A REFORM STRATEGY

Low-income countries' progress in integrating their recurrent and development budgets has been very limited. One factor that helps maintain the status quo is antiquated economic development theory, emphasising capital spending for faster economic growth.

Another is institutional incentives. Donor practices have also tended to reinforce dual budgeting practices. Donors have traditionally focused on capital investments, and a desire to attract donor funding gives a country a strong incentive to maintain a separate development budget process, even though donors' use of budget support over project aid and multi-donor involvement in financing recurrent expenditures may increasingly change that incentive. The failure to ensure resources for ongoing maintenance of capital investments gives some agencies an incentive to seek earmarked or extrabudgetary revenues. On the other hand, some ministries pursue activities through the development budget that would otherwise be treated as recurrent spending, due to the budgetary incentives that are at work.

It seems that some practical recommendations for achieving budget integration in low-income countries would be useful. In summary, the following benchmarks for budgeting for public investment can be suggested, however it should be noted that these recommendations represent what LICs might be able to attain over a period of years.

Capital Budget Planning, Prioritisation and Implementation

(i) Determining the resource envelope

1. Capital expenditure decisions should be based on a consolidated budget approach, incorporating all revenues and expenditures, in particular foreign-financed projects and extrabudgetary funds with investment activities.
2. Capital expenditure decisions should be based on a medium-term budget perspective.
3. Decisions regarding capital expenditures should be taken in the context of a hard budget constraint. There should be explicit ceilings for guarantees and commitments beyond the budget year.
4. Governments should have clear policies regarding which capital expenditures should be financed by the budget, which may be realised through public-private partnerships and which should be handled by public or private enterprises.

(ii) Efficient prioritisation and selection

1) The budget calendar and the procedures for integration of capital expenditures in the budget must be clear, transparent and stable.
2) All projects should be subject to cost-benefit analysis. If the subjection of all projects to cost-benefit analysis is too costly, the focus could firstly be on the larger projects, with using a simplified methodology for smaller projects.
3) A public investment agency, with strong links to the Ministry of Finance, should prepare guidelines for project development and analysis.
4) The Ministry of Finance should give the cabinet recommendations for which investment projects should be realised within the available resource envelope.
5) The decision to implement an investment project should be independent of the financing and procurement modalities for the

project. PPPs can improve risk allocation, but the benefits must be substantial to compensate for increased financing and transaction costs.

(iii) Efficient implementation

a) Rules for budget adjustments should give incentives for realistic initial capital cost estimates. Cost overruns during project implementation should be partly covered by reallocation within ministry's existing budgets.

b) Capital investment project proposals should only be considered when they include a detailed disclosure of the expected operating costs, indicating how these will be accommodated within existing resource envelopes or making an explicit proposal for additional financing of the operating costs.

c) apital investment project proposals should only be considered after the ministry has explained how it will fully cover the maintenance of its existing capital stock.

d) Governments should avoid excessive targeting of capital expenditures for budget cuts.

e) There should be project completion reports for all capital expenditure projects.

The Dominance of Net Present Value

A capital budgeting decision is characterised by costs and benefits that are spread out over several time periods. This leads to a requirement that the time value of money be considered in order to evaluate the alternatives correctly. There are sufficient difficulties in just taking the time value of money into consideration.

Rate of Discount

We shall use the term time value of money to describe the discount rate. One possibility is to use the rate of interest associated with default-free securities. This rate does not include an adjustment for the risk of default; thus risk, if present, would be handled separately from the time discounting. In some situations, it is convenient to use the firm's borrowing rate. The objective of the discounting process is to take the time value of money into consideration. We want to find the present equivalent of future sums, neglecting risk considerations.

Dependent and Independent Investments

In evaluating the investment proposals presented to management, it is important to be aware of the possible interrelationships between pairs of investment proposals. An investment proposal will be said to be economically independent of a second investment if the cash flows expected from the first investment would be the same regardless of whether the second investment were accepted or rejected.

In order for investment A to be economically independent of investment B, two conditions must be satisfied. First, it must be technically possible to undertake investment A whether or not investment B is accepted. Second, the net benefits to be expected from the first investment must not be affected by the acceptance or rejection of the second. In the extreme case where the potential benefits to be derived from the first investment will completely disappear if the second investment is accepted, or where it is technically impossible to undertake the first when the second has been accepted, the two investments are said to be mutually exclusive.

Statistical Dependence

It is possible for two or more investments to be economically independent but statistically dependent. Statistical dependence is said to be present if the cash flows from two or more investments would be affected by some external event or happening whose occurrence is uncertain. For example, a firm could produce high-priced yachts and expensive cars. The investment decisions affecting these two product lines are economically independent. However, the fortunes of both activities are closely associated with high business activity and a large amount of discretionary income for the "rich" people.

Incremental Cash Flows

Investments should be analysed using after-tax incremental cash flows. Although we shall assume zero taxes so that we can concentrate on the technique of analysis, it should be remembered that the only relevant cash flows of a period are after all tax effects have been taken into account.

The definition of incremental cash flows is relatively straightforward: If the item changes the bank account or cash balance, it is a cash flow. This definition includes opportunity costs

In choosing the methods of analysis and implementation, it is assumed that the objective is to maximise the wellbeing of stockholders, and more wealth is better than less.

Two Discounted Cash Flow Methods

The two primary discounted cash flow investment evaluation procedures are net present value (NPV) and internal rate of return (IRR). We shall conclude that the net present value method is better than the other possible methods of analysing investments.

Net Present Value

The two most important measures of investment worth are called the discounted cash flow (DCF), measures. It is desirable to explain the concept of the present value of a future sum because in one way or another this concept is utilised in both these measures.

The present value of $100 payable in two years can be defined as that quantity of money necessary to invest today at compound interest in order to have $100 in two years. The rate of interest at which the money will grow and the frequency at which it will be compounded will determine the present value. Assume that we are given a 0.10 annual rate of interest. Let us examine how the present value of a future sum can be computed by using that rate of interest.

Suppose that an investment promises to return a total of $100 at the end of two years. Because $1.00 invested today at 10% compounded annually would grow to $1.21 in two years, we can find the present value at 10% of $100 in two years by dividing $100 by 1.21 or by multiplying by the present value factor, 0.8264. This gives $82.64. Therefore, a sum of $82.64 that earns 10% interest compounded annually will be worth $100 at the end of two years. By repeated applications of this method, we can convert any series of current or future cash payments into an equivalent present value.

The net present value method is a direct application of the present value concept. Its computation requires the following steps:

1. Choose an appropriate rate of discount.
2. Compute the present value of the cash proceeds expected from the investment.
3. Compute the present value of the cash outlays required by the investment.
4. Add all the present value equivalents to obtain the net present value.

The sum of the present values of the proceeds minus the present value of the outlays is the net present value of the investment. The recommended accept or reject criterion is to accept all independent investments whose net present value is greater than or equal to zero and to reject all investments whose net present value is less than zero.

With zero taxes, the net present value of an investment may be described as the maximum amount a firm could pay for the opportunity of making the investment without being financially worse off. If no such payment must be made, the expected net present value is an unrealised capital gain from the investment, over and above the cost of the investment used in the calculation.

The following example illustrates the basic computations for discounting cash flows—that is, adjusting future cash flows for the time value of money, using the net present value method.

We want first to compute the net present value of this investment using 0.10 as the discount rate. The present value of $1 due zero periods from now discounted at any interest rate is 1.000. The present value of $1 due one period from now discounted at 0.10 is 0.9091 or (1.10) The present value of $1 due two periods from now discounted at 0.10 is 0.8264 or (1.10).

The net present value is positive, indicating that the investment is acceptable. Any investment with a net present value equal to or greater than zero is acceptable using this single criterion. The net present value calculation is a reliable method for evaluating investments.

Internal Rate of Return

Many different terms are used to describe the internal rate of return concept. Among these terms are: yield, interest rate of return, rate of return, return on investment, present value return on investment, discounted cash flow, investor's method, time-adjusted rate of return, and marginal efficiency of capital. IRR and internal rate of return may be used interchangeably.

The internal rate of return method utilises present value concepts. The procedure is to find a rate of discount that will make the present value of the cash proceeds expected from an investment equal to the present value of the cash outlays required by the investment. Such a rate of discount may be found by trial and error. For example, with a conventional investment, if we know the cash proceeds and the cash outlays in each future year, we can start with any rate of discount and find for that rate the present value of the cash proceeds and the present value of the outlays.By a process of trial and error, an approximately correct rate of discount can be determined. This rate of discount is referred to as the internal rate of return of the investment, or its IRR.

The IRR method is commonly used in security markets in evaluating bonds and other debt instruments. The yield to maturity of a bond is the rate of discount that makes the present value of the payments promised to the bondholder equal to the market price of the bond. The yield to maturity on a $1,000 bond having a coupon rate of 10% will be equal to 10% only if the current market value of the bond is $1,000.

The internal rate of return may also be described as the rate of growth of an investment. This is more easily seen for an investment with one present outlay and one future benefit. For example, assume that an investment with an outlay of $1,000 today will return $1,331 three years from now.

The internal rate of return of a conventional investment represents the highest rate of interest an investor could afford to pay, without losing money, if all the funds to finance the investment were borrowed and the loan was repaid by application of the cash proceeds from the investment as they were earned.

We want to find the rate of discount that causes the sum of the present values of the cash flows to be equal to zero. Assume that our first choice is 0.10. In the preceding situation, we found that the net present value using 0.10 is a positive $886. We want to change the discount rate so that the present value is zero. Since the cash flows are conventional, to decrease the present value of the future cash flows we should increase the rate of discount.

The net present value is negative, indicating that the 0.20 rate of discount is too large. We shall try a value between 0.10 and 0.20 for our next estimate.

The net present value is zero using 0.16 as the rate of discount, which by definition means that 0.16 is the internal rate of return of the investment.

Although tables give only present value factors for select interest rates, calculators and computers can be used for any interest rate.

Net Present Value Profile

The net present value profile is one of the more useful devices for summarising the profitability characteristics of an investment. On the horizontal axis we measure different discount rates; on the vertical axis we measure the net present value of the investment. The net present value of the investment is plotted for all discount rates from zero to some reasonably large rate. The plot of net present values will cross the horizontal axis at the rate of discount that is called the internal rate of return of the investment.

The net present value profile for the investment discussed in the previous two sections. If we add the cash flows, assuming a zero rate of discount, we obtain

#$12,337 + $10,000 + $5,000 = $2,663

The $2,663 is the intersection of the graph with the Y axis. We know that the graph has a height of $886 at a 0.10 rate of discount and crosses the X axis at 0.16, since 0.16 is the internal rate of return of the investment. For interest rates greater than 0.16, the investment's net present value is negative.

Note that for a conventional investment the net present value profile slopes downward to the right.

The Rollback Method

On a simple hand calculator that lacks a present value button, it is sometimes convenient to use a rollback method of calculation to compute the net present value of an investment. One advantage of this procedure is that the present values at different moments in time are obtained.

References

Jones, K., "The Finance Function Knocks at Your Door", *Intelligent Enterprise*, June 28, 2002.

Levinson, Mark, *Guide to Financial Markets*, London: The Economist (Profile Books), 2006, pp.145-6.

Markowitz, Harry M, "The early history of portfolio theory: 1600-1960," *Financial Analysts Journal*, Vol. 55, No. 4, 1999.

9

Financial Transactions

Corporate finance tends to become more narrowly focused when one talks to an investment banker or investment bank. Corporate finance departments advertise their abilities to provide advice and complete transactions in the following areas:

— Mergers, Acquisitions and Divestitures (M&A).

— Financial Advice (capital structure and fairness opinions).

— Flotations/Initial Public Offerings (IPOs).

— Further Equity Offerings.

Corporate finance is about building relationships with companies as much as it is about transactions. The roles of the corporate financier in the above transactions, we need to place the corporate finance department in the context of an investment bank.

Role of Chinese Walls

Corporate financiers are said to work behind Chinese Walls - separating them from other members of the firm, in particular those who have daily contact with investors. The name, presumably, is taken from the Great Wall of China. Chinese Walls are established arrangements in the form of procedures, systems, management and physical location which act as barriers within a firm to ensure that confidential information which is generated by one part of the firm or obtained from a client in one part of the firm does not penetrate another part of the firm. They exist (or should do) in any integrated securities firm, investment bank, accounting firm or any other organisation where some members of the firm have access to and deal with information that could affect the share price of clients.

Strengthening Chinese Walls became increasingly important in the aftermath of the 'Internet Bubble' of the late 1990s and early 2000s. Research analysts, particularly in the US, became highly involved in IPOs and further equity offerings, where they should not have done. Corporate finance departments in large investment banks are almost always located on a separate floor than other departments.

In some cases, at the largest banks, the corporate finance team may even reside in another building. At the very least, access is restricted in the corporate finance area to those who work there or escorted visitors who are signed in and out. Chinese Walls provide a mechanism for firms to function as multi-disciplinary operations. Without Chinese Walls, a firm could not offer both corporate finance advice and research, sales and trading with clients. They work like porous membranes that allow information to flow only in one direction as illustrated in Figure 1.

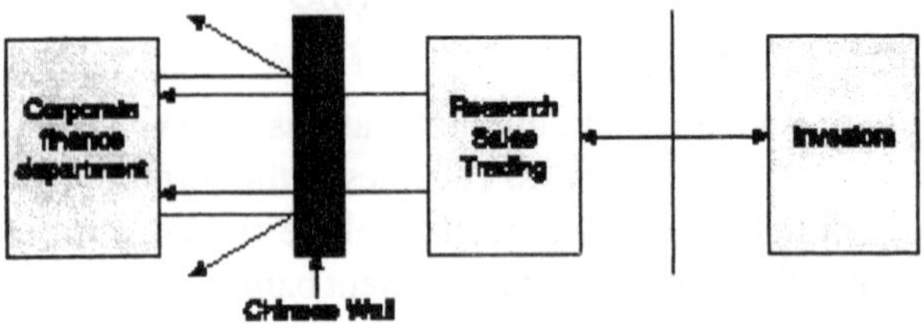

Figure 1. Information flow through the Chinese Wall – arrows represent the flow of information, and its direction.

Corporate financiers' work involves 'price-sensitive' information. Knowing that Company A plans to bid for Company B would send B's share price shooting up if the information found its way to the market. If a sales-man in the investment bank working on the bid discovered the potential bid as a result of weak Chinese Walls, he or she potentially could feed the information to selected clients who would benefit illegally from this inside information on announcement of the bid. If Company C plans to raise funds through a new equity issue, the Chinese Wall should be maintained until announcement, as share prices typically drop on announcement of new issues. A party with inside information, gained from a leaky Chinese Wall, would be able to sell shares prior to the announcement of a new issue and buy them back at a lower price following the offering's announcement.

In order to advise clients, corporate financiers must receive information regarding the market, investors' attitudes, etc. from research analysts and salesmen who are in contact with investors. However, the confidential corporate information received by corporate financiers must not flow in the other direction as it could have an impact on the price of the shares.

Corporate Finance Assignment

Flotations/IPOs

The IPO of any company is one of the most important moments in its corporate life - it only happens once, and while companies can become skilled at acquisitions and divestitures, they do not get practice of IPOs. Thus, the role of the corporate financier in guiding companies and their management to market is crucial. Many investment banks have specialist departments that sit alongside corporate finance - called Equity Capital Markets (ECM). ECM professionals specialise in the flotation of companies and any subsequent equity offerings.

The corporate finance team co-ordinates the flotation process from start to finish. Figure 2 provides a schematic of the interested parties in a flotation.

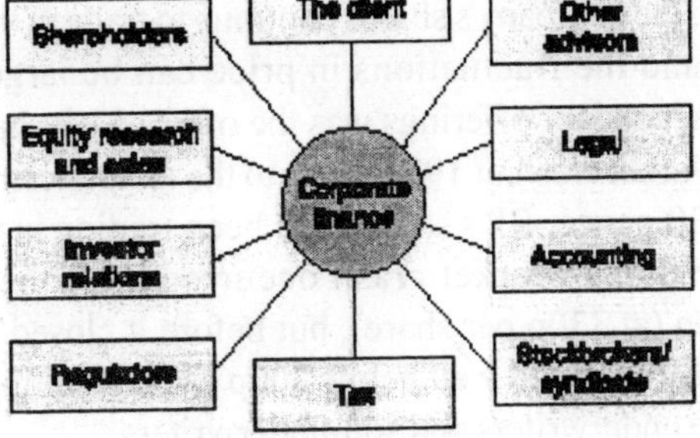

Figure 2. Parties involved in flotations and M&A.

The corporate financier keeps everything together: he or she is the main interface with the company, although solicitors, accountants and investor relations people also sit around the meeting table.The corporate finance team is usually the first appointed external advisor. It then aids the company in selecting the other advisors to work on the transaction. Corporate financiers provide advice on the capital structure, developing the investment story, appointing external directors, determining the timing of an issue and, generally, managing the project. The team then co-ordinates the new issue timetable. From start to finish, the flotation process takes from 3 to 6 months, sometimes longer if there are particularly difficult corporate structuring issues to be resolved. Corporate financiers deal with documentation and the regulators. They are also responsible for the coordination of the different departments in their investment bank and members of the syndicate.

Finally, junior members of the corporate finance team are responsible for the organisation of the closing dinner; a gala affair for all the participants in the transaction that usually takes place a month or so after the shares have been trading on the Stock Exchange.

Rights issues

Corporate financiers and their equity capital markets colleagues perform much the same role in rights issues and secondary offerings as they do in flotations. They coordinate the work of the other advisors, lead the preparation of documentation, advise the issuer or vendor on the pricing of shares and so on.

There is one complication, and it can be a large one. During a rights issue, the company's shares continue to trade in the stock market every day and the fluctuations in price can be large. The biggest disaster in secondary offerings was the offer of BP shares just before the Stock Market crash of 1987. Prior to the announcement of a sale of shares at 330 pence, BP's shares had been trading in the 345p-355p range. The Stock Market crash occurred after the offering was underwritten (at 330p per share), but before it closed. Following the crash, BP shares traded well below 300p each, resulting in significant losses to the underwriters and sub-underwriters.

Mergers, Acquisitions and Divestitures

After flotation, a merger or acquisition is the most significant corporate event that most companies go through. Corporate financiers, acting alone or alongside strategy consultants, help senior management with planning for the future. They may recommend a divestiture, acquisition or joint venture, depending on the client's strategic, operational and financial criteria. Once the client has decided what course of action to pursue, corporate financiers help in the execution of the transaction. Whatever the recommendation, the corporate finance team will co-ordinate all parties involved in the transaction. Figure 2 is also appropriate to describe the corporate finance role in mergers, acquisitions and divestitures.

Acquisitions and mergers

If the client has determined that growth through acquisition or merger is its preferred strategy, the corporate finance team swings into action. The corporate financier will conduct a search of domestic and international businesses that fit his client's criteria. In most instances, the client will know its industry well enough to identify the most likely targets without the assistance of an investment bank. Corporate financiers add value in analysing potential targets, as well as in broadening the search to international markets, if required.

Working with the client, corporate financiers evaluate potential candidates to determine a short-list based on potential fit and the receptiveness to an offer. The friendly welcome of an offer is vital. Only in the Anglo-Saxon economies are hostile takeover bids common and commonly successful. The vast majority of transactions are 'friendly', although the press given to hostile bids makes them seem to be more prevalent. Once the client has agreed a short-list, the bankers analyse each target's business, competitive position and future prospects. Valuations on a stand-alone and merged entity basis are conducted.

Corporate financiers (the senior ones) can act as confidential intermediaries in approaching the potential vendor. Depending on the experience and inclination of his client, the corporate financier can take the lead in negotiations throughout the transaction. In any event, he will help to develop a bidding strategy and assist in structuring and negotiating terms and conditions.

In integrated securities houses, the corporate financier will bring in his colleagues in funding departments who can arrange financing (both short-term and permanent). Investment banks are increasingly providing loans to help complete deals; competing with banks. From the agreement to negotiate exclusively with his client through closing, the corporate financier coordinates the activities of the lawyers, accountants and other advisors in managing the due diligence effort and the documentation required to support and close the deal. Of course, not all transactions happen in such a structured manner.

In some instances, an offer can be devised, proposed and accepted over the course of a frantic weekend. Such speedy transactions are usually in contested situations, where the client is second into the battle over a target which has great strategic importance.

Orderly divestitures

Organised sales of divisions, subsidiaries or businesses make up the majority of M&A transactions. Investment bankers are hired in order to maximise the value received by the vendor, minimise the length of the process and minimise the disruption caused to management of the business that is for sale. On the other side of the transaction, interested purchasers hire investment banks to aid in valuation, deal structuring and negotiation.

The first stage in an orderly divestiture is to determine the most likely purchaser(s). To add value at this stage, the corporate finance team should decide on a short-list of the most likely purchasers based on business fit and the strategic rationale for the acquisition. Private equity houses are now included as potential purchasers in most transactions, as are international businesses.

At the same time as the team is assembling a list of potential bidders, others will conduct a valuation to determine the worth of the business. The valuation helps the vendor in deciding whether an offer should be accepted or not. Corporate financiers also recommend whether a negotiated transaction or an auction should be held. The auction process best serves larger businesses that are likely to elicit a high degree of interest. The extra work should result in a higher sale price.

The corporate finance team prepares a confidential information memorandum that describes the operations of the business, its markets and prospects, contains historical financial results and often includes management's forecasts for the next year. Letters are sent to prospective purchasers, followed by telephone calls from corporate financiers attempting to determine their interest. Those who are interested receive a copy of the information memorandum.

In an auction, prospective buyers are given several weeks to submit an initial bid based on the information contained in the memorandum. Once the preliminary, non-binding 'expressions of interest' are submitted, the corporate financiers assist the vendor in determining the short-list of potential purchasers. Bidders on the shortlist then have access to a 'data room', which has more information than contained in the information memorandum and site visits, if appropriate. Data rooms, which were once an actual room with reams of corporate information, now are often 'virtual'.

PDF files, with confidential information are posted on a secure Internet site, accessible to potential bidders via a password. Throughout the process, corporate financiers manage the distribution of information, contact with management and aim to maintain competitive tensions between/among potential bidders. When the final bids are submitted, corporate financiers aid in evaluation of the offers and assist in negotiations over the terms and conditions until the sale is complete.

Importance of Financial Advice

A good corporate financier monitors his clients' share price and reputation among investors. When the market persistently undervalues a company, the corporate financier provides advice regarding actions his client might take. These actions might include disposal of certain divisions, a 'carve-out' (IPO of part of a subsidiary) or increasing the gearing of the balance sheet through share buybacks or special dividends. Corporate financiers also provide fairness opinions to boards of directors. This typically involves the preparation of an independent valuation of potential acquisitions, divestitures or restructuring proposals.

The opinion assures directors that the proposed transaction is fair, from a financial perspective, to all shareholders. In the UK, all quoted companies must have a named financial advisor. The named advisor provides continuing advice in return for an annual retainer. The advisor also tends to be the investment bank that executes the majority of a client's transactions. However, companies are not bound to use their advisor on all or any transaction.

Table 1. Leading UK corporate finance advisors.

Rank	Advisor	Number
1	UBS Investment Bank	117.0
2	Seymour Pierce	86.0
3	Dresdner Kleinwort Wasserstein	79.5
4	KBC Peel Hunt	76.0
5	Brewer Dolphin Securities	70.0
6	Panmure Gordon & Co.	68.0
7	Evolution Securities	67.5
8	NM Rothschild 64.5	
9	Collins Stewart	55.5
10	Teather & Greenwood	47.5

Many companies will reward other investment banks with a leading role if the bank provides compelling ideas. Table 1. lists the top financial advisors as of mid-2005.

Corporate Finance Professional

According to established bankers, a corporate finance professional has the cunning of a snake, the stamina of a camel, the creativity of a chameleon, the memory of an elephant, the work ethic of a beaver, the negotiating finesse of a mouse sharing a bed with an elephant and so on. To join the corporate finance zoo is not easy. Applications exceed the number of positions by multiples. The two main entry points are as executives/analysts and managers/associates. To get these sought-after positions investment banks universally demand:

— academic excellence;
— ability to work in teams;
— ability to work under pressure;
— quantitative skills;
— verbal and written communication strength. The main entry points into corporate finance are as a graduate, following the completion of an accountancy designation, or following an MBA.

Table 2 sets out illustrative job titles within a corporate finance department of a UK and a US investment bank. The paragraphs following the table provide more detail of the actual responsibilities held by the corporate financier at each level.

Table 2. Typical career progression of a corporate financier.

Years of experience	Title(s)
0–2	Executive/Analyst
3–4	Manager/Associate
5–8	Assistant Director, Associate Director, Vice President
8+	Director
Too many	Managing Director

Banks try to fill corporate finance with people who have the attention to detail, quantitative skills and stamina to successfully gather information, conduct valuations and carry out other tasks during the early years of their career. After being in the bank for 4 to 6 years, the most important skills gradually change, ultimately becoming the ability to manage existing clients and attract new ones. The above is not meant to be a definitive list of titles.

Banks are different; some have Assistant Managers, others both Assistant and Associate Directors. Titles change. Many organisations suffer from 'title inflation', a disease that occurs when too many big egos clash with a bonus pool that is too small.

Executives and Analysts are typically hired for corporate finance positions on completion of a degree. A small percentage may join a bank as an executive after a short stint at another job. Most larger banks have comprehensive induction/training programmes to ensure that all their employees start working life on an even footing. The role of the Executive/Analyst is to collect information, prepare valuations, keep notes of meetings, and aid in the drafting and proof-reading of prospectuses and takeover circulars. The days are long, the pressure high.

American investment banks have a tradition of chucking out all their analysts at the end of 2 years. The traditional analyst will then go to business school to get an MBA in the hopes of returning to the bank as an Associate; the sane ones go to Hawaii and take up surfing.

Managers and Associates are Executives who have put in around 3 years of hard graft. In addition, there is a large intake of recently qualified accountants at this level. In American banks, Associates arrive with MBAs. The Associate's job is similar to that of the Executive's, except there is more. Most Associates and Managers are assigned to industry teams, where they reside for 3 to 4 years.

The Corporate Finance role may be defined as one of project management. Mid-ranking corporate financiers, Associate Directors and Vice Presidents are expected to keep two, three or even four deals on the go at any one time. At this level the job entails: making sure that the lawyers draft the documentation, accountants prepare financial statements and conduct due diligence, ensure that the PR team gains favourable press coverage and all the while 'holding the client's hand'. At this stage, the corporate financier is also spending more time marketing the firm's capabilities. After approximately 4 years in this role, the corporate financier can be expecting his next promotion.

The smart, some might say Machiavellian, corporate financier will make a habit of socialising and developing relationships with company managers who are 5 to 10 years older. Assuming that some of these friends and acquaintances are competent, they should be reaching senior corporate positions as the corporate financier becomes a director/managing director. These relationships should then bear fruit. A lucky corporate financier is one who has older siblings who are able to make appropriate introductions.

Directors and Managing Directors are generally responsible for client acquisition and retention. They go to the important meetings where decisions are taken, but they leave the day-to-day running of transactions to the people at the level below. There are few corporate financiers who remain in the City after the age of 50 or so. Most switch to less pressurised jobs at client corporations, while a lucky few are able to retire at an early age in order to take up organic farming or purchase a vineyard.

References

Adams, Peter S. and William A. Harrison, ed., *Essentials of Cash Management*, MD: Treasury Management Association, 1998.

Bathory, Alexander, *The Analysis of Credit: Foundations and Development of Corporate Credit Assessment*, London: McGraw -Hill Book Company (UK) Limited, 1987.

Bear, Larry A. and Rita Maldonado-Bear, *Free Markets, Finance, Ethics, and Law*, Upper Saddle, NJ: Prentice Hall, 1994.

Block and Hirt, *Foundations of Financial Management*, 6th edition, Richard Irwin & Co, 1992.

Brealey, Richard A., *Principles of Corporate Finance*, NY: McGraw Hill, 2000.

10

Risk and Return

As a prelude to examining different models for risk and return, it is worth exploring the ingredients that make a model a good one. A good risk and return model should do the following:

— Come up with a universal measure for risk. To be useful, a risk measure has to apply to all investments, whether stocks or bonds or real estate, because they all compete for the same investment dollar. A good risk and return model will came up with one measure of risk that applies to all investments, financial as well as real.

— Specify what types of risk are rewarded and what types are not. It is an accepted part of investment that not all risks are rewarded. A good model should be able to distinguish between risk that is rewarded and risk that is not and provide an intuitive rationale far the distinction.

— Standardize risk measures, to allow for analysis and comparison. While risk is always relative, a good risk measure should be standardized in such a way that an investor, when looking at the measure of risk far anyone investment, should be able to came to a conclusion about the riskiness of that investment relative to others.

— Translate the risk measure into an expected return. One of the objectives in measuring risk is to came up with an estimate of an expected return far an investment. This expected return then becomes the benchmark that determines whether the investment is a "good" or "bad" one. It is not sufficient far a model to say that higher risk investments should yield higher expected returns without providing a specific estimate of the risk premium.

— Work. The ultimate test of a good model is that it works; that is, it provides a measure of risk, which, at least in the long term and across the cross section of investments, is positively correlated with returns. A stronger test would be to examine whether the actual returns, again in the long term, match the expected returns derived from the model.

General Models

The awareness that risk matters is nat new. Until recently, however, models far risk and return were largely subjective and varied widely among investors. Starting in the 1950s, with the development of modern portfolio theory, risk and return models have been formulated which, in addition to being mare quantitative and specific in their predictions, have also been mare widely accepted.

Capital Asset Pricing Model (CAPM)

The capital asset pricing model (CAPM) is the standard against which other risk and return models are measured. Given its wide use an Wall Street and in corporate policy making, the CAPM has also became a magnet far criticism, same warranted and same not. The advantages of the model are that it is simple and intuitive and provides same very strong and testable implications.

Variance in Returns

This is a measure of the squared difference between the actual and expected returns as an investment. The capital asset pricing made I is built an the premise that the variance in returns is the appropriate measure of risk but that only that portion of variance that is not diversifiable is rewarded. The model measures the nondiversifiable variance and relates expected returns to this measure of risk.

Measuring Risk

In the capital asset pricing model, investments are measured an two dimensions:

(1) the "expected return" an the investment comprises the reward; and

(2) the variance in anticipated returns comprises the risk an the investment.

The variance an any investment measures the disparity between actual and expected returns. In statistical terms, the variance can be captured in the return distribution. Given a choice between two investments with the same standard deviation but different expected returns, investors will always pick the one with the higher expected return.

Although the concept that investors choose on the basis of expected return and variance may seem intuitive, it is not as straightforward as it seems. In the real world, investors often consider other dimensions of risk and return beyond just the mean and the variance in making their decisions. For instance, an investor may accept a higher variance investment (over a lower variance investment with the same expected returns) because it offers a higher probability of extraordinary pay-offs. In statistical terms, this probability of a high payoff is measured by the "skewness" of returns, and there is some evidence that investors like positively skewed distributions.

The assumptions about risk and return made by the capital asset pricing model are central to its derivation and have been defended by its proponents on two levels. On a theoretical level, the assumption that expected return is traded off against variance can be justified if investors possess utility functions where nothing else matters. This is more an assumption of convenience than one that can be defended on empirical grounds, however, for there is no evidence that investors have such utility functions. The other way in which the expected return/variance trade-off can be justified is by assuming that returns follow a normal distribution, in which case the entire distribution can be described in terms of the first two moments-the expected return and the variance. This assumption is also difficult to justify on empirical grounds because the investors' limited liability will result in return distributions that are positively skewed.

The other defence provided for the assumption that variance is the appropriate measure of risk is more believable because it is based on the empirical evidence relating average returns and variances on classes of assets over long time periods. For instance, the investment class with the highest average returns (small stocks) had the highest standard deviation, whereas the investment class with the lowest average returns (Treasury bill) had the lowest standard deviation. A leap in logic is still required, however, to arrive at the CAPM assumption that variance is the only measure of risk that matters. Many analytical services also use the standard deviation to measure risk

Risk is Rewarded

Although the capital asset pricing model defines variance as risk, not all variance is rewarded by financial markets with higher returns. The CAPM is built on the tenet that some of the risk in any individual asset can be eliminated through diversification across large numbers and classes of assets, such as stocks, bonds, real estate, and other real assets. Because prices on these different asset classes do not always move together, investing in them should result in substantial savings in risk while not reducing expected returns substantially. The notion that diversification can reduce risk can be backed up on both intuitive and statistical grounds.

Diversification

This is the process of holding multiple investments in a portfolio, either across the same asset class (stocks) or across asset classes. On an intuitive level, the risk in any asset comes from two sources-firm-specific actions that affect primarily the prices of that asset, and marketwise movements that affect the prices of all assets. The effects of firm-specific and marketwise actions can be either positive or negative. There is a key difference between the two effects, however: the effects of firm-specific risk on the prices of individual assets in a portfolio can be either positive or negative for any period. Thus, in large portfolios, it can be reasonably argued that this risk will average out to be zero and thus not impact the overall value of the portfolio.

The effects of market wide movements are likely to be in the same direction for all investments in a portfolio, although some assets may be affected more than others. For instance, other things being equal, an increase in interest rates will lower the values of most assets in a portfolio. Being more diversified does not eliminate this risk, although holding assets in different classes may reduce the impact.

Firm-Specific Risk

This is risk that affects only one asset or a small group of similar assets. In the case of a stock, it is risk that is specific to the company issuing the stock or to the industry in which the company operates. The argument that diversification reduces risk is incontestable, but the assumption that CAPM makes-that diversifiable risk does not matter-is debatable. This argument is based on the presumption that the marginal investor in the market, who sets prices and therefore determines how risk is viewed, is well diversified and expects to be rewarded only for the nondiversifiable risk. If the marginal investor is not well diversified, however, diversifiable risk may affect prices and expected returns.

More on diversifiable and nondiversifiable risk A number of examples of actions can be cited that affect the returns of the firm taking those actions and, hence, create firm specific risk. Some of these actions may have positive consequences: a consumer product company may profit because management introduced a successful product or revamped its marketing strategy, or an oil company may gain because it finds new oil reserves. Some actions may have negative consequences: a company's products may carry a defect that causes unexpected costs for the company, or the natural resource used by the company to manufacture its products may become more expensive. The risk associated with these actions should be diversifiable.

This definition can even be extended to actions that affect the returns of one specific sector of the economy. For instance, as a consequence of actions taken by the U.S. government to restrict the import of Japanese cars into the United States, all U.S. automobile companies may gain in terms of profitability. Alternatively, pollution laws directed primarily at auto emissions may make these same firms much less profitable. For a diversified investor who holds stocks across a wide variety of sectors and industries, this is still diversifiable risk.

Risk that is nondiversifiable affects all investments, although the degree of impact may vary across investments. One example would be an announcement by the Federal Reserve that it plans to raise interest rates. If, as a result of this announcement, market interest rates go up, all investments are affected, though to varying extents. Holding a diversified portfolio is not going to provide protection against this type of risk. A statistical analysis of diversification-reducing risk The effects of diversification on risk can be illustrated by examining the effects of increasing the number of assets in a portfolio on variance.

The variance in a portfolio is determined by the variances of the individual assets in the portfolio and the covariances between pairs of assets in that portfolio. It is the covariance term, which captures how asset prices move together, that provides an insight into why and by how much diversification will reduce risk.

Covariance

This is a measure of how two assets or investments move together. A positive covariance suggests that their prices move in the same direction most of the time, whereas a negative covariance suggests that their prices move in opposite directions. Correlation coefficients and portfolio variance The variance of the two-asset portfolio is clearly a function of the correlation in returns between the two assets. The greater the correlation in returns between the two assets, the smaller the benefit from diversification.

The standard deviation of the portfolio is halfway between the standard deviations of the individual assets when the correlation coefficient is 1. As the correlation coefficient declines, so does the standard deviation of portfolio. From two assets to three assets to n assets If there is in fact a diversification benefit of going from one asset to two, as the preceding discussion illustrates, there must be a benefit in going from two assets to three and from three to more assets. The variance of a portfolio of three assets can be written as a function of the variances of each of the three assets, the portfolio weights on each, and the correlations between pairs of the assets. The number of covariance terms in the variance formulation has increased from one to three.

The covariance of an asset with itself is the variance of that asset. The number of terms in this formulation increases exponentially with the number of assets in the portfolio, largely because of the number of covariance terms that have to be considered. In general, the number of covariance terms can be written as a function of the number of assets:

$$\textit{Number of covariance terms} = n\,(n - 1)\,/2$$

Where n is the number of assets in the portfolio:

Number of Assets	Number of Covariance Terms
2	1
5	10
10	45
20	190
100	4,950
1,000	499,500

This formulation can be used to estimate the variance of a portfolio and the effects of diversification on that variance. For simplicity, assume that the average asset has a standard deviation in returns of er and that the average covariance in returns between any pair of assets is <Tjj. Furthermore, assume that the portfolio is always equally weighted across the assets in that portfolio. The variance of a portfolio of n assets can then be written as To illustrate, assume that the average: asset has a variance in returns of 50% and that the average covariance in returns between any two assets is 10%. The variance of a portfolio of five assets can then be written as

a2p = (1/5) (50%) + (4/5) (10%) = 18%

The variance of a portfolio of 10 assets can be written

as a2p = (1/10) (50%) + (9/10) (10%) = 14%

The number of assets in the portfolio increases, the variance of the portfolio approaches the average covariance, and the first term in the equation approaches zero. The marginal benefits of diversification decrease with the addition of each new asset to the portfolio.

The variance of the portfolio drops from 50% to 11.60% as the number of assets increases from 1 to 25. Increasing the number of assets further pro. vides only a small additional benefit, for the variance can drop to 10% at the minimum. Given that diversification can be costly, in terms of transactions and information costs, this provides a rationale for why most investors do not carry diversification to its logical limit and hold, as many assets as there are available.

Markowitz Portfolio

This is the portfolio that yields the highest expected return for a specified level of risk or the minimum standard deviation for a specified expected return.

Return optimization-Markowitz portfolios: The fact that variances can be estimated for portfolios made up of a large number of assets suggests an approach to optimizing portfolio construction in the mean/variance framework on which the CAPM is devised. If an investor can specify the maximum amount of risk he is willing to take on (in terms of variance), the task of portfolio optimization becomes the maximization of expected returns subject to this level of risk. Alternatively, if an investor specifies her desired level of return, the optimum portfolio is the one chat minimizes the variance subject to this level of return.

These portfolios are considered efficient because they maximize expected returns given the standard deviation; the entire set of portfolios is referred to as the efficient frontier. The Markowitz approach to portfolio optimization, though intuitively appealing, suffers from two major problems. The first is that it requires a very large number of inputs, since the covariances between pairs of assets are required to estimate the variances of portfolios. This may be manageable for small numbers of assets, but it becomes less so when the entire universe of stocks or all investments are considered.

The second problem is that the Markowitz approach ignores a very important asset choice that most investors have-the choice of investing their money risklessly in default-free government securities-in coming up with optimum portfolios. The CAPM addresses these limitations and comes up with a far simpler approach to constructing optimal portfolios, while considering the riskless asset simultaneously.

Both the CAPM and Markowitz portfolio optimization make one assumption that exposes them to some criticism: they both assume that there are no transactions or information costs associated with diversification. Optimum portfolios with the riskless asset most investors have the choice of investing some or all of their money in a riskless asset, as a way of managing risk. By itself, the addition of one asset to the universe may seem trivial, but the riskless asset has some special characteristics that affect optimal portfolio choice for all investors.

Riskless Asset: A riskless asset is one for which the actual return is equal to the expected return.

1. The risklessasset, by definition, has an expected return that will always be equal to the actual return. For example, consider an investment in a shortterm government security. The investment has no default risk and provides a guaranteed cash flow (at least in nominal terms) at the end of its maturity. The expected return is known when the investment is made, and the actual return should be equal to this, if the investor holds until maturity.
2. While returns on risky assets vary, the absence of variance in the riskless asset makes it uncorrelated with returns on any of these risky assets. Consequently, combinations of any risky asset or portfolio with the risk less asset will yield linear results for the standard deviation. To prove this, assume that the variance of the risky portfolio is u / and that Wr is the proportion of the overall portfolio invested in these risky assets. The balance is invested in a riskless asset, which has no variance, and is uncorrelated with the risky asset. The variance of the overall portfolio can be written as

2-22

U portfolio - Wr U r

Uportfolio = Wr Ur

The other two terms drop out and that the standard deviation of the overall portfolio is linearly related to the proportion of the portfolio invested in the risky portfolio.

Effect of Market Portfolio

This is the portfolio of all risky assets, held in proportion to their market value. If this seems abstract, consider M to be an extremely well diversified mutual fund that holds both financial and real assets, and Treasury bills to be the riskless asset. In the CAPM, all investors will hold combinations of Treasury bills and the same mutual fund and adjust for risk through their allocation decisions. They will put more of their money in the mutual fund if they want to take risk, and less into it if they want to decrease their risk exposure. At the limit, if they feel that putting all their money in the mutual fund does not expose them to enough risk, they can borrow money and invest it in the mutual fund.

These results are predicated on two assumptions. First, there exists a riskless asset, with the characteristics described earlier. Second, investors can lend and borrow at this riskless rate to arrive at their optimal allocations. Some variations of the CAPM allow these assumptions to be relaxed and still permit conclusions consistent with the CAPM. Adding the riskless asset to the risky portfolios, developed using the Markowitz optimization techniques, yields very strong implications for optimal investment strategy. All investors will hold combinations of the riskless asset and the market portfolio. The only difference across investors is in the allocation decision; more risk averse investors will invest more in the riskless asset, and less risk-averse investors will invest more in the market portfolio.

Capital Market Line

This is the line that plots the expected return on an efficient portfolio as a function of the standard deviation of that portfolio. The efficient portfolios are all combinations of the riskless asset and the market portfolio.

Defenders of the capital asset pricing model should undoubtedly be troubled by the fact that investors in the real world hold wide variety of portfolios and do not hold just the market portfolio. Some of these variations can be ascribed to the presence of transactions costs and others to differences in the information available to investors and to expectations about future returns. The question that remains, however, is whether these deviations from the predictions of the CAPM are serious enough to call into question its conclusions about how risk is measured.

Measuring nondiversifiable risk with the market portfolio as the standard In a world in which investors hold a combination of only two assets-the risk less asset and the market portfolio-the risk of any individual asset will be measured relative to the market portfolio. In particular, the risk of any asset will be the risk it adds on to the market portfolio. To arrive at the appropriate measure of this added risk, assume that a2 m is the variance of the market portfolio prior to the addition of the new asset, and that the variance of the individual asset being added to this portfolio is a2j. The market value portfolio weight on this asset is Wi> and the covariance in returns between the individual asset and the market portfolio is aim' The variance of the market portfolio prior to and after the addition of the individual asset can then be written as

Variance prior to asset i being added = a2 m

Variance after asset i is added = a2 m' = Wi~ a2i + (1 - Wi)2 a2 m + 2 Wi (1 - Wi) COVim

The market value weight on any individual asset in the market portfolio should be small since the market portfolio includes all traded assets in the economy. Consequently, the first term in the equation should approach zero, and the second term should approach a2 m' leaving the third term (COVim, the covariance) as the measure of the risk added by asset i. To illustrate, assume that the market portfolio includes 1,000 assets, a total market value of $1,000 billion, and a standard deviation of 20%. A new asset is added on, witb a market value of $1 billion, a standard deviation of 80%, and a correlation of 0.5 with the market portfolio. To examine the marginal impact of adding this asset to the portfolio, the variance of the market portfolio has to be computed both before and after adding the asset:

Market Value weight of the new asset = 1/1001

Variance of market portfolio before addition = (.20)2 =.04

Variance of market portfolio after addition = a2 m'

= (1/1001)2 (.80? + (1O00/1O01? (.20? + 2 (1/1001)(1000/ 1001)(.5) (.80)(.20) = 0 +.04 + (2/1001) (.08)

Thus, the risk added by the new asset is proportional to its covariance with the market portfolio.

Beta of Investment

The beta of any investment in CAPM is a standardized measure of the risk it adds to the market portfolio. Standardizing covariances Since the covariance of the market portfolio with itself is the market variance, the covariances ol individual assets with the market portfolio can be standardized by dividing by the market variance. This standardized measure of nondiversifiable risk is the beta of the asset.

Beta of an asset i = COVim/a2m

The beta of the market portfolio is 1 (since Covmm = a2m); assets that are riskier than average (using this measure of risk) will have betas that exceed 1, and assets that are safer than average will have betas that are lower than 1. The riskless asset will have a beta of zero. The expected return as an asset is linearly related to the beta of the asset. In particular, the expected return on an asset can be written as a function of the risk-free rate and the beta of that asset:

Expected Return on asset i

= Risk-free rate + Beta of asset i (Risk premium on market portfolio)

= Rf + ~i [E(Rm) - Rf]

where

E(Ri) = Expected Return on asset i

Rf = Risk-free Rate

E(Rm) = Expected Return on market portfolio

~i = Beta of investment i

If the CAPM is correct, all assets should fall on the security market line, which provides the expected return for any given beta.

CAPM Implications

The capital asset pricing model does make some strong assumptions, but it provides equally strong and testable implications.

1. All investors will allocate their wealth across two assets-the riskless asset and a market portfolio of all risky assets, held in proportion to their market value.
2. The risk of any asset will be measured by how much risk it adds on to the market portfolio; this added risk can be estimated using the covariance between the returns on the asset and the returns on the market portfolio. This covariance can be standardized by dividing by the market variance to arrive at a beta for the asset.

3. The expected return on any asset is linearly related to its beta.

E(Rj) = Rf + ~j[E(Rm) - Rf]

where

E(Rj) = Expected Return on asset i

Rf = Risk-free Rate

E(Rm) = Expected Return on market portfolio

~i = Beta of investment i

Testing the CAPM Does the CAPM work? Is beta a good proxy for risk, and is it correlated with expected returns? The answers to these questions have been debated widely in the last two decades. The first tests of the model suggested that betas and returns were positively related, although other measures of risk (such as variance) continued to explain differences in actual returns. This discrepancy was attributed to limitations in the testing techniques.

In 1977, Roll, in a seminal critique of the model's tests, suggested that since the market portfolio could never be observed, the CAPM could never be tested. Therefore, all tests of the CAPM were joint tests of both the model and the market portfolio used in the tests. It could therefore be argued that in any empirical test that claimed to reflect the CAPM, the rejection could be of the proxy used for the market portfolio rather than of the model itself Roll noted that there was no way to prove that CAPM worked and, thus, no empirical basis for using the model.

Book-to-Market Ratio

This is the ratio of the book value of equity to the market value of equity. In a damning indictment, Fama and French examined the relationship between betas and returns between 1963 and 1990 and concluded that there was no relationship between the two. They also noted that two other variables-size and book-to-market ratio-explain differences in returns across firms much better than does beta and may in fact be better proxies for risk. These results have been contested on two fronts.

First, Amihud, Christensen, and Mendelson, using the same data, performed different statistical tests and showed that betas did, in fact, explain returns during the time period. Second, Chan and Lakonishok examined a much longer time series of returns from 1926 to 1991 and found that the positive relationship between betas and returns broke down only in the period after 1982. They attribute this breakdown to indexing, which they argue has allowed the larger, lower-beta stocks in the S&P 500 to outperform smaller, higher-beta stocks. They also find that betas are a useful guide to risk in extreme market conditions, with the riskiest firms performing far worse than the market as a whole, in the 10 worst months for the market between 1926 and 1991.

Arbitrage Pricing Model

The failure of the capital asset pricing model to explain adequately differences in returns across assets using betas opened the door for other asset pricing models. The leading candidate for an alternative model is the arbitrage pricing model (APM). The logic behind the APM is much the same as that behind the capital asset pricing model: investors are rewarded for taking on nondiversifiable risk. In the capital asset pricing model, one factor captures this nondiversifiable risk. In contrast, the measure of this nondiversifiable risk in the APM can come from multiple factors. The number and identity of the factors are determined by the data on historical returns.

The arbitrage pricing model is built on the simple premise that investors take advantage of arbitrage opportunities. In other words, if two portfolios have the same exposure to risk but offer different expected returns, investors will buy the portfolio that has the higher expected returns and, in the process, adjust the expected returns to equilibrium. Decomposing returns into anticipated and unanticipated components The return on any asset can be decomposed into two parts-a normal, or expected, return component that is predictable, and an unanticipated component that is not:

$$R = E® + U$$

where E® is the expected component and U is the unexpected component of return It is the unanticipated component that creates the risk in investments. The source of unanticipated returns-firm-specific and market wide risk The "surprise" in returns comes from two sources. The first is firm-specific and covers information that primarily affects the firm. The second is marketwide and affects most or a investments and includes unanticipated changes in a number of economic variable including gross national product, inflation, and interest rates. Incorporating this into the return model above

R − E® + m + e

where

m is the marketwide component of unanticipated risk and e is the firm-specific component. Note that this distinction is very similar to the distinction between firm specific and market risk made in the capital asset pricing model.

The sources of marketwide risk Although both the capital asset pricing model and the arbitrage pricing model make a distinction between firm-specific and marketwide risk, they W,rt ways when it comes to measuring the market risk. The CAPM assumes that the market risk is captured in the market portfolio, whereas the arbitrage pricing model sticks with economic fundamentals allowing for multiple sources of marketwide risk, such as unanticipated changes in gross national product, interest rates, and inflation, and measures the sensitivity of investments to these changes with factor betas. In factors:

R:R+m+e l

E[R] + (131 F1 + 132 F2 +.... + 13n Fn) + e

where

13j = Sensitivity of investment to unanticipated changes in factor j

Fj= Unanticipated changes in factor j

Suppose that investment j is expected to have a return of 7% next year. There are four economic factors that drive returns, and the betas of investment j to each factor are given below:

Beta relative to factor 1 = 2.5 Beta relative to factor 2 = 0.5

significant economic factor driving expected returns in the 1970s but are not as significant in other time periods. Using the wrong factor(s) or missing a significant factor in a multifactor model can lead to inferior estimates of cost of equity.

PORTFOLIO RISK MEASURING

The standard statistical measures of spread are variance and standard dilution. The variance of the market return is the expected squared deviation m the expected return. In other words,

Variance (1" m) = the expected value of (f m - r m)2

where f_m is the actual return and r_m is the expected return. The standard deviation is simply the square root of the variance:

Standard deviation of f m = Ovariance (f m)

Standard deviation is often denoted by s and variance by s2. Example. Here is a very simple example showing how variance and standard deviation are calculated. Suppose that you are offered the chance to play the following game. You start by investing $100. Then two coins are flipped. For each head that comes up you get back your starting balance plus 20 percent, and for each tail that comes up you get back your starting balance less 10 percent. Clearly there are four equally likely outcomes:

— Head + head: You gain 40 percent.
— Head + tail: You gain 10 percent.
— Tail + head : You gain 10 percent.
— Tail + tail : You lose 20 percent.

There is a chance of 1 in 4, or 25, that you will make 40 percent; a chance 2 in 4, or 5, that you will make 10 percent; and a chance of 1 in 4, or 25, U. you will lose 20 percent. The game's expected return is, therefore, a weighted average of the possible outcomes:

Expected return = (.25 x 40) + (.5 x 10) + (.25 x -20) = +10%

One way of defining uncertainty is to say that more things can happen than will happen. The risk of an asset can be completely expressed, as we did for coin-tossing game, by writing all possible outcomes and the probability of each. For real assets this is cumbersome and often impossible. Therefore we use variance or standard deviation to summarise the spread of possible outcomes.

These measures are natural indexes of risk. The standard deviation would have been sero. The acril standard deviation is positive because we don ' know what will happen. Or think of a second game, the same as the first except that each head meals a 35 percent gain and each tail means a 25 percent loss. Again, there are four equally likely outcomes:

— Head + head: You gain 70 percent.

— Head + tail: You gain 10 percent.

— Tail + head: You gain 10 percent.

— Tail + tail: You lose 50 percent.

For this game the expected return is 10 percent, the same as that of the first game. But its standard deviation is double that of the first game, 42 versus 21 percent. By this measure the second game is twice as risky as the first.

In principle, you could estimate the variability of any portfolio of stocks or bonds by the procedure just described. You would identify the possible outcomes, assign a probability to each outcome, and grind through the calculations. But where do the probabilities come from? You can't look them up in the newspaper; newspapers seem to go out of their way to avoid definite statements about prospects for securities.

The market currently appears to be undergoing a period of consolidation. For the intermediate term, we would take a constructive view, provided economic recovery continues. The market could be up 20 percent a year from now, perhaps more if inflation moderates. On the other hand,... The Delphic oracle gave advice, but no probabilities. Most financial analysts start by observing past variability. Of course, there is no risk in hindsight, but it is reasonable to assume that portfolios with histories of high variability also have the least predictable future performance. The annual standard deviations and variances observed for the four portfolios over the period 1926-1988 were:

Portfolio	Standard Deviation	σVariance σ2
Treasury bills	3.3	10.9
Long-term government bonds	8.5	72.3
Corporate bonds	8.4	70.6
Common stocks	20.9	436.8

As expected, Treasury bills were the least variable security, and common stocks were the most variable. Government and corporate bonds hold the middle ground. You may find it interesting to compare the coin-tossing game and the stock market as alternative investments. The stock market generated an average annual return of 12.1 percent with a standard deviation of 20.9 percent.

The game offers 10 and 21 percent, respectively-slightly lower return and about the same variability. Your gambling friends may have come up with a crude representation of the stock market. Of course, there is no reason to believe that the market's variability should stay the same over more than 60 years. For example, it is clearly less now than in the Great Depression of the 1930s. Here are standard deviations of the returns on. We should be cautious about reading too much into standard deviations calculated from 10 or so annual returns.

Over the 1980s were below average on the volatility front. However, there were brief episodes of extremely high volatility. On Black Monday, October 19, 1987, the market index fell by 23 percent on a single day, Tit standard deviation of the index for the week surrounding Black Monday was equivalent to 89 percent per year. Fortunately, volatility dropped back to normal levels within a few weeks after the crash. We can calculate the measures of variability equally well for individual security and portfolios of securities. Of course, the level of variability over 63 years is less interesting for specific companies than for the market portfolio-it is a rare Company that faces the same business risks today as it did in 1926.

Table presents estimated standard deviations for 10 well-known company stocks for a recent 5-year period. 10 Do these standard deviations look high to you They should remember that the market portfolios standard deviation was about 20 percent over the entire

1926-1988 period and somewhat less in later years. Of the individual stocks only Exxon and Bristol Myers Squibb had standard deviations of less than 20 percent. Most stocks are substantially more variable than the market portfolio; only a handful are less variable.

Even a little diversification can provide a substantial reduction in variability. Suppose you calculate and compare the standard deviations of randomly chosen one-stock portfolios, two-stock portfolios, five-stock portfolios, etc. But you can get most of this benefit with relatively few Corporate stocks: The improvement is slight when the number of securities is increased beyond, say, 20 or 30. Diversification works because prices of different stocks do not move exactly together.

Statisticians make the same point when they say that stock price changes are less than perfectly correlated. Look, for example. You can see that an investment in either Delta Air Lines or Polaroid would have been very variable. But on many occasions a decline in the value of one stock was cancelled by a rise in the price of the other. Therefore there was an opportunity to reduce your risk by diversification. The risk that potentially can be eliminated by diversification is called unique risk. Unique risk stems from the fact that many of the perils that surround an individual company are peculiar to that company and perhaps its immediate competitors. But there is also some risk that you can't avoid, regardless of how much you diversify. This risk is generally known as market risk.

Market risk stems from the fact that there are other economy wide perils which threaten all businesses. That is why stocks have a tendency to move together. And that is why investors are exposed to "market uncertainties," no matter how many stocks they hold. If you have only a single stock, unique risk is very important; but once you have a portfolio of 20 or more stocks, diversification has done the bulk of its work.

Risk and Return Practicals

Cost of Equity

The cost of equity is the rate of return that investors require to make an equity investment in a firm. There are two approaches to estimating the cost of equity: the first is to use a risk and return model; the second is to apply a dividend growth model.

Capital Asset Pricing Model

The capital asset pricing model (CAPM) measures risk in terms of nondiversifiable variance and relates expected returns to this risk measure. The non-diversifiable risk for any asset is measured by its beta, which can be used to yield an expected return.

$$\text{Expected Return} = Rf + \text{Equity Beta}\,[E(Rm) - Rf]$$

where

Rf = Risk-free rate

$E(Rm)$ = Expected Return on the Market Index

The return that investors expect to make on an equity investment, given its risk, becomes the cost of equity to managers in that firm.

Risk premium measurement

The risk premium used in CAPM is generally on historical data. The premium is defined as the difference between average return on stocks and average returns on risk-free securities over the measurement period measurement questions remain. First, how long should the measurement period be? Second, should arithmetic or geometric averages be used to compute the risk premium? In answer to the first question, whereas measurement periods ranging from 10 years to longer are used in practice, the use of the longest possible historical period seems justified absent any trend in premiums over time. In much of the analysis in this book, the average premiums based on data from 1926 to 1990 will be used for U.S. stocks.

Geometric mean

The geometric mean of a series is the average of the series, taking into account the effect of compounding on the data. There is just as much disagreement among practitioners over the usage of the arithmetic versus geometric means. The arithmetic mean is the average of the annual returns for the period under consideration, whereas the geometric mean is the compounded annual return over the same period. The contrast between the two measures can be illustrated with a simple example containing two years of returns:

Year	Price	Return
0	50	-
1	100	100%
2	60	-40%

The arithmetic average return over the two years is 30%, whereas the geometric average is only 9.54% (1.2°.5-1=1.0954). Those who use the arithmetic mean argue that it is much more consistent with the mean-variance framework of the CAPM and a better predictor of the premium in the next period. The geometric mean is justified on the grounds that it takes into account compounding and that it is a better predictor of the average premium in the long term. There can be dramatic differences in premiums based on the choices made at this stage, as illustrated in Table.

Magnitude of the Risk Premium

Historical Period	Stocks-Treasury Bills		Stocks-Treasury Bonds	
	Arithmetic	Geometric	Arithmetic	Geometric
1926-1990	8.41%	6.41%	7.24%	5.50%
1962-1990	4.10%	2.95%	3.92%	3.25%
1981-1990	6.05%	5.38%	0.13%	0.19%

The geometric mean generally yields lower premium estimates than does the arithmetic mean. In the context of corporate finance, where expected returns are compounded over long time periods, the geometric mean provides a better estimate of the risk premium. Thus, the premium of 5.50% (the geometric mean of the premium over Treasury bonds) is used throughout this book for calculating expected returns for U.S. stocks. Historical data on stock returns are easily available and accessible in the United States; for other countries reliable historical data are not available for as long a time period as is available for the United States, Table here summarised premiums from 1970 to 1990.

The premium earned by stocks over Treasury bonds has typically been much lower in the European markets (not counting Britain) than in either the United States or Japan. Three fundamental principles determine the size of this premium:

1. *Variance in the underlying economy*: Risk premiums will be larger in economies that have more volatility associated with them. Thus, the premiums for emerging markets, with their higher-growth, higher-risk economies, will be larger than the premiums for developed markets. The higher uncertainty associated with future economic growth in China, for instance, would lead us to use a larger premium in the Chinese market than we would in the Singapore market, where there is much less uncertainty about future economic growth.
2. *Political risk*: Risk premiums will be larger in those markets where there is potential for political instability, which translate to economic instability. Although concrete measures of political risk remain difficult to come by, The Economist, for instance, provides measures of political risk for any countries on a regular basis. In early 1995, its measure of political risk, which goes from zero (least risk) to 100 (most risk) placed Iraq at the top (most risky) and Singapore at the bottom (least risky) of the nations surveyed. Ratings agencies, like Standard and Poor's, take an alternative approach; they assign bond ratings to countries that capture, among other factors, the political risk in these countries.
3. *Structure of the market*: In some markets, the risk premium for investing in stocks will be lower because the companies that are listed on the exchange are large, diversified, and stable. In general, as smaller and riskier companies are listed on the market, as is the case in the United States and the United Kingdom, the average risk premium for investing in stocks will increase.

Using the U.S. premium for stocks over bonds of 5.50% as the benchmark, we see that these fundamentals point toward a larger premium for markets that are riskier than those of the United States on any or all of these counts and a smaller premium for less risky markets.

Risk-free Rate

Variant 1 A short-term government security rate is used as the risk-free rate, and the historical premium earned by a broad equity market index over and above this security rate is used to estimate the expected return on the market. The cost of equity, thus obtained, is then used as the discount rate for each year's cash flows.

Standard Procedures for Estimating CAPM

The standard procedure for estimating betas is to regress stock returns (R/f against market returns (Rm)5:

$$Rj = a + bRm$$

where

a = Intercept from the regression

b = Slope of the regression = Covariance (Rj, Rm)/a2 m

The slope of the regression corresponds to the beta of the stock and measures the riskiness of the stock. The intercept of the regression provides a simple measure of performance during the period of the regression, relative to the capital asset pricing model.

Rj = Rf + 13(Rm - Rf)

= Rj.1 - 13) + Rm Capital asset pricing model

Rj = a + bRm Regression equation

Thus, a comparison of the intercept (a) to Rf(1 - 13) should provide a measure of the stock's performance, at least relative to the capital asset pricing mode1.6.

If

a>RJ.1 - 13).... stock did better than expected during regression period

a = RJ.1 - 13) stock did as well as expected during regression period

a<RJ.1 - 13).... stock did worse than expected during regression period

The difference between a and Rf(1 -13) is called Jensen's alpha and provides a measure of whether the asset in question under or outperformed the market, after adjusting for risk, during the period of the regression.

Jensen's Alpha

This is the difference between the actual returns on an asset and the return expected from it during a past period, given what the market did, and the asset's beta. The final statistic that emerges from the regression is the Rsquared (R2) of the regression. Although the statistical explanation of the R-squared is that it provides a measure of the goodness of fit of the regression, the financial rationale for the R-squared is that it provides an estimate of the proportion of the risk (variance) of a firm that can be attributed to market risk. The balance (1 - R2) can then be attributed to firm-specific risk.

R-squared

The R-squared measures the proportion of the variability of a dependent variable that is explained by an independent variable or variables.

— The first concerns the length of the estimation period. Most estimates of betas, including those by Value Line and Standard and Poor's, use five years of data, while Bloomberg uses two years of data. The trade-off is simple: a longer estimation period provides more data, but the firm itself might have changed in its risk Characteristics over the time period. For instance, using data from 1985 to 1994 to estimate betas for Microsoft might increase the amount of data available, but it will lead to a beta estimate that is much higher than the true beta, since Microsoft was a smaller and riskier firm in 1985 than it was in 1994.

— The second estimation decision relates to the return interval. Returns on stocks are available on an annual, monthly, weekly, daily, and even intraday basis. Using daily or intraday returns will increase the number of observations in the regression, but it exposes the estimation process to a significant bias in beta estimates related to nontrading 10 For instance, the betas estimated for small firms, which are more likely to suffer from nontrading, are biased downward when daily returns are used. Using weekly or monthly returns can reduce the nontrading bias significantly For example, the beta for America Online, the online service provider, was 1.20 using daily returns from 1990 and 1994, while it was 1.80 using monthly returns.

— The third estimation issue relates to the choice of a market index to be used in the regression. The standard practice used by most beta estimation services is to estimate the betas of a company relative to the index of the market in which its stock trades. Thus, the betas of German stocks are estimated relative to the Frankfurt DAX, British stocks relative to the FTSE, Japanese stocks relative to the Nikkei, and U.S. stocks relative to the NYSE composite. Although this practice may yield an estimate that is a reasonable measure of risk for the parochial investor, it may not be the best approach for an international or cross-border investor, who would be better served with a beta estimated relative to an international index.

— The fourth estimation issue relates to whether the betas obtained from regressions should be adjusted to reflect the likelihood of estimation errors and the tendency of betas to regress toward the average. Most published betas use variants of a statistical technique that shrinks betas toward 1, based on the standard error of the regression beta estimate-the larger the error, the greater the shrinkage. The gains from using these techniques are large when daily returns are used to estimate betas, but they become smaller as longer return intervals are used.

Beta Determination

The beta of a firm is determined by three variables:

— the type of business(es) the firm is in;

— the degree of operating leverage in the firm; and

— the firm's financial leverage.

Cyclical nature of the business Since betas measure the risk of a firm relative to a market index, the more sensitive a business is to market conditions, the higher its beta. Thus, other things remaining equal, cyclical firms can be expected to have higher betas than noncyclical firms.

Cyclical Firm

A cyclical firm has revenues and operating income that tend to move strongly with the economy-up when the economy is doing well and down during recessions. Building on this point, we would also argue that the degree to which a product's purchase is discretionary will affect the beta of the firm manufacturing the product. Thus, the betas of firms such as General Foods and Kellogg's, should be lower than the betas of speciality retailers, since consumers can defer the purchase of the latter's products during bad economic times.

Degree of operating leverage The degree of operating leverage is a function of the cost structure of a firm and is usually defined in terms of the relationship between fixed costs and total costs. A firm that has high operating leverage will also have higher variability in earnings before interest and taxes (EBIT) than would a firm producing a similar product with low operating leverage. Other things remaining equal, the higher variance in operating income will lead to a higher beta for the firm with high operating leverage. This relationship between beta and operating leverage has consequences for a firm's major strategic decisions regarding future direction.

Although much good comes from updating plants and getting the latest technology, there might also be a hidden cost. By reducing the firm's flexibility to respond to economic downturns, it may make the firm riskier. Although operating leverage affects betas, it is difficult to measure the operating leverage of a firm, at least from the outside, since fixed and variable costs are often aggregated in income statements. It is possible to obtain an approximate measure of the firm's operating leverage, however, by looking at changes in operating income as a function of changes in sales. Degree of Operating leverage = % Change in Operating Profit / % Change in Sales For firms with high operating leverage, operating income should change more than proportionately when sales change.

Weighted Average Cost of Capital (WACC)

Intuitively, the cost of capital is the weighted average of the costs of the different components of financing-including debt, equity, and hybrid securities-used by a firm to fund its financial requirements. The weighted average cost of capital (WACC) is defined as the weighted average of the costs of the different components of financing used by a firm:

WACC = k/E/ (D + E + PS" + kiD/(D + E + PS" + kp.(PS/(D + E + PS"

where

W ACC = Weighted Average Cost of Capital
ke = Cost of Equity
kd = After-tax Cost of Debt
kps = Cost of Preferred Stock
E/(E + D + PS) = Market Value proportion of Equity in Funding Mix

Cost of Debt

The cost of debt measures the current cost to the firm of borrowing funds to finance projects. In general terms, it is determined by the following variables:

1. The current level of interest rates: As the level of interest rates increases, the cost of debt for firms will also increase.
2. The default risk of the company: As the default risk of a firm increases, the cost of borrowing money will also increase. One way of measuring default risk is to use the bond rating for the firm; higher ratings lead to lower interest rates, and lower ratings lead to higher interest rates.
3. The tax advantage associated with debt: Since interest is tax deductible, the after-tax cost of debt is a function of the tax rate. The tax benefit that accrues from paying interest makes the after-tax cost of debt lower than the pretax cost.

References

Campsey and Brigham, *Introduction to Financial Management*, 3rd edition, Dryden Press, 1991.

Carmichael, Shenna, *Business Ethics: The New Bottom Line*, London: Demos, 1995.

11

Finance Functions

Corporate Finance deals with the financial aspects of a corporate enterprise, right from the stage of promotion of the organization. It includes administration during initial stages, stages of growth and expansion. It also deals with financial restructuring during financial crisis. Corporate Finance includes financial environment, strategies of financial planning, financial markets, capital formation & financial institutions.

Finance is omnipresent and is intimately associated with other functions in an organization. Finance is related to marketing in formulating credit and collection policies. Each aspect of marketing function—sales promotion, advertising, channels selection etc.—has a bearing on finance as well.

In the purchase function, procurement cost, inventory carrying cost etc. are the financial aspects. In Production function also, finance plays an important role when decisions like make or buy, maintenance cost, transportation cost, acquisition & replacement of assets etc. Production function takes the greater part of capital investment in fixed assets which should pass through capital budgeting. As regards personnel function, decisions like over-time payment, incentive schemes, promotions, bonus schemes, retirement schemes, affect finance. Each activity of an organization has to be financed. The thread of finance is woven into the fabric of the enterprise so well that it is difficult to identify the separate strands of finance.

Organization of the Finance Function

Finance function is very vital for every type of organization, it is necessary to set up a sound and efficient organization. The organization varies depending upon the nature, size of the organization, Though we can not have a standard organization for all the enterprises.

Share holders determine the following while approving the Articles of Association and the bye -laws:

1. The amount and kind of capital
2. Rules governing issue and transfer of stock
3. Powers of directors to declare a dividend, choose a bank, create reserves
4. Sale of firm's assets
5. Plans for reorganization, liquidation, consolidation and mergers etc.

Board of Directors approve the financial policy, declare dividends and translate the aspiration of shareholders into specific goals and objectives and select & appoint the senior officers. The Controller is concerned primarily with the Planning, Accounting and Control activities. The Treasurer is responsible mainly for financing, management of cash & receivables and investment activities

The organization of financial function depends on the needs each organization. The financial needs of each organization varies from the other. In some organization working capital requirements may be more, as in the case of manufacturing organizations as compared to service organizations. In some organization the gestation period may be longer before they start generating revenues and earn profits.

Financial Objectives

Financial objectives of a firm must be set within and in congruence with the Corporate Mission & Goals of the business. Most of the organizations, irrespective of the form, seek to maximise immediate Profit for survival and growth. This provides immediate return also to the share holders in the form of better dividend and it increases the value of the share in the stock market. Many firms look for improving the value of the firm including profit maximisation, as the objective. So, essentially we have two major financial objectives:

1. Profit Maximisation
2. Wealth Maximisation

Profit maximisation

Share holders have invested their money in the organization losing the alternative investment opportunities in anticipation of getting better return here. Other creditors also lent their money in anticipation of getting interest on their money in time. The organization can meet their expectations only when it maximises its profits.

Profit earning is the main aim of every economic activity. Profits are required to cover the costs & survive, to run the business smoothly taking care of contingencies and to provide funds for growth. Profits serve as the measure of efficiency of an organization and indicate the risk bearing ability during unfavourable times. The objective of Profit maximisation is in congruence with most of the businesses. It helps to maximise the socioeconomic welfare.

The following are the drawbacks of Profit Maximisation as the objective of finance:

i. The term 'Profit' is vague and is not clear. It means different things. It is not clear as to profits before tax or after tax or total profit or earnings per share. It leaves considerations of timing and duration undefined.
ii. Profit maximisation objective ignores the time value of money.
iii. It does not consider the element of risk
iv. It exploits employees, customers and others

Wealth maximisation

Wealth maximisation, also called Value Maximisation, is the appropriate financial objective of an enterprise since maximising the value of the firm benefits all the stake holders in the organization—the shareholders, employees, customers, creditors, management and the society. Wealth Maximisation implies the maximisation of the market price of shares. The share's market price serves as a performance index.

The stock holders wealth is the number of shares held by the stock holders multiplied by the stock price per share. Since higher the price per share means greater as the wealth, the firm should aim at maximising the current stock price. Value maximisation is simply the extension of profit maximisation to a world that is uncertain and multi-period in nature. Value maximisation may be achieved through increase in profits, reduction in cost, judicious choice of funds, minimum risks, long-run value approach.

Advantages of Wealth Maximisation Objective are:

— It considers the present value of cash in flows & outflows and the net effect of investment and benefits.

— It considers the risk factor by considering discount rate while calculating net present value.

Financial Decision Making

You must be aware that basically management is concerned with Decision making. Management of finance function or Financial Management is concerned with financial decisions. A business may require funds either for funding the long-term assets which yield return over a period of time in future or for day-to-day operations. However the total fund requirement is to be looked at.

When the total funds requirement is being considered, it becomes the Investment Decision to be taken. When the sources of finance are tapped for funding the investments, it becomes the Financing Decision. When the profits, as a result of Investment and Financing decisions, are considered for ploughing back into the business or for distributing as dividend, it becomes the Dividend Decision.

Investment decision

Investment decision involves deciding about investments to be made in the assets—long-term assets or short-term or current assets which are normally convertible into cash within a year. Deciding about the long-term assets involve Capital Budgeting and the short-term or current assets involve Working Capital Management.

Capital budgeting

The investment proposals are appraised in terms of relative benefits & returns and magnitude, timing, risk / uncertainty of cash flows associated with it. The standard broadly expressed in investment appraisals is the cost of capital.

Working capital management

Working capital management or short-term financial management refers to the day-to-day financial activities involving current assets (inventories, trade debtors, short-term holding of marketable securities, and cash) and current liabilities (shortterm debts, trade creditors and accruals). It is important because short-term survival is pre-requisite for long-term success. A proper balance needs to be maintained between liquidity and profitability. Inadequate funds for day-to-day activities renders illiquid and more funds kept for day-day-day activities means not investing the surplus funds in more profitable options.

Financing decision

Financing decision is concerned with identification of various sources of finance for funding the investment decisions. Longterm / Capital assets are financed through long-term funds and the current assets are financed through short-term funds. Funds are raised from primary market, financial institutions and commercial banks.

Capital structure

Capital structure refers to the proportion of Debt and Equity capital. A proper balance between debt and equity (optimal capital structure) is required to ensure a trade-off between risk and return with maximum returns to the shareholders.

Dividend decision

Declaring more dividend will enhance the image of the enterprise in the stock market, instill confidence in creditors etc. but will reduce the opportunity to plough back the income which may be required considering the cost of capital of other sources of financing. Optimum dividend pay out ratio needs to be arrived at considering the preference of shareholders and the investment opportunities available.

FUNCTIONS OF FINANCIAL MARKETS

Financial markets play a pivotal role in allocating resources in an economy by performing three important functions:

1. Financial markets facilitate price discovery: the continual interaction among numerous buyers and sellers who throng financial markets helps in establishing the prices of financial assets. The value of a financial asset can be obtained just by looking at its price in the financial market.
2. Financial markets provide liquidity to financial assets: Investors can readily sell their financial assets through the mechanism of financial markets. Companies can raise long term funds from investors by negotiation and transferability of securities through financial markets
3. Financial markets considerably reduce the cost of transacting. The major costs associate with transacting are search costs and information costs. Search costs includes explicit costs such as the expenses incurred on advertising when one wants to buy or sell an asset and implicit costs such a s the effort and time one has to put in to locate a customer. Information costs refer to çosts incurred in evaluating the investment merits of financial assets.

Classification

There are different ways of classifying financial markets.

— The debt market is the financial market for fixed claims(debt instrument) and equity market is the financial market for residual claims (equity instruments)

— Money market is the market for short term financial claims. Capital market is the market for long term financial claims. Since short term financial claims are almost invariably debt claims, the money market is the market for short term debt instruments and the capital market is the market for long term debt instruments and equity instruments.

— Third way to classify financial markets is based on whether the claim represents new issues or outstanding issues. The market where issuers sell new claims is referred to as the primary market and the market where investors trade outstanding securities is called the secondary market.

— A cash or spot market is one where the delivery occurs immediately and a forward or futures market is one where the delivery occurs at a pre-determined time in future.

— An exchange-traded market is characterized by a centralized organization with standardized procedures. An over the counter market is a decentralized market with customized procedures.

Methods of Floatation

Initial issues are those floated by new companies for the first time, while further issues are subsequent issues floated by the existing companies. Issues can be classified as those given for cash, for exchange of technical know-how, exchange of shares of another company or exchange for any other services rendered by the agencies or promoters.

The placement of the issues may be through:

(i) prospectus

(ii) offer of sale

(iii) private placement

(iv) rights issue

Offer through prospectus

Offer through prospectus involves inviting subscription from the public through issue of prospectus. The price at which the securities are offered for sale is at the face value of the share in the case of new companies and may be at a premium or discount in the case of old companies. The prospectus is a document, which is a notice, or circular or advertisement inviting offers for subscription or purchase of any shares or debentures from the public.

The prospectus should contain authentic data such as name of the company, address, activities, board of directors, location of industry, authorized, subscribed and paid up capital, dates of opening and closing of the subscription list, names of brokers and underwriters etc. and should be delivered to the Registrar of Companies for registration. The draft of the prospectus should be approved by board, solicitors, lending financial institutions and the stock exchanges in which they are to be listed.

Offer of sale

This method consists of outright sale by the company instead of offering shares to the public to through intermediaries such as issuing houses or share brokers. The company sells shares en bloc at an agreed price to brokers or merchant bankers who in turn resell them to the investing public. Offer of sale of shares takes place in the case of existing shareholders purchasing en bloc and then reselling them to the public. Similarly, foreign collaborators or promoters may sell their shares to the Indian public through offer of sale which may be either through brokers or through prospectus.

Private placement

Private placement is defined as sale by the issuing house or broker to his own clients of securities previously purchased by him. The issuing houses or financial intermediaries buy them outright with the intention of placing them with their clients afterwards. The brokers would make their profit in the process of reselling to the public. This method of private placement is used to a limited extent in India but is very popular abroad. Before the issues are placed in the market by the promoters, they sell to their friends and well wishers as the Govt. guidelines require a minimum contribution from the promoters and their friends.

Private placement is also made by bargaining with financial institutions for their share of contribution. Private placement in India is mostly of equity or equity related instruments of unlisted companies and debt instruments of listed companies.

Appeal of private placement: The phenomenal growth of private placement of debt may be attributed to the following reasons.

1. *Accessibility*: Private placement market can accommodate issues of smaller size whereas the public issues market does not permit an issue below a certain minimum size.

2. *Flexibility*: There is greater flexibility in working out the terms of issue. e.g. When a non-convertible debenture issue is privately placed, a discount may be given to institutional investors to make the issue attractive. There may be more latitude to renegotiate the terms of the issue and even roll over the debt.
3. *Speed*: A private placement requires lesser time, perhaps a month or two, as the elaborate procedure followed in a public issue is largely bypassed.
4. *Lower issue costs*: The issue cost for a private placement is substantially less as a public issue entails several statutory and non- statutory expenses associated with underwriting, brokerage, printing, mailing, announcements, promotion and so on. whose costs are quite high.

Institutional investors, before participating in a private placement, need to look into a number of factors like the net worth of the company, the interest cover, the level of profit before tax, the asset cover, the debt equity ratio, the dividend record, the percentage of unsecured deposits/ borrowings, the price history of the company's stock, and the existence of carried forward loss.

Rights issue

It is an offer with a preemption right to the shareholder of existing companies to contribute to the share capital or its debt capital in the form of debentures. An existing company can issue rights to augment its equity base, if necessary. These are offered to the existing shareholders in a particular proportion to their existing share ownership. The rights are themselves transferable and saleable in the market.

Under the Companies Act, where a company increases its subscribed capital by the issue of new shares either after two years of its formation or after one year of the first issue of shares whichever is earlier, these have to be first offered to the existing shareholders with the right to reserve them in favour of a nominee. A company issuing rights is required to send a circular to all existing shareholders. The circular letter should provide information on how the additional funds would be used and their effect on the earning capacity of the capital.

The company may normally give a time limit of at least 1 month or two to shareholders to exercise their exercise their right before it is offered to the public. Rights may also be offered through underwriters. If the company is doing well, rights will be received well by the shareholders and the need for underwriting may not be felt. Main condition is that the shareholders be given an opportunity to apply for additional shares. If the rights are not fully taken up, the balance is to be distributed among the applicants for additional shares. Any balance still left over after making such allotment is required to be disposed of by the company in the market at the ruling price or the issue price.

Capital Market

The capital market is a market in which the securities with maturities of more than one year are bought and sold. The capital market refers to the market for long term securities, such as corporate stocks and bonds, for financing long term assets. The major players being Corporates, Banks, Financial Institutions, Mutual Funds etc. The capital market is further classified as follows:

Primary Capital Market: The 'primary capital market' is one in which new issues of common stock, bonds and preferred sotck are sold by companies. The proceeds raised in this market is the new capital funds.

Secondary Capital Market: The secondary capital markets are also called 'stock markets: In the secondary markets, the outstanding issues are permitted to trade. In this market, a stock or bond issue which has already been sold to the public, and it is traded between current and potential owners. The proceeds from a sale in the secondary market do not go to the issuing organisation but to the current owner of the security. The stock markets are classified as follows:

i. *Stock Exchanges*: The Stock Exchanges will have a physical location where stocks buying and selling transactions take place in the stock exchange floor.

ii. *Over the Counter Exchange*: Where shares, bonds, and money market instruments are traded using a system of computer screens and telephones is called 'Over the Counter Exchange

Capital market is the barometer of the economy and represents the macro economic affairs of the country. It is an index of economic and industrial development of the country. Capital market discounts the future and it is reflection of future of the economy. In the long run it is a true measure of the health of any economy. In the capitalistic economy, the capital markets playa pivotal role by bring the common investor to invest in corporate securities.

The global trend is that even socialist countries like China and Russia are moving towards capitalistic economy by inviting the private investments into the industry. Financial disintermediation along with diversification of financial sector is one of the important developments in the era of liberalisation world over. The term financial disintermediation' refers to the transformation of a financial system from institution based to market based. In an institution based financial system, the role of financial intermediaries like Bank is prominent in mobilisation and allocation of financial resources.

In the current capital market system, the role of banks as intermediaries is diluted in the market based system where the investor and user of funds are expected to come into direct contact with the borrowers i.e. the corporates. A tendency was developed among the corporate houses to access savings directly through public deposits, commercial paper, Equity and Debenture issues etc. This process of transformation has been further facilitated by the introduction of a set of new financial instruments with varied degrees of liquidity, risk and returns.

Among the instruments, mutual funds, bonds and derivative instruments are more active which have grasped a substantial share in resource mobilisation giving a challenge to traditional monetary assets such as bank deposits. Similarly, instruments like deep discount bonds, zero coupon bonds and other bonds with very long maturity period compete with traditional term saving instruments. The nature, extent, and efficiency of disintermediation varies from country to country. The USA and UK have a market based system while economies like Germany and Japan are dominated by bank based financial system.

In the era of globalisation and liberalisation, the capital markets assume a greater importance. The smooth functioning of the capital market depends on the regulators, participants and investors. The past decade has been a golden age for securities market in India. It is now a far more important source of finance than traditional financial intermediaries for corporate sector. It is poised to dominate the future of corporate finance in India. The process of reforms has led to a pace of growth of markets almost unparalleled in the history of any country.

Securities market in India has grown exponentially as measured in terms of amount raised from the market, number of stock exchanges and other intermediaries, the number of listed stocks, market capitalisation, trading volumes and turnover on stock exchanges, and investor population. Along with this, the profiles of the investors, issuers and intermediaries have changed significantly. Indian market is now comparable to many developed markets.

The state of primary market of late has not been very encouraging as for as the industry is concerned. The number of issues and the amounts mobilised through the primary market is predominantly by financial institutions and banks as opposed to industry. This is a clear reflection of recessionary trends in the economy over the 5 years.

Indian capital market scenario

Reforms in the securities market, particularly the establishment and empowerment of SEBI, determined allocation of resources, screen-based nation-wide trading, dematerialisation and electronic transfer of securities, rolling settlement and ban on deferral products, sophisticated risk management and derivatives trading, have greatly improved the regulatory framework and efficiency of trading., settlement.

Indian market is now comparable to many developed markets in terms of a numbers, qualitative parameters. Over the past several years the securities market has witnessed a sea change. The market has been more in terms of infrastructure, adoption of best international practices and introduction of competition. With the maturity of the regulatory framework and increased market surveillance, the market has also' become safer and investor is better protected.

The extensive reforms introduced by SEBI over the last few years have enhanced the integrity, transparency and efficiency of the operations of the securities market. The introduction of electronic trading and order matching system in all the 23 stock exchanges, have led to reduction in transaction costs, speedier execution of trades and gains in liquidity.

Transaction costs

Transaction cost for a market is important for several reasons. It is a key parameter to measure the impact of modernisation of market infrastructure, institutionalisation of the market and market regulation. Transaction costs can be classified into two categories viz.,

Explicit costs are observable and measurable. They can be easily measured and are directly borne by the investors. These costs include:

— Brokerage commission

— Stamp duty

— Service tax

— Custody charges

— Regulatory charges etc.

Some of these charges, such as stamp duty and service tax are also levied in few other markets also.

The Implicit costs include:

— Bid-ask spreads

— Realised spreads

Opportunity cost of delayed execution (timing costs) or nonexecution. Like implicit costs, certain additional explicit costs also arise from the nature of the trading and settlement systems, existence of physical paper and the registration process. The transaction costs are influenced by the following important factors:

— Trading, Clearance and Settlement

— Systems Physical and

— Dematerialised Shares Investor

— Profile

— After- Trade Practices

— Margins

— Rolling Settlement

In the Indian capital market, transaction costs in respect of most of the components especially brokerage, are charges as a "percentage of the value of trade" (ad valorem) as is the practice in several other markets, viz. Hong Kong, Australia, Singapore, UK and not on "per transaction "basis as in the US markets. Both principles of charging are valid and have their own logic and merit.

The components of explicit transaction costs for institutional investors include brokerage, stamp duty, safe keeping which includes custody charges for physical stock and charges for dematerialisation. Each of these components vary depending on whether:

— The stock which is traded is in compulsory dematerialisation list, which implies that trading and safe keeping have necessarily to be in the dematerialised form or,

— The stock which is traded is in the physical segment, in which case both trading/delivery will be in physical form while safe keeping may be in the physical or dematerialised form or,

— The existing stock has not been fully dematerialised and hence is still being held in the physical form.. The transaction cost is different for each of the above situations. Variations on account of squaring off or carry forward of transactions do not occur for institutional investors as they have to operate on delivery basis.

International Financial Market System

Foreign Exchange as a subject deals with the means and methods by which rights to income and wealth in one country's currency are converted into similar rights in terms of another country's currency. It involves the investigation of the methods by which the currency of one country is exchanged for that of another, the causes which render such exchange necessary, the forms in which exchange may take place and the ratios or equivalent values at which such exchanges are effected.

Such exchange may be in the form of one currency to another or of conversion of credit instruments denominated in different currencies such as cheques, drafts, airmail transfers, fax and telegraphic transfers, cable transfers, bills of exchange, trade bills, bankers' bills or any promissory notes. It is through these instruments and foreign currency accounts of banks that the banks are able to effect such exchange of currencies or claims to currencies.

RBI has, however, responded to emerging situation in the foreign exchange market quickly and promptly. Since rupee convertibility was launched in March 1992, RBI is publishing a reference rate around which it operates in the market to stabilise the rate of exchange of rupee in terms of US dollar.

International and Foreign Exchange Market

One of the important components of the international financial system is the foreign exchange market. The various commercial and financial transactions as between countries result in receipts and payments as between them. The items of balance of payments leading to receipts and payments are trade, travel, transportation, royalties, fees, investment income, unilateral transfers, short-term and long- term capital receipts and payments etc. Such receipts and payment involve exchange of one currency for another.

Each economy has a foreign sector representing that economy's external transactions. All such external transactions are either economic and commercial or financial transactions. These result in receipts into and payments out of the domestic economy. Such receipts and payments involve exchange of domestic currency as against all foreign currencies of countries with which domestic economy has dealings.

Such exchange transactions are put through in the exchange market for that currency. For each nation, therefore, there is an exchange market for that country's currency vis-a vis other currencies. These national foreign exchange markets are components of the international financial system There are three major components of this market, depending upon the level at which transactions are put through:

1. Transactions between the public and the market at the base level involve receipts from any payments to the public or purchases from and sales to public.
2. Transactions as between the banks dealing in foreign exchange involving conversion of currencies taking place in the same centre or as between centres in the same country (inter-bank market) or as between countries involving the correspondent or agent banks abroad or branches of the domestic banks abroad.

3. Transactions between banks and central bank involving purchase and sale of foreign currencies for cover or final disposal of excess foreign balances The rate of exchange is determined at any moment by the forces of demand for and supply of a currency, which in turn depends on the demand for and supply of commodities and services as between India and the USA.

Features of International Markets

1. Both investors and borrowers are well-known names in the international market.
2. These loans are unsecured and no government guarantee either. Only creditworthy borrowers are generally approaching this market.
3. Country's credit rating and borrowing party's credit rating rate being looked into; rating by standard and poor or moody's are popular for assessing the creditworthiness of borrower.

Regulations

The market is functioning outside the countries and is offshore in nature. No regulation of any national and international nature exists. The market practices in the secondary market trading are based on the rules laid down by Association of International Bond dealers.

Same parent companies and some foreign governments do guarantee the interest and payment of principal. The interest payment is provided in the agreement itself and stricter controls are exercised in the collection of interest, although these rates are lower than those on national bonds of any country.

Euro currency market

The Euro currency market refers to funds channelled via financial intermediaries from international lenders to international borrowers. The Eurocurrency markets provide the short to medium term debt required by banks, corporate and government borrowers. The source of these funds is domestic bank deposits whose ownership is transferred to bank outside the controlled domestic monetary systems.

The deposits are in large denominations, frequently $ 100,000 or more, and the banks use them to make Eurocurrency loans to quality borrowers. The Eurocurrency deposit rate is usually slightly higher than the rate paid by the domestic banks. The Euro Currency loans in a particular currency are priced according to a 'LIBOR (London Inter Bank Offering Rate) plus basis' with the margin over LIBOR depending on market conditions and the credit quality standing or riskiness of the borrower.

The banks generally arranges syndicated loans in this market. Thus the risk of a particular borrower are distributed across several banks. The Euro currency market is not regulated by any government and therefore, is an international currency. The 'Euro' prefix refers to the high volume of these funds circulating in Europe, mainly through London. However, this market is world wide, and sectors of the market exist in the Middle East and Far East (Asia dollar market)

Functions of Eurocurrency Markets:

The Euro currency markets serve three basic functions.

— They are extensively used for foreign exchange hedging purposes as the banks seek to balance out their foreign assets and liabilities. The banks, therefore, take positions in the Eurocurrency markets to cover the forward commitments they have made with their customers.

— Euro currency markets can at times bypass domestic channels of financial 'intermediation' especially when governments impose tight credit policies. For example, US Corporation can acquire Eurodollars in London. These deposits may be US domestic dollar deposits that have been transferred abroad during a US domestic credit squeeze.

— Function of the market is the full international intermediation role of channellising surplus liquid resources from, say, OPEC countries or corporations who need to borrow.

The most important Euro currency markets are Eurodollar, Euromark and Eurosterlling. Eurocurrency market operates only in currencies that are freely convertible into other currencies, such as the US dollar and the German mark, and only outside those currencies-Country of

Origin. Eurobanks are, therefore, located in countries which do not regulate their foreign currency banking activities.

The Eurocurrency markets are money markets rather than foreign exchange markets. Their importance in the context of international financial management is that they provide an alternative source of funds to domestic banks. A wide range of participants make use of the Eurocurrency markets. Types of Eurocurrency Loans—The following types of Eurocurrency loans are available in the Eurocurrency markets:

— Fixed interest loans are usually over a medium term of up to five years, and the borrower knows in advance what the interest payments will be.

— Stand-by credits are overdraft facilities offered by banks to customers in Eurocurrency.

— Most Eurocurrency loans are roll-over loans, where the bank agrees to make funds available over a given period of time, say five years, but the interest rate is open to renegotiation every three or six months.

— A number of banks may form themselves into a syndicate in order to provide a large loan to a single customer over a period that is longer than usual. Such loans are called syndicated loans:

The advantages to the borrower of using Euromarket are that lenders on the domestic market may discriminate, or larger sums may be required than are available in the home markets, or it may be deemed necessary to avoid the possibility of exchange control barriers.

Eurobond Market

The second major sector of the unregulated capital market is the Eurobond market. The Eurobond market is characterised by direct transaction between borrowers and lenders, although the large banks playa major role in underwriting and placing the bonds. The market permits lenders to lend directly to borrowers across national borders, without the intermediation of a bank. Bank can, however, plays a major role in arranging the transaction.

Eurobonds differ from foreign bonds in that the latter are issued in one country in its currency by a foreign borrower. By contrast, the

Eurobond is issued in one currency such US $, the yen, the pound, the mark or the Swiss franc for sale in many capital markets with the sale managed by an international syndicate of bank Underwriters. The borrowers or issuers of the bonds include public sector organisations and commercial banks, established bluechip companies.

The lenders or purchasers of the bond securities are individual and institutional investors, with the latter group dominating. A secondary market for Eurobonds has grown rapidly as these financial institutions continuously seek to adjust their portfolios, and as a result the original lenders are not committed to a borrower until the final maturity of the bond issue. Generally, purchasers buy Eurobonds in currencies other than their own, and a major attraction of these bonds for individuals is that in most currencies they are exempt from withholding taxes.

Further more, the unregulated nature of the market means that its costs are lower and its issuing process is much faster domestic or foreign bond counter parts. These bonds market provide a wide variety of medium to funds of 3 to 15 years maturity. Fixed coupons or interest rates are common but floating rate notes are also important.

The distinctive features of Eurobonds issues are as follows:

- The issue of Eurobonds is in the form ' placing' rather than formal issuing, to avoid national regulations on new issues
- Eurobonds are placed simultaneously in many countries through multinational syndicates of underwriting banks who sell them to an investment clientele throughout the world.
- Euro bonds are sold principally in countries other than the country of issue.
- The interest on Eurobonds is not subject to withholding tax, which is an advantage over domestic bonds owned by non-residents, on which tax deduction is made before interest is paid.

Brief Procedure in Eurobonds Issues is arranged as follows:

- The managing banks try to ensure the success of the bond issue by inviting a group of banks and other financial institutions to underwrite the issue.
- Once the issue is underwritten, the managing banks will try to place the issue with a number of selling banks and other financial institutions.

— The selling banks will in turn try to place all or some of their allotment with clients. The 'Placing Power' of the selling banks will be a vital factor in the successful launch of a new issue, i.e., it is crucial that the selling banks should be able to place the bonds with buyers. To help the selling process, a 'Prospectus' will be issued giving information about the terms and conditions of the bond, the name and details of the issuer, the purpose of the loan and selling information.

— Eurobond issues in the UK are usually constituted under a trust deed. The bank which is responsible for making payments to the bondholders will act as their trustee

FINANCIAL INSTITUTIONS

Unit Trust of India (UTI)

Main objectives are:

— To mobilize savings particularly from the low and middle income groups

— To channelise these savings into productive investment

— To provide an assured income to savers

It provides the savers with expert investment service, portfolio management and assured income. The UTI mobilizes the savings through the sale of its units and operates a number of schemes with varied characteristics to suit the requirements of savers and investors. These characteristics include income, capital appreciation, liquidity through repurchase, an element of insurance etc.

Activities of UTI includes:

— Underwriting new issues

— Make direct subscription to public issues or private placements

— Keep deposits with banks and companies

— Operate in the money market by subscribing to Treasury bills, commercial bills etc

It can partake in the inter bank market as a lender or borrower of short term funds. It can borrow from RBI or the Government in case of need.

UTI schemes

1. *Unit Scheme 1964*: is a perpetual scheme, each unit with a face value of Rs.10, transferable and repurchased by the UTI. Dividend income from the UTI qualifies for deduction of income tax under Section 80L of the Income Tax At and eligible for Wealth Tax exemption up to Rs.5 lakhs. Reinvestment facility as an alternative to dividend distribution is available.
2. *Unit-linked Insurance Plan(ULIP) 1971*: Schemes of 10 year and 15 year periods are available both with life insurance and accident insurance. The target amount is a maximum of Rs.60,000 and the age limit is 55 years. The life coverage is secured from the LIC by the contributions of UTI. The contributions of the insured are payable yearly or half yearly.
3. *Capital Gains Unit Scheme(CGUS)*: Investment in part or in full of the capital gains due to sale of any long term capital assets in the Capital Gains Units Scheme would qualify for exemption from capital gains tax under Section 54A of the Income tax Act. This investment is to be made within 6 months of the date of the sale of capital assets and there is no maximum limit. This is to be held for a minimum period of 3 years. Dividend income along with others is exempt under Section 80L of Income tax Act up to Rs.115,000 and from the wealth tax up to Rs.5 lakhs
4. *Children's Gift Growth Plan*: Units with a face value of Rs.10 are gifted to a minor child under this scheme, maturing at the age of 21 by the child. Gifts up to Rs.20,000 were exempt from gift tax, at that time and Rs.30,000 now.
5. *Various Close ended Schemes*: Such schemes as monthly income unit scheme, growing income unit scheme etc, were started in various years since 1982 for meeting the varying needs of investors.
6. *Master Shares floated for Indian investors and India Fund and India Growth Fund etc. for foreign investors*: The Mutual Fund Subsidiary Unit Scheme (Master Shares) 1986 are quoted on the stock exchanges and are treated as shares. A third offshore fund was initiated in 1989-90 with the help of a Japanese securities firm and AB, in addition to the above two.

The first 3 schemes account for 70 % of the total investible funds of the UTI. The second venture capital fund managed by the Technology Development and Information Company of India Ltd. Was set up in 1990 with a contribution of Rs.35 crores from the UTI and contributions from other financial institutions. This helps the financing of Greenfielɗ ventures from new entrepreneurs to promote industrial growth.

Industrial Development Bank of India (IDBI)

IDBI is the leader in the Indian capital market. It has both regulatory and developmental functions. The role of IDBI in the market is to promote and develop industries as per the planned projections of the Government, to provide technical and consultancy assistance for the expansion and modernisation of industry and for rediscount and refinance facilities to financial institutions.

IDBI as the leader in the market coordinates guides and monitors the credit facilities by all India and State level financial institutions and development corporations. It undertook the responsibility for promoting and financing the small and cottage industries and also the import-export trade of the country until separate bodies namely Exim Bank and Small Industries Development Bank of India (SIDBI) were set up.

Major schemes of IDBI are:

i. Textile Modernisation Fund Scheme for the purpose of promoting modernisation of jute and cotton textile industries

ii. Venture capital Fund Scheme for the purpose of developing new ventures and promoting risky ventures by new technicians and new entrepreneurs

iii. Technology upgradation Scheme for the purpose of upgrading technology in selected capital goods industries

iv. Energy conservation Scheme for the purpose of financing of energy saving proposals of industries and

v. Seed Capital Scheme for the purpose of providing initial seed capital in the form of promoters' contribution to new ventures. The IDBI operates direct assistance schemes whereby project appraisal and financing for medium and large scale projects is undertaken. It provides refinancing under the Industrial Loans Scheme for the loans extended by commercial and cooperative banks and SFCs. This refinancing is for assisting SSIs, transport operators and units in the backward areas etc.

IDBI also borrows abroad and seçures funds under arrangements with foreign financial institutions, foreign banks and foreign governments and operates foreign lines of credit, secured by the Government.

Industrial Credit and Investment Corporation of India (ICICI)

The objectives are:

— To encourage industrial investment in the private sector and to promote participation of private capital, both external and internal with a view to widening the base of industrial development and of capital market in India.

— Full merchant banking services, venture capital financing and allied financial services.

— Assistance to the private and joint sector enterprises with rupee and foreign currency loans and advances, underwriting, guaranteeing of loans from other agencies, equity participation and other forms of assistance particularly to the new enterprises.

— Services to the development of backward areas through industrial growth, promotion of investment priorities of the Government and for the growth of private corporate sector.

Venture capital funds for the promotion of green field companies ad risk capital investment and joined other financial institutions in setting up SHCI, CRISIL and OTC Exchange of India Ltd.

Its paid up capital, borrowing from Government, IDBI, RBI etc. and raises funds from the capital market by issuing bonds or equity and borrow from abroad with the permission of the Government. It has set up its own bank and a mutual fund like UTI.

Industrial Finance Corporation of India (IFCI)

IFCI was as set up for the purpose of assisting the medium and long term projects for capital expenditure on projects, expansion, modernisation and technological upgradation etc. It plays a promotional and developmental role, particularly in relation to the small and medium scale entrepreneurs.

Main functions are providing:

— Underwriting and guaranteeing facilities to the industrial concerns.

— Term loans or contribute to the debentures or equity

— Rupee loans and foreign currency loans are through foreign credit lines from foreign banks and foreign governments etc.

— Financial assistance to limited companies either in the private, public or joint sectors and cooperative societies engaged in

  a. manufacturing, preservation and processing of goods
  b. shipping
  c. mining
  d. hotel industry
  e. electricity generation and distribution etc

It concentrates mostly on medium and large scale projects. By an agreement with other Financial Institutions and IDBI, the IFC specialises in financing of certain industries like jute, cement, sugar etc.

Industrial Reconstruction Bank of India (IRBI)

Main purpose is to provide assistance to sick but potentially viable units and extend finance for their modernisation, expansion or diversification. Government, borrowing from the IDBI, RBI etc. issue of debentures or bonds to the public or raise deposits from he public or raise deposits from the public.

Industrial Investment Bank of India (IIBI)

It has shed off its outfit of financing sick industries into one financing industrial investment for growth, expansion, diversification etc. It has now become a development financial institution with a five year tax holiday in addition to completely restructured capital structure.

In addition to the above development institutions, we have National Housing Bank that is the apex bank for Housing Finance to provide finance and refinance to Housing Finance Corporations like HDFC. Shipping Credit and Investment Corporation of India (SCICI) help financing and refinancing shipping companies.

Insurance Companies

Life Insurance Corporation (LIC)

LIC provides cover of risk of life, retirement, disability etc.

Sources of Funds: Paid up capital, premium collections, borrowing from government and the RBI ad now the mobilisation of savings by insurance companies accounts for 79% of the financial savings of the household sector.

The proportion of funds to be deployed at their discretion was hardly 25% of the total investible funds, while the rest are earmarked for specified government and semi government securities (50%) ad for lending or socially desirable projects like housing finance loan, mortgage loans, loans to approved bodies for electricity, housing, water etc (25%) LIC invests in shares/debentures of companies, provide rupee loans to companies, makes initial subscription and underwriting of new issues of shares etc. It as set up a Mutual Fund for operating various schemes for mobilisation of savings from the public, particularly from the rural and urban areas and channel these funds to the stock market and capital market.

General Insurance Corporation (GIC)

Sources of Funds: Paid up capital, reserves, profits and premium income. It operate in the money and capital markets, earn on underwriting and making of long term loans and investments.

Main Objectives are:

— To carry on the general insurance business other than life such as accident, fire etc. to aid and advise the subsidiaries to conduct insurance business and to help the conduct of investment strategy of the subsidiaries in an efficient and productive manner.

SFCs/SIDCs

Sources of Funds: Issue of bonds and debentures in the market, fixed deposits from the public, borrowings from RBI, IDBI, state Government etc.

These bodies assist small scale industries, units in backward areas, new entrepreneurs etc. Industrial Development Corporations, Industrial Investment Corporations were set up by some states for promotion, infrastructural development, financial, managerial and entrepreneurial guidance to the industrialists, provision of indstrial sheds/plots for setting up of small units etc.

Stock Holding Corporaton of India Ltd. (SHCIL)

It was intended to facilitate quicker share transfer among financial institutions, and their transfers with other investors, members of stock exchanges etc. It is offering its services to its own seven promoter institutions. It acts on the basis of Letter of Authority/Power of Authority issued by the financial institutions and render the following services:

a. Clearing services—It receives and/or delivers the securities on behalf of the institutions after each settlement of the Stock Exchange. Monitors the execution of the purchase/ sale orders of the institutions by the brokers.
b. Depository services-including services related to the collection of dividend warrants, and interest cheques; it attends to the necessary consolidation or splitting of shares, redemption and collection of bonus and rights and other privileges attached to shares, debentures and other instruments.
c. Support services-arranges to monitor interest/dividend payments due to the institutions and ensure that the warrant
d. Management/Information services
e. Development services

Credit Rating and Information Services of India Ltd

Main objective is to rate the debt obligations of Indian companies on a voluntary basis with a view to providing the investors a guide as to the risk of timely payment of interest and principal by the company. The rating is confined to fixed deposits, debentures, preference shares and short term instruments like commercial paper. CRISIL does not rate equity shares or the performance of the company as a whole.

Investors

Investors should be familiar with the ratings given by the Credit Rating and Information Services of India Ltd. (CRISIL) for protecting their interests. The CRISIL ratings are given only for debt instruments of companies, namely, Commercial Papers (CP), debentures, bonds and fixed deposits. Since early 1992, the ratings of Investment Information and Credit Rating Agency (ICRA) are also used by companies.

The ratings in use by the companies are published by the CRISIL in their "CRISIL Rating Scan." The companies use them only when the ratings are favourable to them and when they are making any public offer for deposits or debentures, etc. The investors should examine these symbols with regard to their benefits and their implication. Since a rating given can be revised upwards or downwards, the investors should keep a watch on any such revisions.

Information and Credit Rating Agency (ICRA)

Another Credit Rating Agency was set up later; namely, The Investment Information and Credit Rating Agency of India Limited, registered in 1991, sponsored by the IFCI and a number of other financial institutions. It has its headquarters at Delhi, while the CRISIL has its headquarters in Mumbai. Credit Rating is now mandatory for all debt instruments—issued by the companies both short-term and long-term. The debentures of both convertible and non-convertible nature require credit rating, if they are not convertible within 18 months. Debentures, bonds, preference shares and fixed deposits are eligible to be rated. The rating is instrument wise but not for the whole company. The ratings given by the credit rating agency like ICRA are indicators of the correct opinion of the relative capability of timely servicing of debts and obligations by the company.

The ratings given are AAA, AA or A for safety, BBB, BB or B for less safe investments C and D indicate no safety and default respectively. But as equities are essentially risky and investor is willingly entering the risky investment of equity, credit rating for equity is neither possible nor necessary. Only in respect of debt instruments, investor wants to avoid risk and so he should know the extent of the risk, he is taking. Equity holder is the owner and takes risk voluntarily while the debenture holder is creditor and he does not want to take risk in respect of interest or in payment of the principal.

In evaluating the instruments in question, CRISIL takes into account the various risks involved in servicing of instruments. They undertake business analysis, financial analysis, management evaluation and fundamental analysis. They also take into account the regulatory and competitive environment faced by the company and other relevant factors.

The CRISIL also evaluates the management risk as judged by the track record of the management, planning and control system, managerial expertise, tax planning and expansion plans of the company.

Ratings

All the above types of analysis will be done by experts after discussions with the company executives, its suppliers, customers and market competitors. The information is gathered on a confidential basis and assessed with a view to examine the capacity of the company to service the instruments issued to the public.

Broadly, there are three categories of ratings:

a. Long-term Instruments

b. Medium-term Instruments

c. Short-term Instruments

The rating indicates the degree of risk and the highest safety possible is under the rating of AAA or F AAA or P I' The credit worthiness is indicated in the ratings and reflects the capacity of the company to service them adequately with a view to ensure the timely payment of interest and principal.

References

Jones, K., "The Finance Function Knocks at Your Door", Intelligent Enterprise, June 28, 2002.

12

Cash-flow Valuation

Discounted Cash-flow Valuation

A valuation for an investment created by estimating future cash flows using a measure of risk, which can be thought of as the required rate of return, and considering the time of the investment period. To calculate valuations of stocks using discounted cash flows, the value is estimated using some measure of the present value of a cash flow.

Intuitively, the value of any asset should be a function of three variables:

1. How much it generates in cash flows;
2. When these cash flaws are expected to occur; and
3. The uncertainty associated with these cash flows. Discounted cash-flow valuation bring.

These three variables together by computing the value of any asset to be the present value of its expected future cash flaws:

t=n

Value = Σ: CFt

t=1(1+r)t

where

n = Life of the asset

CFt = Cash flow in period t

r = Discount rate reflecting the riskiness of the estimated cash flows
The cash flows will vary from asset to asset-dividends for stocks; coupons (interest) and face value for bonds; and aftertax cash flows for real projects. The discount rate is a function of the riskiness of the estimated cash flows-riskier assets carry higher rates; safer projects carry lower rates.

Equity Valuation versus Firm Valuation

One path to discounted cash-flow valuation is to value just the equity stake in the business; a second is to value the entire firm, including equity and any other claimholders in the firm (bondholders, preferred stockholders, etc.). Although both approaches discount expected cash flows, the relevant cash flows and discount rates are different for each. The value of equity is obtained by discounting expected cash flows to equity-that is, the residual cash flows after meeting all expenses, tax obligations, and interest and principal paymentsat the cost of equity-that is, the rate of return required by equity investors in the firm.

$$\text{Value of Equity} = \sum_{t=1}^{t=n} \frac{\text{CF to Equity}_t}{(1 + k_e)^t}$$

where

$$\text{CF to Equity}_t = \text{Expected Cash Flow to Equity in period } t$$
$$k_e = \text{Cost of Equity}$$

The dividend discount model is a specialised case of equity valuation, whereby the value of a stock is the present value of expected future dividends.

Value of Equity

This is the value of the equity stake in a business; in the context of a publicly traded firm, it is the value of the common stock, warrants and other equity claims in the firm. The value of the firm is obtained by discounting expected cash flows to the firm, that is, residual cash flows after meeting all operating expenses and taxes, but prior to debt payments at the weighted average cost of capital-that is, the cost of the different components of financing used by the firm, weighted by their market value proportions.

t=n CFto Firm t

ValueafFirm = Σ: t=1 (1+ WACCfr

where

CF to Firm t = Expected Cash Flow to Firm in period t

WACC = Weighted Average Cost of Capital

The two approaches use different definitions of cash flow and discount rate 001 will yield consistent estimates of value as long as the same set of assumptions applied for both. It is important to avoid mismatching cash flows and discount rate. Since discounting cash flows to equity at the weighted average cost of capital will lead to an upwardly biased estimate of the value of equity, whereas discounting cash flot! to the firm at the cost of equity will yield a downward biased estimate of the valued the firm.

Value of Firm

The value of the firm is the value of the claims of all investors who gave claims on the firm; thus, it includes lenders and bond holders, who have fixed claims and equity investors, who have residual claims.

Equity Valuation Models

Equity valuation models attempt to estimate the value of equity In firm by discounting cash flows to equity at the rate of return required by equity Investors (cost of equity).

Dividend discount model

When investors buy stock, they generally expect to get two types of cash flow dividends during the holding period and an expected price at the end of the holding period. Because this expected price is itself determined by future dividends, the value of a sioci is the present value of dividends through perpetuity:

t = DPS t

Σ (1+r)t

t=1

where

DPS t = Expected dividends per share

r = Required rate of return on stock

The rationale for the model lies in the present value rule: the value of any asset me present value of expected future cash flows, discounted at a rate appropriate to the riskiness of the cash flows being discounted.

Terminal price

This is the expected price of a stock (or equity) at the end of a specified holding period. What is a stable growth rate? It is difficult to talk about extraordinary growth without first defining what we mean by a stable growth rate. There are two insights to keep in mind when estimating a "stable" growth rate. First, since this growth rate in the firm's dividends is expected to last forever, the firm's other measures of performance (including earnings) can be expected to grow at the same rate. Consider the long-term consequences of a firm whose earnings grow 6% a year forever, while its dividends grow at 8%.

Over time, the dividends will exceed earnings. Similarly, if a firm's earnings grow at a faster rate than its dividends in the long term, the payout ratio will converge toward zero, which is also not a steady state. Thus, although the model's requirement is for the expected growth rate in dividends, if the firm is truly in a steady state, analysts should be able to substitute in the expected growth rate in earnings and get the same result.

Stable growth rate

This is a growth rate that a firm can sustain forever in earnings, dividends, and cash flows. The second issue relates to what growth rate is reasonable as a "stable" growth rate. Again, the assumption that this growth rate will last forever establishes rigorous constraints on "reasonableness." A firm cannot in the long term grow at a rate significantly greater than the growth rate in the economy in which it operates. Thus, a firm that grows at 12% forever in an economy growing at 6% will eventually become larger than the economy.

In practical terms, the stable growth rate cannot be larger than the nominal (real) growth rate in the economy in which the firm operates, if the valuation is done in nominal (real) terms. The nominal growth rate in the economy is determined by expected inflation and the real growth rate in GNP. Thus, in 1995 in the United States, the expected nominal growth in the economy, assuming expected inflation! in the long term of 3% a year and real growth 2 of 3%, would have been:

Expected nominal growth in U.S. economy = Expected
Inflation + Expected real growth = 3% + 3% = 6%

By definition, therefore, a stable firm is one whose growth rate does not exceed 6% by a significant amount. Given the uncertainty associated with estimates of expected inflation and real growth, there can be differences in the benchmark growth rate used by different analysts-analysts with higher expectations of inflation in the long term may project a higher nominal growth rate in the economy. There is another instance in which an analyst may be able to stray from a strict limit imposed on the "stable growth rate." If a firm is likely to maintain a few years of "above stable" growth rates, an approximate value for the firm can be obtained by adding a premium to the stable growth rate to reflect the above average growth in the initial years.

Even in this case, the analyst's flexibility is limited. The sensitivity of the model to growth implies that the stable growth rate cannot be more than 1 % or 2% obey the growth rate in the economy. Can a stable growth rate be much lower than the growth rate in the economy? There are no logical or mathematical limits on the downside. Firms that have a stable growth rate much lower than the growth rate in the economy will become smaller in proportion to the economy over time. Because there is no economic basis for arguing that this cannot happen, there is no reason to prevent analysts from using a stable growth rate that is much lower than the nominal growth rate in the economy.

The assumption that the growth rate in dividends has to be constant over time is a difficult assumption to meet, especially given the volatility of earnings. If a firm has an average growth rate that is close to a stable growth rate, the model can be used with little real effect on value. Thus, a cyclical firm that can be expected to have year-to-year swings in growth rates but has an average growth rate of 6% can be assumed to be in stable growth, without a significant loss of generality. This is because since dividends are smoothed even when earnings are volatile, they are less likely to be affected by year-to-year changes in earnings growth.

Length of the High-growth Period

The length of the high-growth period is a key input to this valuation model, and it does not lend itself easily to a rigid framework. Let us consider the easy cases first. :First, if the firm is growing at a rate close to the stable growth rate right now, no extraordinary growth is anticipated and it can be assumed that the firm is in stable growth already. Second, if the firm is growing at a rate higher than the stable growth rate, but the higher growth is coming from a single product or service for which the firm has a protected position, the extraordinary growth can be expected to last as long as the protection lasts. Thus, a pharmaceutical firm that is generating high growth because of a single patent protected product, whose patent is expected to expire in four years, can be expected to have a fouryear high-growth period.

High-growth period

This is a period during which a company's earnings or cash flows are expected to grow at a rate much higher than the overall growth rate of the economy. In other cases, the estimation is much more difficult. In general, we can make the following assumptions about the length of the high-growth period.

1. The greater the current growth rate in earnings of a firm, relative to the stable growth rate, the longer the high-growth period, although the growth rate may drop off during the period. Thus, a firm that is growing at 40% currently should have a longer high-growth period than one growing at 14%.
2. The larger the current size of the firm-both in absolute terms and relative to the market it serves-the shorter the high-growth period. Size remains one of the most potent forces that push firms toward

stable growth; the larger a firm, the less likely it is to maintain an above-normal growth rate.

At the risk of sounding arbitrary, the following guidelines for defining the length of the high growth period as a function of current growth rates:

Current Growth Rate	Length of High-Growth Period
:5 1 % higher than stable growth rate	No high growth
1-10% higher than stable growth rate	5 years
> 10% higher than stable growth rate	10 years

Again, the sensitivity of value to changes in the length of the high-growth period can always be estimated. Although some analysts use growth periods greater than 10 years, the combination of high-expected growth and long growth periods creates a potent mix in terms of increasing the size of the firm, in many cases well beyond the realm of reasonableness. Required return on stock-discount rates The dividends and terminal price should be discounted back at a rate that reflects their riskiness to stockholders to arrive at the dividend discount model value. To arrive at this rate, we first have to arrive at a measure of the riskiness, using a risk and return model.

If CAPM is used, for instance, the beta of the stock relative to a market index is the measure of risk; if APM is used, the betas of the stock relative to the factors are the measures of risk. We then have to arrive at an expected return based on the risk measure. In CAPM, this requires an estimate for the riskless rate and the risk premium.

Required Return on Equity = Riskless Rate + Beta (Risk Premium) A similar estimate can be made using APM.

Expected dividends

The first step in estimating expected dividends during the high growth period is to estimate the expected earnings for each period. This is done using the current earnings and the expected growth rates in earnings, which may either be constant or vary across the high-growth period. The expected earnings are paired with estimated dividend payout ratios in each period, which again may change over the high-growth period. This may seem to be an wake procedure, since expected dividends could well be estimated using the current dividends and applying a dividend growth rate, but it is used for two reasons.

First, analyst projections for growth are stated in terms of earnings rather than dividends. Second, separating earnings growth from dividend payout provides more flexibility terms of changing dividend payout ratios as earnings growth rates change. In particular, it allows us to raise dividend payout ratios as earnings growth rates decline.

Estimating earnings growth The key input in this model is the expected growth rate in earnings. It can be estimated using one of three approaches:

Historical Growth (in Earnings): This is the growth rate over the past few periods in earnings; it can be calculated either by averaging the year-specific growth rates (arithmetic average) or by estimating the compounded growth rate over the whole period (geometric average).

1. *Historical Growth:* The growth rate in earnings per share over past periods can be used to estimate future growth. In doing so, we assume that firms whose earnings have grown rapidly in the past will continue to do so in the future. There are two considerations in using this measure. The first is how far back to go; the growth rate will be different for different time periods, but it is important that some consistency be maintained across valuations. The other relates to the measurement of the growth rate itself; because earnings growth compounds over time, that geometric average growth rate in earnings, rather than the arithmetic average, should be used: " Geometric average growth rate in earnings = (EPSo/ EPSO-t) l/t - 1
2. *Analyst Projections*: The easiest solution is to use an analyst projection of growth in earnings for the company being valued. For most U.S. companies, such projections are widely available and disseminated by a number of services, including Zacks and I/ B/E/S. They are less widely available for non-U.S. companies, because there are far fewer equity research analysts in other markets.
3. *Fundamentals of the firm*: The most complex-and richest approach relates expected growth to the fundamentals of the firm.

In particular, the expected growth rate should be a function of the proportion of the earnings that are reinvested back into the firm and the returns earned on the projects taken with the money:

Expected Growth Rate = Retention Ratio* Return on Equity we noted that the return on equity is itself affected by the leverage of the firm, and we expanded it to include this effect:

Return on Equity = ROA + DIE [ROA - i (1 - t)]

where

ROA = Return on Assets =

DIE = Debt I Equity Ratio i = Interest rate on Debt t = Marginal tax rate
EBIT (1 - t) I (BY of Debt + BY of Equity)

Fundamental Growth Rate

This is the growth rate in earnings estimated from the company's policy on reinvestment and the quality of its projects. This formulation allows the analyst valuing the firm to bring in the effect of the investment, financing, and dividend decisions of the firm not only in current periods but also in future periods. The return on assets itself is a product of the after-tax operating margin of the firm and the asset turnover ratio:

Return on Assets = After-tax Operating Margin * Asset Turnover Ratio
where

After oo tax Operating Margin = EBIT (1 - t)/Sales Asset Turnover Ratio =
Sales I (BY of Debt + BY of Equity)

The earnings growth rate during the high-growth period can also take one of many paths, ranging from a constant-growth rate to one that changes each year:

Constant-growth rate during the high-growth period: From a purely mechanical standpoint, the simplest assumption is that the earnings growth rate is constant for the high-growth period, after which the growth rate drops to the stable level. The limitation of this formulation is obvious: it assumes that the growth rate is high during the initial period and is transformed overnight to a lower, stable rate at the end of the period. Although these sudden transformations in growth can happen, it is much technically, this could be considered a return on capital rather than a return on assets. That might be true, but the formulation takes a different view of assets than the traditional balance sheet.

If assets are viewed as fixed assets plus working capital, then adding together the book values of debt, equity, and preferred stock (if any) should provide a measure of these assets more realistic to assume that the shift from high growth to stable growth occurs gradually over time. The assumption that the growth rate drops precipitously from its level in the initial phase to a stable rate also implies that this model is more appropriate for firms with modest growth rates in the initial phase.

For instance, it is more reasonable to assume that a firm growing at 12% in the high-growth period will see its growth rate drop to 6%, than it is for a firm growing at 40% in the high-growth period. If we assume that the growth rate and payout ratio are fixed for the high-growth period, the present value of the dividends during the high-growth period can be estimated as follows:

Constant growth for the initial part of the high-growth period, followed by gradually reduction to stable growth: In this case, the growth rate does not drop precipitously at the end of the high-growth period to the stable rate; rather, it adjusts more gradually to it, This model allows for growth rates and payout ratios to change at least during the transition period. Thus, it may be more appropriate for firms that are expected to grow at very high rates, say 30% to 40% for the next few years.

Growth rates chat change every year for the high-growth period: In the most general formulation, the growth rates and payout ratios can be different in each year of the high growth period, reflecting changes in investment opportunities and firm size. Under this scenario, the value of a stock is the present value of the dividends each year during the high-growth period added on to the present value of the terminal price at the end of the high-growth period. Estimating dividend payout ratios The other input needed to estimate expected dividends during the high-growth phase is the dividend payout ratio, since the expected dividends in period t can be written as

Expected Dividends in period t = Expected Earnings t * Payout Ratio t

The payout ratio should reflect changes in expected growth. As growth declines, the payout ratio should increase.

Estimating Terminal Price

The terminal price-the price at the end of the high-growth period-can be estimated from expected dividends in the first time period following the high-growth period, the required rate of return on the stock in the stable phase, and the expected stable growth rate in dividends as follows:

$$Value\ of\ Stock = \frac{DPS\,n+1}{r-gn}$$

where

DPSn + 1 = Expected dividends one year after end of high growth period
r n = Required rate of return for equity investors in stable phase
gn = Growth rate in dividends forever

A stable growth rate is assumed to be fairly close to the growth rate of the economy in which the firm operates. In addition, the payout ratio and risk should reflect the stable growth assumed for the firm, since stable firms payout more of their earnings as dividends and have lower risk. One way of estimating this new payout ratio is to use the fundamental growth model.

$$g = b\,[ROA + DIE\,(ROA - i\,(1 - t)]$$

where

b = Retention ratio = 1 - payout ratio
ROA = Return on assets = [Net Income + Interest Expense (1 - t)] / Total Assets DIE = Debt / Equity (in book value terms)
i = Interest Expense / Book Value of Debt

Manipulating this growth rate equation yields the payout ratio as a function of the expected growth rate:

$$Payout\ ratio = 1 - b = 1 - [g / (ROA + DIE\,(ROA - i-(1 - t))]$$

Where the inputs for this equation will be those for the stable growth period. Once estimated, the terminal price has to be discounted back to the present and added back to the present value of dividends. To illustrate, assume that a firm has the following parameters for the ROA, debt/equity ratios, payout ratios, and interest rates in the initial high-growth phase and in the stable-growth phase:

	Initial Growth Phase	Stable Period
ROA	20%	16%
Payout ratio	20%	?
DIE	1.00	1.00
i	10%	8%
Growth rate	?	8%

The tax rate for the firm is 40%.

Growth rate in first five years = (1 - 0.2) [.20 + 1 (.20 -.10*(1 - 0.4))] = 27.2 %

Payout ratio after year five = 1 - [.08/(.16 + 1 (.16 -.08*(1 - 0.4")] = 70.59 %

As the growth rate drops in the stable-growth period, the payout ratio increases from 20% to 70.59%.

Once the expected dividends and the terminal price have been estimated and the discount rate has been obtained from the risk measure for the firm, the present value of the dividends and terminal price is calculated, providing a measure of the value of the stock using the dividend discount model.

FCFE Valuation Model

This model estimates the value of equity as the present value of the expected free cash flows to equity over time. Briefly, the FCFE is the residual cash flow left over after meeting interest and principal payments and providing for capital expenditures to maintain existing assets and create new assets for future growth. The free cash flow to equity is measured as follows:

FCFE = Net Income + Depreciation - Capital Spending
Working Capital - Principal Repayments + New Debt Issues

In the special case where the capital expenditures and the working capital are expected to be financed at the target debt ratio &, and principal repayments are made from new debt issues, the FCFE is measured as follows:

FCFE = Net Income + (1 - &) (Capital Expenditure., - Depreciation) + (1 - &) ~ Working Capital

In the general version of the FCFE model, we allow for two stages in growth-an initial period of extraordinary growth, followed by stable growth forever. Extraordinary growth period Stable growth: **g** n forever

Value of the Stock = PV of FCFE during extraordinary phase + PV of terminal price

Just as in the dividend discount model. There are four basic inputs needed for this model to be usable.

— First, the length of the high-growth period is defined.
— Second, the free cash flow to equity each period during the growth period is specified; this means that net capital expenditures, working capital needs and the debt-financing mix are all estimated for the high-growth period.
— Third, The rate of return that stockholders will demand for holding the stock is estimated.
— Finally, the terminal price at the end of the high growth period is estimated based on the estimates of stable growth, the free cash flows to equity and required return after the high growth ends.

Of the four inputs, the length of the high-growth period and the rate of return required by stockholders are the same for the dividend discount and FCFE valuation models. The differences in the other two inputs are minor but still worth emphasizing.

FCFE during the High-growth Period

As in the dividend discount model we start with the earnings per share and estimate expected growth in earnings. Thus the entire discussion about earnings growth in the dividend discount model applies here as well. Once the earnings are estimated the net capital expenditures, working capital needs and debt-financing needs have to be specified in order to arrive at the FCFE. Just as the dividend payout ratio was adjusted to reflect changes in expected growth, the net capital expenditure and working capital needs should change as the growth changes. In particular, high-growth companies will have relatively higher net expenditures and working capital needs. As the growth rate declines, these requirements should also decline.

Net Capital Expenditures

This is the difference between capital expenditures and Depreciation A similar point can be made about leverage. High-growth, high-risk firms generally do not use much leverage to finance investment needs. As the growth tapers ofhowever, the firm will be much more willing to use debt; thus, debt ratios will likely increase I growth rates drop.

Estimating the Terminal Price

The terminal price in the FCFE model is also determine by the stable growth rate and the required return. The difference between this model and the dividend discount model lies primarily in the cash flow used to calculate the terminal price: the dividend discount model uses expected dividends in the period after the high growth period, whereas the FCFE model uses the free cash flow to equity in that period:

$$Value\ of\ Stock = \frac{FCFE\ n+1}{r - gn}$$

In estimating that cash flow, the net capital expenditures and working capital needs should be consistent with the definition of stability. Many analysts assume that stable growth firms have no net capital expenditures. FCFE valuation versus dividend discount model valuation The FCFE discounted cash-flow model can be viewed as an alternative to the dividend discount model. Because the two approaches sometimes provide different estimates of value, however, a comparison is in order.

There are two conditions under which the value obtained from using the FCFE in discounted cash-flow valuation will be the same as the value obtained from using the dividend discount model. The first condition is obvious: when the dividends are equal to the FCFE, the value will be the same. The second condition is more subtle: when the FCFE is greater than dividends, but the excess cash (FCFE - Dividends) is invested in projects with net present value of zero, the values Will also be similar. For instancc, investing in financial assets that are fairly priced should yield a net present value of zero. More often, the two models will provide different estimates of value.

First, when the FCFE is greater than the dividend and the excess cash either earns below-market interest rates or is invested in negative net present value projects, the value from the FCFE model will be greater than the value from the dividend discount model. This is not as unusual as it might seem. There are numerous case studies of firms that, having accumulated large cash balances by paying out low dividends relative to FCFE, chose to use this cash to finance unwise takeovers. Second, the payment of smaller dividends than the firm can afford lowers debt equity ratios; accordingly, the firm may become under leveraged, reducing its value.

When dividends are greater than FCFE, the firm will have to issue either new stock or new debt to pay these dividends. At least three negative consequences for value are possible. One is the flotation cost on these security issues, which can be substantial for equity issues. Second, if the firm borrows the money to pay the dividends, the firm may become over leveraged (relative to the optimal), leading to a loss in value. Finally, paying too much in dividends can lead to capital rationing constraints, whereby good projects are rejected, resulting in a loss of wealth. When the two models yield different values, two questions remain:

(1) What does the difference between the two models tell us?

(2) Which of the two models is the appropriate one to use in evaluating the market price?

More often, the value from the FCFE model exceeds the value from the dividend discount model. The difference between the value obtained from the FCFE model and the value obtained from the dividend discount model can be considered one component of the value of controlling a firm that is, it measures the value of controlling dividend policy. In a hostile takeover, the bidder can expect to control the firm and change the dividend policy (to reflect FCFE), thus capturing the higher FCFE value.

In the more infrequent case-the value from the dividend discount model exceeds the value from the FCFE the difference has less economic meaning but can be considered a warning on the sustainability of expected dividends. As for the question as to which of the two values is more appropriate for evaluating the market price, the answer lies in the openness of the market for corporate control. If there is a good probability that a firm can be taken over or its management changed, the market price will reflect that likelihood. In that case, the value from the FCFE model would be a more appropriate benchmark. As changes in corporate control become more difficult, either because of a firm's size and/or legal or market restrictions on takeovers, the value from the dividend discount model will provide a more appropriate benchmark for comparison.

FCFF Valuation

The free cash flow to the firm (FCFF) is the sum of the cash flows to all claimholders in the firm, including stockholders, bondholders, and preferred stockholders. There are two ways of measuring the free cash flow to the firm. One is to add up the cash flows to the claimholders:

FCFF = Free Cash Flow to Equity
+ Interest Expense (1 - tax rate) + Principal Repayments - New Debt Issues
+ Preferred Dividends

The other involves using earnings before interest payments and taxes (EBIT) as a base for the calculation:

FCFF = EBIT (1 - tax rate) + Depreciation - Capital Expenditure - working Capital

Both approaches should provide the same estimates of the cash flow. The differences between FCFF and FCFE arise primarily from cash flows associated with debt-interest payments, principal repayments, and new debt issues-and other non equity claims, such as preferred dividends.

One widely used measure in valuation is the earnings before interest, taxes, depreciation, and amortisation (EBITDA). The free cash flow to the firm is a closely related concept, but it takes into account the potential tax liability from the earnings as well as capital expenditures and working capital requirements. Another common measure is the net operating income (NOI)-the income from operations, prior to taxes and nonoperating expenses. If nonoperating expenses are deducted, the resulting figure is the earnings before interest and taxes (EBIT). Each of these measures is used in valuation models, and each is a variant of the free cash flow to the firm. Each, however, makes some assumptions about the relationship between depreciation and capital expenditures.

Growth in FCFE and FCFF

The primary cause of differences in the growth rates in FCFF and the FCFE is the existence of leverage. Leverage generally increases the growth rate in the FCFE, relative to the growth rate in the FCFF. This can be illustrated using the formulation relating the growth rate to financial fundamentals. The growth rate in earnings per share is defined as

$$g_{EPS} = b\,[ROA + DIE\,(ROA - i\,(1 - t)]$$

where

g_{EPS} = Growth rate in Earnings per share

b = Retention ratio= 1 - Payout ratio

ROA = Return on Assets = (Net Income + Interest Expense (1 - t"/(BV of Debt + BV of Equity)

D/E = Book Value of Debt/Book Value of Equity

i = Interest Expense / Book Value of Debt

As long as the return on assets earned by a firm on its projects exceeds the after-tax interest rate, increasing leverage will increase the growth rate in earnings per share. The cash flow to the firm is a pre-debt cash flow and is not affected by increased leverage. Thus, the growth rate in EBIT, for the same firm, will be a function of just the retention ratio and the return on assets and will generally be lower:

$$g_{EBIT} = b\,(ROA)$$

The growth rates in capital expenditures, depreciation, and capital spending will be identical for purposes of calculating the FCFE and FCFF.

General Model

In the general version of the FCFF model, we allow for two \tip in growth-an initial period of extraordinary growth, followed by stable growth forever. Just as in the dividend discount model, there are four basic inputs in this model.

— First the length of the high-growth period is defined.

— Second, the free cash flow to the firm each period during the growth period is specified; this requires estimating net capital expenditures and working capital needs for the high-growth period.

— Third, the cost of capital that investors demand for holding stock, debt, and other securities is estimated, based on their market value weights.

— Finally, the terminal value of the firm at the end of the high-growth period is estimated, based on the estimates of stable growth, free cash flows to the firm, and required return after the high growth ends.

The FCFF model therefore uses much of the same information needed for the FCFE model, but it differs in certain respects. The free cash flow to the firm is before cash flows to debt holders and is thus based on operating income growth rather than net in come growth. In addition, the discount rate is the cost of capital rather than the cost of equity. Finally, the present value of the cash flows provides an estimate of the value of the firm rather than just the equity.

FCFF Model

The FCFF model estimates the value of the firm as the present value of the expected FCFF, discounted back at the cost of capital. That said, all of the caveats relating to FCFE valuation apply here as well. The assumptions about net capital expenditures and working capital should be consistent with assumptions about growth. The debt ratios matter here. not because they affect the cash flows, but because they help determine the cost of capital and should be changed to reflect the changing characteristics of the firm.

Firm valuation versus equity valuation unlike the dividend discount model or the FCFE model, the FCFF model values the firm rather than equity. The value of equity, however, can be extracted from the value of the firm by subtracting out the market value of outstanding debt.

The advantage of using the firm valuation approach is that cash flows relating to debt do not have to be considered explicitly, since the FCFF is a pre-debt cash flow. By contrast, they have to be taken into account in estimating FCFE. In cases where the leverage is expected to change significantly over time, this can be a significant saving. At the same time, the firm valuation approach requires information about debt ratios and interest rates to estimate the weighted average cost of capital. The value for equity obtained from the firm valuation and equity valuation approaches will be the same if two conditions are met:

— *If consistent assumptions are made about growth in the two approaches*: This does not mean that the same growth rate is used in both approaches, and it may require that the growth rates in earnings be adjusted for the effect of leverage. This is especially true for the calculation of the terminal value, whereby a stable growth rate is assumed in both FCFE and FCFF.

— *If bonds are correctly priced*: The value of equity in the FCFF approach is obtained by subtracting out the market value of the debt from the value of the firm. If the firm's debt is overvalued, the value of equity obtained from the FCFF model will be lower than the value obtained from the equity valuation approaches. Similarly, the value of equity will be higher if the firm's debt is undervalued.

References

Emery and Finnerty, *Principles of Finance with Corporate Applications*, West, 1991.

Eun, Cheol S. and Bruce G. Resnick, *International Financial Management*, New York: Irwin McGraw-Hill, 1998.

Fabozzi, Frank, *Assessing Capital Market Through Securitization*, New Hope, PA: Frank J. Fabozzi Associates, 2001.

Flannery, Mark J., "Using Market Information in Prudential Bank Supervision: A Review of U.S. Empirical Evidence," *Journal of Money*, Credit and Banking, pp. 274-305, August 1998.

French, Warren A. and John Granrose, *Practice Business Ethics*, Upper Saddle River, NJ: Prentice Hall, 1995.

Gitman, and Joehnk, *Fundamentals of Investing*, 4th edition, Harper & Row, 1990.

Bibliography

Agrawal V. and D. Farrell, *Who Wins in Offshoring*, The McKinsey Quarterly, Speech Edition; Global Directives, 2003.

Alexander, David, *Principles of Emergency Planning and Management*, Oxford University Press: New York, NY, 2002.

Block and Hirt, *Foundations of Financial Management*, 6th edition, Richard Irwin & Co, 1992.

Brealey, Richard A., *Principles of Corporate Finance*, NY: McGraw Hill, 2000.

Campsey and Brigham, *Introduction to Financial Management*, 3rd edition, Dryden Press, 1991.

Carmichael, Shenna, *Business Ethics: The New Bottom Line*, London: Demos, 1995.

Desanctis, Gerardine and Janet Fulk (eds.), *Shaping Organizational Form: Communication, Connection, and Community*, Thousand Oaks, CA: Sage Publications, 1999.

Eckerson, Wayne W., *Performance Dashboards*, Hoboken, NJ: John Wiley & Sons, 2005.

Emery and Finnerty, *Principles of Finance with Corporate Applications*, West, 1991.

French, Warren A. and John Granrose, *Practice Business Ethics*, Upper Saddle River, NJ: Prentice Hall, 1995.

George Steiner, *Strategic Planning: What Every Manager Should Know*, Free Press, 1979.

Gibson, J.W., "Satisfaction with Upward and Downward Organizational Communications: Another Perspective. *Proceedings of the Southwest Academy of Management* (March), 1985.

Gibson, J.W., and R.M. Hodgetts, *Organizational Communication – A Managerial Perspective*, 2nd Edition. New York: HarperCollins Publishers, 1991.

Gordon, Thomas, Dr. *L.E.T.: Leader Effectiveness Training,* New York: Bantam Books, 1977.

Gray, S. J., "Towards a Theory of Cultural Influence on the Development of Accounting Systems Internationally", *Abacus,* March, 1998.

Greenleaf, Robert K., *Servant Leadership: A Journey into the Nature of Legitimate Power and Greatness,* Paulist Press, March 1983.

Grover, V. and Davenport, T.H., "General perspectives on knowledge management: fostering a research agenda", *Journal of Management Information Systems*, 2001.

Grover, Varun and William J. Kettinger, *Business process change: reengineering concepts, methods and technologies,* Harrisburg, PA: Idea Group Publishing, 1995.

John M. Bryson, *Strategic Planning for Public and Nonprofit Organizations,* Jossey-Bass, 1995.

Jones, K., "The Finance Function Knocks at Your Door", *Intelligent Enterprise*, June 28, 2002.

Joseph L. Bower, *Managing the Resource Allocation Process,* Harvard Business School Press, 1970.

Karl M. Wiig, *Knowledge Management Methods: Practical Approaches to Managing Knowledge,* July 1994.

Kotter, John P., *Leading Change,* Harvard Business School Press, September 1996.

Kouzes, James M. and Barry Z. Poser, *Credibility: How Leaders Gain and Lose It, Why People Demand It,* San Francisco: Jossey-Bass, May 1995.

Kreiger, Lee T. A., and R. H. Parker, *The Evolution of Corporate Financial Reporting,* London: Nelson, 1979.

Lee, H. L., V. Padmanabhan, and S. Whang, "Information Distortion in a Supply Chain: The Bullwhip Effect," *Management Science*, April 1997.

Levinson, Mark, *Guide to Financial Markets*, London: The Economist (Profile Books), 2006, pp.145-6.

Lucey, T., *Management Information Systems* (9th edn), Thomson Learning, London, 2005.

McCall, Morgan W., *High Flyers: Developing the Next Generation of Leaders,* Harvard Business School Press, September 1997.

McFarland, Lynne Joy, Larry E. Senn and John R. Childress, *21st Century Leadership: Dialogues with 100 Top Leaders,* New York: The Leadership Press, 1994.

Modigliani, F.; Miller, M., "The Cost of Capital, Corporation Finance and the Theory of Investment", *American Economic Review* 48 (3): 261–297, 1958.

Nagle, Thomas T. and Reed K. Holden, *The Strategy and Tactics of Pricing: A Guide to Profitable Decision Making*, NJ: Pearson, 1994.

Nash, Robert C. and Joseph F. Sinkey, Jr., "On Competition, Risk, and the Hidden Assets in the Market for Bank Credit Cards," *Journal of Banking and Finance*, pp. 89-112, (January 1997), January 1997.

Neher, W.W., *Organizational Communication – Challenges of Change, Diversity, and Continuity*, Boston: Allyn and Bacon, 1997.

Niven, Paul R., *Balanced Scorecard Step-by-Step*, second edition, Hoboken, NJ: John Wiley & Sons, 2006.

Ongkrutaraksa, Worapot, *Financial Modeling and Analysis: A Spreadsheet Technique for Financial, Investment, and Risk Management*, 2nd Edition, Frenchs Forest: Pearson Education Australia, 2006.

Paladino, Bob, *Five Key Principles of Corporate Performance Management*, Hoboken, NJ: John Wiley & Sons, 2007.

Petty, Keown, Scott, and Martin, *Basic Financial Management*, 6th edition, Prentice Hall, 1993.

Ross, Stephen A., "The Capital Asset Pricing Model (CAPM), Short-sale Restrictions and Related Issues," *Journal of Finance*, 32 (177), 1977.

Schall and Haley, *Introduction to Financial Management*, 5th edition. McGraw-hill, 1988.

Seitz, Neil E. and Mitch Ellison, *Capital Budgeting and Long-term Financing Decisions*, TX: Dryden Press, 1995.

Tobin, James, *Liquidity preference as behavior towards risk*, The Review of Economic Studies, 25, 1958.

Van Horne, *Financial Management and Policy*, 8th edition, Prentice Hall, 1989.'

Yee, Kenton K., "Aggregation, Dividend Irrelevancy, and Earnings-Value Relations", *Contemporary Accounting Research* 22 (2): 453–480, 2000.

Index